Daphnes A Practical Guide for Gardeners

TIMBER PRESS

Thank you for choosing this Timber Press book. Our books are widely available at good bookstores and garden centers.

To receive our free catalog or e-mail announcements, complete and return this card, or visit our Web site at: **www.timberpress.com/rr**

Name (please print)

Address

City State Zip

E-mail address

- ☐ I prefer not to receive e-mail announcements.
- ☐ Do not share this information with any other company or organization.

We'd also welcome your comments on this book.

Title of book:

Comments:

Please check your areas of interest:

- ☐ Annuals (45AN)
- ☐ Architecture (45AC)
- ☐ Art of Plants (45AR)
- ☐ Bonsai/Penjing (45BO)
- ☐ Botany (4400)
- ☐ Bulbs (45BU)
- ☐ Cacti/Succulents (45CA)
- ☐ Climbers/Vines (45CL)
- ☐ Ethnobotany (44ET)
- ☐ Grasses & Groundcover (45GA)
- ☐ Growers/Professional (45GR)
- ☐ Herbs (45HE)
- ☐ Landscaping & Design (45LA)
- ☐ Literature (45LT)
- ☐ Low-Water Gardening (45LW)
- ☐ Mosses, Ferns & Fungi (45MO)
- ☐ Native Plants (45NP)
- ☐ Natural History (45NH)
- ☐ Natural Resource Mgmt. (4800)
- ☐ NW Regional (4100)
- ☐ Orchids (45OR)
- ☐ Perennials (45PE)
- ☐ Regional (45RE)
- ☐ Rhododendrons/Azaleas (45RH)
- ☐ Rock Gardening (45RG)
- ☐ Roses (45RO)
- ☐ Trees & Shrubs (45TR)
- ☐ Tropicals & Exotics (45TO)

NO POSTAGE
NECESSARY
IF MAILED
IN THE
UNITED STATES

BUSINESS REPLY MAIL

FIRST CLASS MAIL PERMIT NO. 717 PORTLAND, OR

POSTAGE WILL BE PAID BY ADDRESSEE

TIMBER PRESS, INC.
The Haseltine Building
133 S.W. Second Avenue, Suite 450
Portland, OR 97204-9743

Daphnes A Practical Guide for Gardeners

Robin White

Timber Press

Dedication

To Sue, with love and thanks for her patience and hard work transferring my scribble to the word processor, and her encouragement and support running our nursery.

Author's acknowledgements

A special thank you to Chris Brickell for writing this book's Foreword and providing much helpful advice. I am grateful to the following for their help and information: The Alpine Garden Society, The Daphne Society, John Bieber, Abby Jane Brody, Andree Connell, Kath Dryden, Peter Erskine, Jochen Herdramm, Harry Jans, Michael Kammerlander, Joann Knapp, Fritz Kummert, the late Lord Latymer (Hugo Money-Coutts), Melcourt Industries Ltd., David Mowle, Professor David Rankin, Robert Rolfe, and Brenda and Peter Stillwell.

Published in 2006 by
Timber Press, Inc.
The Haseltine Building
133 S. W. Second Avenue, Suite 450
Portland, Oregon 97204-3527, U.S.A.
www.timberpress.com
For contact information regarding editorial, marketing, sales, and distribution in the United Kingdom, see www.timberpress.com/uk.

ISBN 978-0-88192-752-8 ISBN-10: 0-88192-752-X

Designed by Dick Malt
Printed in China

Library of Congress Cataloging-in-Publication Data

White, Robin, 1943 Sept. 4-
Daphnes : a practical guide for gardeners / Robin White.
p. cm.
Includes bibliographical references and index.
ISBN-13: 978-0-88192-752-8
ISBN-10: 0-88192-752-X
1. Daphnes. I. Title.
SB413.D25.W55 2006
583'.76--dc22
2005018825

A catalogue record for this book is also available from the British Library.

Previous page: *Daphne bholua* 'Alba'; opposite: *Daphne calcicola* 'Sichuan Gold'.

Contents

Foreword

This is a book that very many gardeners, particularly those with a keen interest in growing a wide range of daphnes in their gardens, have long awaited. However, it is certainly not a book for specialists but will have much wider appeal to gardeners generally, as it provides a very clear and detailed guide to all aspects of the cultivation of the wide range of species and hybrids of this beautiful and fascinating genus now available in the nursery trade.

Above all it is an intensely practical account based on the long experience of the author, whose acute observation of the growth, flowering characteristics and foibles of the many daphnes he has grown, as well as his great skill in their cultivation and propagation, have now been made available to gardeners in this well illustrated and very informative book on the genus.

Daphnes, in the past, have often been considered as somewhat unpredictable and sometimes perverse and moody garden plants but this reputation is, to a large extent, undeserved. Some, like *D. petraea*, require more attention to thrive than others, but few are very difficult to grow successfully in ordinary garden soil given the common courtesies one would afford to other shrubs, such as good drainage and adequate site preparation.

Robin White, apart from his reputation as a fine plantsman and nurseryman, is also well known as a very successful hybridizer, and during the last fifteen or more years has produced and introduced a considerable number of excellent garden plants including hellebores, epimediums and, of course, daphnes.

His aims in hybridizing have always been to ensure that any cultivars introduced by Blackthorn Nursery are vigorous, free-flowering garden plants with a good constitution that are tolerant of a wide range of soil conditions and may be propagated with relative ease. Breeding and selection of new *Daphne* cultivars is a long-term process involving careful choice of parent species as well as rigorous evaluation of the progeny to cull any seedlings that do not attain the high standards required by the breeder.

Robin White's success in achieving these aims with daphnes has been considerable, as may be judged by the range of first-rate cultivars of the hybrids *D.* ×*hendersonii*, *D.* ×*susannae*, *D.* ×*whiteorum* and *D.* ×*napolitana* that have been made available by Blackthorn Nursery during recent years.

While using the smaller species of *Daphne* as parents in his hybridization programme has been his main focus, Robin has also crossed some of the larger growing daphnes to good effect, including the much valued winter-flowering *D. bholua*. This is a parent of the recently introduced 'Spring Beauty' and 'Spring Herald', both of which show much promise as fine early-flowering shrubs for the future, as may be seen from the illustrations in this book.

It may be noted that in a number of instances the nomenclature of some of the hybrids is at variance with that given in the most recent monograph on the genus (Halda, 2001). The name *D.* ×*susannae* (*D. collina* × *D. arbuscula*) has been retained as it has not been possible to examine the type specimen on which the name *D.* ×*medfordensis* is based. It has not been located in the herbarium where it was deposited and, as it has been impractical to check whether the two taxa are identical, the name in current usage is maintained in this book.

In addition the names *D.* ×*rollsdorfii* (*D. collina* × *D. petraea*), *D.* ×*jintyae* (*D. petraea* × *D. rodriguezii*) and *D.* ×*latymeri* (*D. sericea* × *D. rodriguezii*) are preferred in this book. It has been possible to examine the type specimens of the three equivalent taxa, *D.* ×*kazbali*, *D.* ×*pudica* and *D.* ×*lepida*, which, it appears, pre-date the epithets used here. As these types do not match the type specimens of *D.* ×*rollsdorfii*, *D.* ×*jintyae*, and *D.* ×*latymeri* respectively, these latter names are used instead.

Robin White has very effectively blended his long experience of growing, propagating and observing daphnes in this excellent and very informative book that will prove an invaluable aid to all gardeners and will certainly stimulate further interest in cultivating this most attractive genus of garden plants. It will undoubtedly remain the standard work on daphnes and their cultivation for many years to come.

Chris Brickell C.B.E., V.M.H.
(former Director General of the RHS 1985-1993 and Director RHS Gardens, Wisley 1969-1985)

Preface

When I left school in 1961, I started work at a large, traditional nursery; their catalogue contained about 2500 items, mostly home-grown. By traditional I mean that the majority of the trees, shrubs and perennials were grown in the ground, to be lifted and sold between October and March. I started work in September, and was soon involved in the busy time of the lifting season which entailed digging up plants to fulfil orders and packing them for dispatch by post, road or rail. I was lucky to be made assistant to a man not far off retirement, who had been growing plants all his life. His name was Archibald Joyce: I knew him as "Arch"; he called me "young'un". All these plants with their Latin names were a mysterious new world to me, so I, keen to learn, bombarded Arch with questions which he was always patient and generally knowledgeable enough to answer.

At the nursery there were special areas enriched with manure and old potting compost, reserved for choice and difficult plants. When plants were dug from these areas they were given what in those days was considered star treatment by having their roots wrapped in burlap. Two of these stars always seemed to excite Arch especially—*Daphne odora* 'Aureomarginata' and *D. blagayana*—but to me, these spindly plants with only one or two branches seemed miserable specimens compared to the lusty, bushy plants we generally handled. However, it was noticeable that stocks of these plants sold quickly, so I wanted to know from Arch what was special about these daphnes. He said I should wait until spring and then he would show me. I had to walk past Arch's bungalow on my way to and from the nursery, and one sunny afternoon the following April, he suggested I call in to see his daphnes. Against the west side of the house was a superb plant of *D. odora* 'Aureomarginata', and in a shady spot a wide area of *D. blagayana*. The scent of the former is still my favourite, and I would always want a plant in my garden. Needless to say, I was very impressed and, later in the season, Arch showed me his wonderful plants of *D. collina* of gardens, *D. retusa* and *D. cneorum*. Compared to the earlier-flowering species, here was real flower power as well as scent, so I was hooked for life.

After three years at the nursery, I left to go to college and I never saw Arch again. I wish he were able to visit me today to see my daphnes; I can picture him now, pushing his cap back to scratch his head while answering one of my questions. Thank you Arch. I like to think that this book will kindle the interest of one or two "young'uns" who will learn to grow these wonderful plants better than I do, and in due course share their knowledge to all with another book on daphnes.

This book is by a grower of daphnes for the benefit of those who grow daphnes, to encourage those people who would like to grow daphnes, and to spread the word far and wide that these rewarding plants can be grown without undue difficulty. I have avoided getting too involved in botany and taxonomy as far as possible, and tried not to be too technical. I have done my best to include all the species and hybrids which would justify their place in a garden, conservatory or alpine house, but there are species in the Far East, China in particular, which may prove to be of merit if they can be introduced into cultivation; *D. macrantha* is top of my wants list.

I have been propagating and growing daphnes for nearly thirty years now, with varying degrees of success. Some problems have been solved; others have arisen and remain to be answered! Most of this book is written from my own experience, though where relevant, I have included outside information. All timing and methods of cultivation relate to my garden and nursery at Kilmeston in Hampshire, in southern England, unless stated otherwise. Since living here we have experienced a minimum temperature of –17°C (0°F) in 1986, but temperatures seldom drop below –10°C (14°F). Summer temperatures above 24°C (75°F) are higher than normal. The climate is essentially maritime with fluctuating winter temperatures and annual rainfall of around 635 MM.

My "Daphnetum"

I use this word to describe an area I have constructed principally to grow a selection of the smaller daphnes. I started work in late summer of 1999 on the sunny, southwest-facing slope of a mound which consisted largely of subsoil from our house foundations, grassed over since 1986. My decision to make the "daphnetum" was triggered by sharing a lorryload of tufa rock with Peter

The "daphnetum", mid-April 2004.

Erskine, a fellow daphne enthusiast who cultivates a wide range of alpines and regularly challenges my grafting skills with new introductions from Europe and Asia. He has used this material successfully in his West Sussex garden for many years. Until this point, our poor soil dictated that many of the small, choice daphnes were grown in raised beds in a polythene tunnel. The "daphnetum" is my first large-scale attempt at growing them in the garden; as such I shall refer to it regularly when writing on species and hybrids.

There are excellent articles on the use of tufa for growing alpine plants in the Alpine Garden Society bulletins (Erskine 1990 and Jans 1993). Tufa is formed from leached carbonates of calcium and magnesium accumulating in organic matter and hardening to form a porous rock of varying hardness. Holes chipped or drilled in this material make an excellent habitat for many alpine plants difficult to grow under more natural lowland conditions.

I used lumps of tufa rock cemented together to make the retaining wall at the bottom of the slope, and also to construct a gully about 30 cm wide running the length of the slope with a southwest to northeast orientation. Preparation of the ground consisted of removing the turf, which had been sprayed with glyphosate, a non-persistent herbicide, and putting it to one side. The ground was then dug over to a depth of 25–30 CM, removing the worst of the clay subsoil as I went. I then incorporated the chopped-up old turves and a generous quantity of old potting compost mixed with 1–6 MM grit. On top of this went a 12.5–15 CM layer of Cotswold limestone pea gravel that ranged in size from 6 to 12 MM, chosen primarily because it matched the greyish cream colour of the tufa. The tufa gully was filled with a free-draining mixture of loam, peat, grit and tufa chippings and topped with 2.5 CM of limestone pea gravel.

To date the project has proved fairly successful in growing daphnes and a range of alpines, the former mainly planted in the pea gravel, the latter in holes or cracks between tufa. One of the main problems to contend with is the fact that tall trees to the south and our house to the west shade the site when the sun is low in the sky from autumn to spring; this, coupled with our recent wet autumns and the fact that tufa holds water like a sponge, has resulted in dank, humid conditions, particularly in the gully, which have not been to the liking of *D. petraea* clones on their own roots and to a lesser extent *D. arbuscula* forms. Plants are defoliated by winter wet and have suffered dieback. In contrast, plants of these species planted clear of the gully have not suffered from leaf drop. These problems were noticeably improved in the drier autumn of 2003, so quite clearly they needed a more buoyant atmosphere. *Daphne blagayana* 'Brenda Anderson' and seedlings of *D. glomerata* have grown well in the shadier part of the gully, while *D. calcicola*, *D. juliae* and *D.* ×*thauma* do well in the sunnier part. The main open areas are a success: all the smaller species and hybrids have established and grown well.

Following the problems with *D. petraea* forms on their own roots in the gully, I decided to try a sunnier spot. Peter Erskine has had considerable success in growing *D. petraea* on its own roots by burying relatively small pieces of tufa so that the tops are just below surface level, with a gap of 5–7.5 CM between them. Young plants are then put into the gap. I have replicated this method with a selection of clones, and to date they are growing and flowering well. Peter has also grown *D. petraea* in lumps of tufa, both free-standing and placed in troughs, which have survived well for many years, making slow growth, but not flowering very freely. In an effort to improve on this I have made holes right through some of the tufa blocks of the retaining wall, and planted young specimens of *D. petraea* in the hope that they will establish in the tufa and then root into the richer soil of the main bed to make stronger-growing plants which will flower more freely.

I do not want to give the impression that the success of my "daphnetum" depended on the use of the tufa rock. Many of the plants are not in contact with it anyway. Tufa does have water-retentive properties that make it particularly suitable for use in troughs, but this property does make it unsuitable for areas which get prolonged, heavy frosts, as the expansion of water as it freezes in the tufa will cause a steady breakdown of the rock.

It is important to stress that all the daphnes in the main bed areas of the "daphnetum" are planted as young plants from 9 or 10 CM pots holding less than a litre of compost. They are therefore planted in pure pea shingle, which is not the easiest of operations, and firming is impossible. Careful watering is essential, but establishment is rapid, and examination of plants growing on their own roots has revealed wide-ranging horizontal roots throughout the pea shingle. I have to assume that roots have also grown downwards in order to benefit from the water and nutrients in the ground below the shingle.

As well as daphnes, many other plants are thriving in the pea shingle bed area of the "daphnetum", making me wish for much more space! These include varieties of corydalis, *Thalictrum orientale*, *Thalictrum tuberosum*, *Viola cazorlensis*, *Crocus goulimyi*, *Crocus banaticus* and various terrestrial orchids.

D. genkwa.
(Photo: John Fielding)

1 Taxonomy, History and Morphology

Taxonomy

The genus *Daphne*, as described by Linnaeus, belongs to the family Thymelaeaceae. Other genera of this family include *Dais*, *Edgeworthia*, *Pimelea*, *Stellera* and *Wikstroemia*. The genus contains about 70 species, all confined to the northern hemisphere, and mainly found in Europe and temperate and subtropical Asia. However, until a careful study is carried out, some confusion will continue to exist over the Chinese species in particular, and opinions also differ over the status of *D. collina* and *D. sericea*.

History

According to Greek mythology Daphne was a nymph who was changed into a tree to escape the attentions of the god Apollo. However, the plant known to the ancient Greeks as daphne was *Laurus nobilis*, the bay tree, the foliage of which was used for making victors' wreaths in their sporting contests. While the origin of the name daphne is generally considered to be Greek, it may be derived from an Indo-European source meaning "odour", in reference to the fragrant flowers (Brickell, Mathew 1976).

Daphne gnidium was certainly used in ancient Greece for its medicinal properties, while in the 17TH century herbalists such as Parkinson and Gerard refer to *D. mezereum*, *D. laureola* and *D. gnidium*. The fact that all parts of these plants are poisonous must have made their use in medicine rather hazardous.

By the middle of the 18TH century, species such as *D. alpina* and *D. pontica* were known, and from then on the list steadily grew, with species from the east such as *D. odora* and *D. genkwa* appearing in European gardens in the first half of the 19TH century. Further introductions by the plant hunters of the late 19TH and early 20TH centuries included *D. aurantiaca* and *D. tangutica*. Among the latecomers were *D. bholua*, *D. jasminea* and *D. jezoensis*.

Morphology

All members of the genus *Daphne* are shrubs. They range in habit from the prostrate, mat-forming *D. cneorum* to *D. bholua*, a tall, upright shrub which may reach 5 metres in height. The mature wood of many of the taller species is soft and pliable, resulting in growth prone to storm or snow damage. In contrast, the wood of small alpine species like *D. arbuscula*, *D. jasminea* and *D. petraea* is brittle.

Roots

Little study has been made of daphne roots. Compared with a wide range of other shrubs that I have grown in plastic pots, many daphnes are unusual in that their fine feeding roots attach themselves to the sides of the pot, to the extent that many are left stuck to it when the plants are turned out. Reasons for this characteristic remain to be discovered. It is noticeable that Asian species such as *D. bholua*, *D. longilobata* and *D. tangutica* produce a compact root system with relatively fleshy roots, while European species such as *D. arbuscula*, *D. cneorum* and *D. petraea* have a wide-ranging system of much finer roots. During the time I have grown them, I have known *D. bholua*, *D. genkwa*, *D. jezoensis* and *D. mezereum* to produce adventitious shoots from their roots.

Leaves

Daphnes may be true evergreens or deciduous, but some of the Asian species which are normally evergreen will drop their leaves in response to low temperatures. Some hybrids, particularly those between deciduous and evergreen species, are semi-evergreen. Leaves are sessile or shortly stalked. They are normally set alternately on the stem, but in *D. aurantiaca* and *D. genkwa* are usually opposite. All leaves are entire (with the exception of those of *D. rodriguezii*, which have small teeth at the apex) but they can vary considerably in shape (see Figure 1), even on the same plant of a species. Their surfaces range from intensely hairy to glabrous.

Figure 1: Leaf shapes and leaf tips

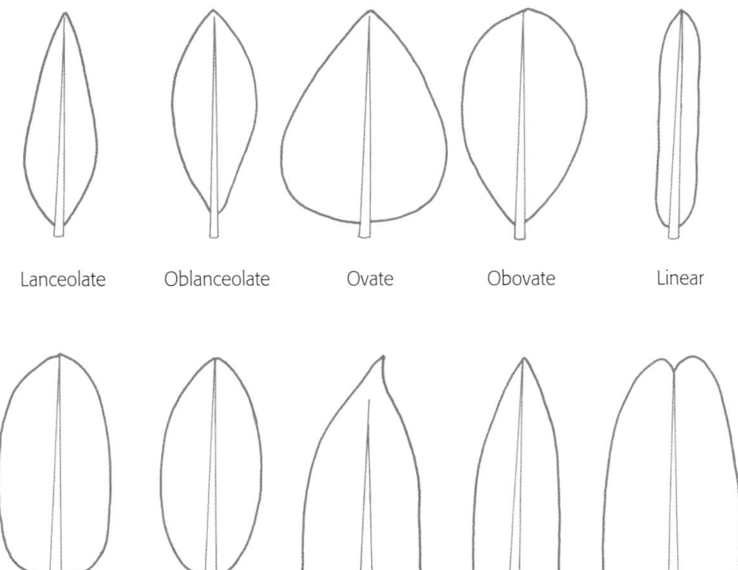

Flowers

The inflorescence may be terminal or axillary, and may be surrounded by an involucre of bracts that are often caducous, dropping off as the flowers develop. The flowers are generally hermaphrodite, but dimorphism may occur in some species, for example *D. jezoensis* and *D. laureola.* I have plants of the former species whose flowers have rudimentary stamens that do not produce pollen.

The individual flowers (see Figure 2, overleaf) do not have petals. Instead they consist of a fleshy tube made up from the calyx, referred to in this book as the perianth tube, which has four spreading lobes. The outer pair of lobes may be wider than the inner pair.

Flower colour may be creamy white, pink, rosy purple, yellow, green or lilac. The intensity of some flower colours can vary from year to year or within a season according to temperature and sunlight; the pinks of *D. petraea* are much deeper given cold night temperatures, while the white flowers of *D. arbuscula* f. *albiflora* soon acquire a pink flush under such conditions, but remain pure white when temperatures are higher later in the year. In most cases the flowers

Figure 2: Diagrammatic representation of a daphne flower

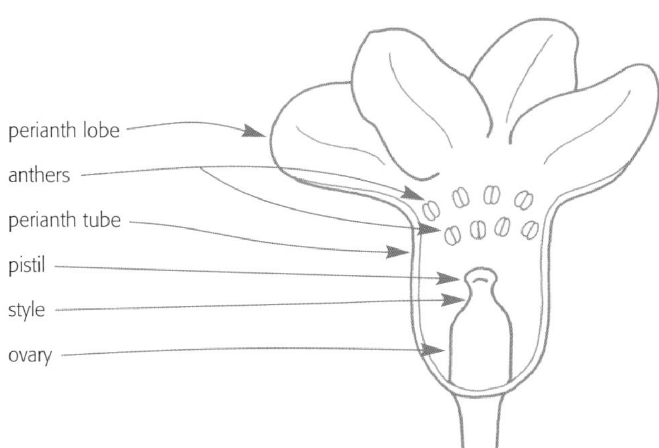

produced on the current season's growth as secondary or tertiary flushes lack the colour intensity of the first spring or early summer flush produced on the previous season's growth. Pink flowers usually turn darker with age, but the flowers of *D. petraea* turn paler and those of *D. sericea* mature to yellowish buff. The flowers are generally pleasantly scented, particularly towards evening, indicating that moths are their main pollinators.

The flower has eight stamens arranged in two whorls of four; the upper whorl may be exserted—protruding from the mouth of the perianth tube, or be inserted—set inside the top part of the tube. The ovary has a single ovule; the style is very short or lacking. The stigma is capitate.

Fertility

Many *Daphne* species are self-fertile to a varying degree. Solitary plants of *D. alpina*, *D. giraldii*, *D. longilobata* and *D. mezereum* set plenty of seed annually, while *D. acutiloba*, *D. caucasica* and *D. tangutica* generally produce a light seed crop. When grown under protection, most species do set seed almost every year, especially on flowers produced during the summer. Whether or not this is due to extra warmth or to the activity of moths, which are the main pollinators of daphne flowers, I am not sure—probably a combination of the two. Forms of *D. genkwa*, *D. jasminea* and *D. odora* that I grow do not seem to be self-fertile, but I have recently heard of a single plant of *D. genkwa* which regularly sets seed.

Fruits

The fruit is a drupe, sometimes surrounded by the dry remains of the perianth tube. The pericarp may be fleshy or dry. When adequate moisture is available, species such as *D. cneorum* and *D. sericea* may produce fruits with a fleshy pericarp which splits the dead calyx tube, but if water is scarce the fruit has a coriaceous pericarp and remains enclosed in the perianth tube. The colour of the fruits may be red, orange, yellow or blackish purple. All daphne fruits should be treated as poisonous to livestock and humans. Ingestion on a large scale is unlikely, however, since they taste bitter and cause a burning sensation in the mouth.

D. acutiloba CD&R 626 'Fragrant Cloud'.

2 *Daphne* Species

This chapter does not contain all *Daphne* species. With the exception of *D. macrantha*, I have omitted those which, as far as I know, are not available to gardeners in the United Kingdom or United States, and those which I think may be a disappointment to all but the most enthusiastic "daphnephile". However, I have included some which do not perform to their best in my garden, but may well prove useful and attractive plants in gardens with a warmer, drier climate than mine; to which end I have given US Department of Agriculture Hardiness Zones (see map, p. 22).

Detailed information on the recommended propagation techniques and cultivation requirements given in each description can be found in Chapters 4 and 5 respectively, while Chapter 6 contains advice on plant problems.

Daphne acutiloba Rheder

Introduced from China early in the 20TH century, this excellent evergreen shrub appears to have been neglected by gardeners, at least in the U.K., and in some cases has been confused with *D. longilobata* (a comparison of the main distinguishing features between the two species is made on page 74). In the early 1990s two introductions from western Sichuan by Compton, D'Arcy and Rix under the numbers CD&R 626 and 2500 were initially grown as *D.* aff. *acutiloba*. The noted Japanese botanist and plant explorer Mikinori Ogisu has had these plants confirmed as *D. acutiloba* by a Chinese botanist. I have therefore based this description on these two clones.

Daphne acutiloba is an evergreen shrub with an upright, bushy habit. Mature plants should reach 1–1.2 M in height and width. Young plants grow strongly, making 20–30 CM of growth in a season, and producing large leaves, 8–10 CM by

US Department of Agriculture Hardiness Zone Map

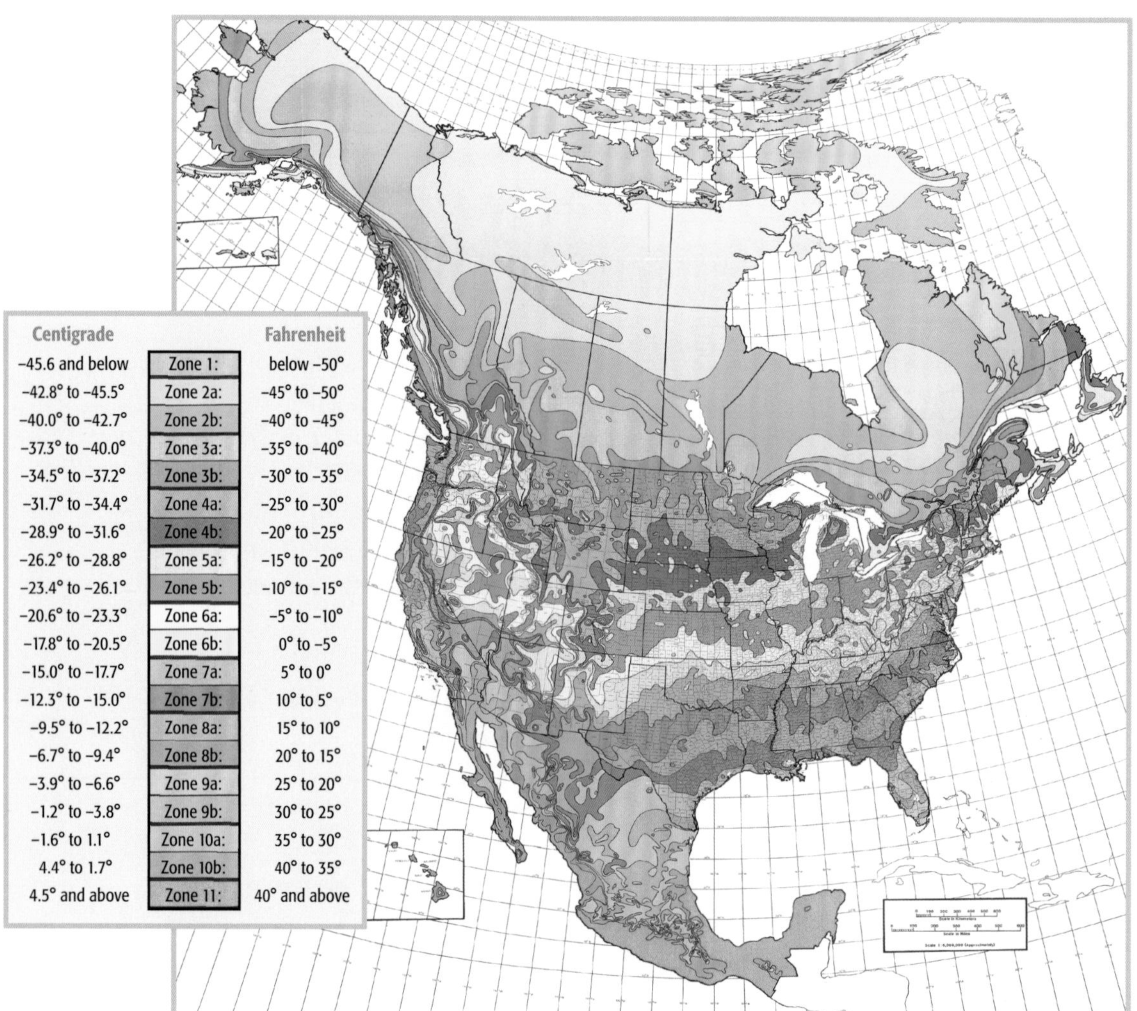

1.5–2 CM, lanceolate to oblanceolate in shape. Growth and leaf size reduce after two or three years. The mature bark is dark brown.

In the open the main flush of flowers is produced in April. The inflorescences are often axillary as well as terminal on strong-growing young plants, but mostly terminal as plants mature. The inflorescence is enclosed by caducous bracts and contains 6–10 flowers. The flower buds are pink-flushed on plants growing without protection, opening to creamy white, with a delicious scent, slightly more spicy than *D. odora*. Some flowers may be produced on new growth in June and July which do not have the substance of earlier blooms. The large, orange-red, elliptical fruits are rarely produced on plants in the garden, but seed is produced regularly by plants grown with protection.

The clone CD&R 626 has been given the cultivar name 'Fragrant Cloud'. It has grown in our garden for a number of years without trouble apart from damage to flowers by late spring frost. It should be given a site shaded from the hottest sun, and is likely to be intolerant of summer drought. This clone is definitely hardy to –12°C/10°F (Zone 8), but open flowers may be damaged by temperatures below –5°C (23°F).

To date this species has crossed with *D. arbuscula*, *D. bholua*, *D. collina* and *D.* aff. *sureil* to produce an interesting group of hybrids.

Propagation

Fresh-sown seed germinates the following spring. Semi-ripe tip cuttings taken in mid-July root well, but are slow to make a substantial plant. Plants grafted onto *D. longilobata* grow well, but need careful pinching to produce a well shaped plant.

D. alpina.

Daphne alpina L.

A small, deciduous shrub from the mountains of Europe, where it is usually found growing in limestone areas. This is a slow-growing plant, especially in the first few years from seed, when extension growth seldom exceeds 5 CM each year. The grey-green leaves are obovate in shape. In April and May terminal inflorescences of creamy white, fragrant flowers are freely produced, followed by generous quantities of orange fruits. Mature specimens may reach 45–60 CM in height and spread.

This is an easy species to grow in any open situation, and could be used more often as a dwarf shrub for the rock garden. In my experience it is tolerant of dry spells during summer, and a plant I saw growing in full sun on Monte Baldo in northern Italy would certainly have had to tolerate summer drought. Plants should be hardy to at least –23°C/–10°F (Zone 6).

Propagation

Seed is easy to germinate, but seedling growth is slow and young plants do not grow well in pots for me; they are best planted out after one season. Grafting produces a good plant in 2 or 3 years if *D. mezereum* is used as the rootstock.

Daphne arbuscula Celak.

All daphne enthusiasts aspire to grow this superb species well. It is native to the Muran Hills in Slovakia; a relatively small area, now a national park which is part of the Carpathian Mountains. Due to its restricted distribution of only 95 square kilometres, this species is considered endangered by industrial pollution, deforestation and collecting, so all plants growing in the wild are protected. *Daphne arbuscula* inhabits limestone areas; it can be found growing in crevices on cliffs or between rocks, in short turf, or among an assortment of alpine plants. The shallow soil seldom exceeds 10 CM in depth; it is humus-rich, with a pH (see p. 186) above 7.0. Plants can be found on both north- and south-facing slopes; the former have a more open, straggly habit and do not bloom so freely. North-facing plants may be covered by snow to the end of April, while south-facing ones may be clear of snow by the end of February.

The forms of *D. arbuscula* that I grow differ slightly in habit. One group has thinner stems which are lax enough to bend towards the horizontal, so branches which touch the ground readily layer themselves. Plants in this group make a flattened dome shape, 10–15 CM high, and mature plants may be 1 M or more across. The other group has sturdier, more rigid growth which results in a plant 15–20 CM high by 45–60 CM across; their leaves cluster towards the apex of the stem and expose more of their tan-coloured bark than the prostrate clones.

The leaves are generally dark, glossy green, but *D. arbuscula* f. *albiflora* and a pink-flowered form I received from the Munich garden of Joseph Mayr have a densely hairy upper surface which gives them a dull green appearance; these may correspond to *D. arbuscula* var. *hirsuta*, which Celakovsky described in 1890 when writing his original account of the species. The leaves are linear or linear-oblong in shape, and on cultivated plants range from 1 to 3 CM in length by 0.2–0.5 CM at their widest point.

The intensely fragrant flowers are always borne in terminal inflorescences which consist of 15–20 blooms. They vary in colour, from white through various shades of pink to deep rose. The colour of the flowers deepens as they

D. arbuscula growing wild in the Muran Hills, Slovakia.
(Photo: Peter Erskine)

D. arbuscula clones in a raised bed.

D. arbuscula thrives in Harry Jans' tufa columns (see p. 26).
(Photo: Harry Jans)

mature. The spring flush of flower can virtually obscure all foliage. Provided that plants are healthy and conditions favourable, a less generous display follows on new growth during the summer. *Daphne arbuscula* f. *albiflora* and 'Diva' are noticeably later to flower than other clones of this species.

Some seed is set every year on the summer flowers of plants grown under protection. The seed remains encased in the dry brown perianth tube until nearly ripe, when the slightly fleshy pericarp, creamy yellow in colour, may swell enough to split it. I believe that the pericarp of fruits that develop on plants grown outdoors has some red coloration that is not apparent on plants under glass or polythene.

Although I have grown *D. arbuscula* successfully in clay pots, either plunged in a sand bed in a polythene tunnel or stood on benching in a glasshouse heavily shaded in summer, my best plants grow in a raised bed two railway sleepers high in a polythene tunnel; most of these are grafted on *D. tangutica*. Until I made my "daphnetum" (see p. 10), I found plants on their own roots difficult to grow in pots or establish in the open, but since 2000 several clones have grown well in the Cotswold pea shingle. The one problem these open-ground plants suffer is partial leaf fall in late autumn, which I have put down to the incessant rain keeping the foliage too damp. I suspect that in their natural habitat they are either kept dry under snow, or a buoyant atmosphere dries leaves quickly after rain. In Holland, Harry Jans, expert grower of a wide range of alpines, is growing *D. arbuscula* very successfully in his columns of tufa; these receive a steady supply of moisture during the growing season via an irrigation system.

Reports suggest that these plants are intolerant of high temperatures in dry conditions. Plants seem tolerant of semi-shade, but their growth habit becomes noticeably more open and flower production is reduced. Apart from some frost scorch to late, unripened growth, I have never seen any damage from cold weather to my plants. This species should be hardy to at least –23°C/–10°F (Zone 6), but snow cover would be an important factor in determining survival in prolonged periods of frost.

Propagation

Most freshly sown seed will germinate the following spring, and a secondary germination may occur if the pot is kept for another year. Semi-ripe basal cuttings taken in June root quickly in a very well drained and aerated compost, allowing them to be potted up and established before winter. Ripewood cuttings of the previous season's growth will also root, but more slowly. This is one of the easiest species to layer; stems that layer themselves naturally always produce their roots from the basal area of the previous season's growth, so this would be the point to pin down to encourage root production. Plants grafted on *D. longilobata* or *D. mezereum* do not grow as well as those on *D. tangutica*. I have also grafted scions of selected clones on rooted cuttings of *D. arbuscula* ex. Sladhova (see p. 29).

Botanical variants and named clones

Daphne arbuscula forma *albiflora* Halda

This form has a prostrate habit. The leaves appear dull green, due to the densely pubescent upper surface, and the bark a grey-brown colour for the same reason. The flowers are pure white when first open, but may become tinged with pink as they age, particularly under cold conditions. After the main spring flush, flowers are freely produced on new summer growth. I do not find it as easy to grow as some of the pink-flowered clones, particularly on its own roots.

Daphne arbuscula forma *grandiflora* Halda

No plant has come to me under this name, but a clone from Slovakia and the clone from Kath Dryden, which originated from Hillier Nurseries and won her three Farrer medals from the Alpine Garden Society, are similar to each other, and correspond to the description in having large flowers up to 2 CM in diameter with perianth lobes 0.5 CM wide. The buds are noticeably crimson before opening to a clear rose pink, ageing to dark rose-purple. The habit is more compact and upright than all other forms. This is always the first clone into flower by several days.

Daphne arbuscula forma *platyclada* Halda

This is perhaps a plant for botanical interest rather than a competitor to the more natural forms. The stems are fasciated and the foliage is bright, glossy green. The plant has a dense, upright habit similar to that of a dwarf conifer. This plant was kindly given to me by Jochen Herdramm, a keen grower of daphnes from Dortmund who has many gardening friends in Slovakia, and I grew it for several years without a flower appearing, but in 2004 bloom was produced. There must have been well in excess of 100 flowers in the inflorescence, but they did not all open together, various areas developing separately. Flower colour is mid-pink. Propagation by grafting a long, narrow wedge of fasciated material is fairly straightforward if raffia is used to bind the graft.

D. arbuscula f. *albiflora*.

D. arbuscula f. *platyclada*.

D. arbuscula 'Muran Pride'.

D. arbuscula f. *grandiflora*.
Mature flowers are deeper pink.

D. arbuscula ex. Sladhova.

D. arbuscula 'Diva' (JJ86).

Daphne arbuscula ex. Sladhova

Over the years I have received what appears to be the same form of *D. arbuscula* from several different sources, so I think of it as the "type" form, corresponding to the Celakovsky description. It has a rather lax habit and small, glossy, dark green leaves, 1.5 CM long by 0.2 CM wide. The lilac-pink flowers are freely produced on both old and new growth; they are slightly smaller than those of other named forms, with a diameter of up to 1.4 CM, and perianth lobes 0.4–0.5 CM wide.

Daphne arbuscula 'Muran Pride'

This is a distinctive clone with the largest leaves of all, measuring 3 CM by 0.5 CM, and thick, rigid stems which give the plant an upright habit. The leaves are clustered near the tips of the new growth, exposing large areas of the reddish-brown bark. The mid-pink flowers are large—up to 2 CM in diameter when mature, with broad perianth lobes up to 0.7 CM wide. The tips of the perianth lobes are more rounded than in f. *grandiflora* or 'Diva'.

Daphne arbuscula 'Diva'

This clone from what was then Czechoslovakia was given to me by Harry Jans in 1994. For ten years I have grown and sold it under the number JJ86, assuming this was a collection reference given by Czech alpine grower Joseph Jurasek. However, during a trip to Slovakia in 2004, Peter Erskine ascertained that Mr. Jurasek had no knowledge of this plant and certainly had no objection to my providing it with a cultivar name. After growing a number of clones together in my "daphnetum", I think this is my favourite.

The habit is prostrate, with deep green, glossy leaves. The flowers are large, with a diameter of 2 CM and with perianth lobes 0.6–0.7 CM wide. The rosy purple buds open to pale rose pink blooms which are freely produced over the whole plant. The contrast between the colour of the bud and that of the open flower is especially good. This is the latest clone to flower, and so might be the best choice for areas prone to late spring frosts.

Daphne aurantiaca Diels. (*D. calcicola* W. W. Smith)

Two forms, one vigorous and one compact, of this fascinating, yellow-flowered species native to the Chinese provinces of Yunnan and Sichuan were recorded in the early part of the 20TH century. The former was named *D. aurantiaca*, the latter *D. calcicola*. Only *D. aurantiaca* survives in cultivation from these early collections, although the fact that it is slightly tender, with a very lax habit, has prevented it from becoming popular.

Now that these areas of China have become more accessible and numerous botanists and enthusiasts have been able to see both vigorous and compact plants together with ones of intermediate habit, all growing in close proximity, confusion and controversy surround these two names. While at present the Flora of China includes *D. calcicola* in *D. aurantiaca*, I have grown *D. aurantiaca* in the glasshouse for many years in its lax, vigorous form, and I do not consider it garden-worthy. Therefore, without wanting to state a botanical opinion,

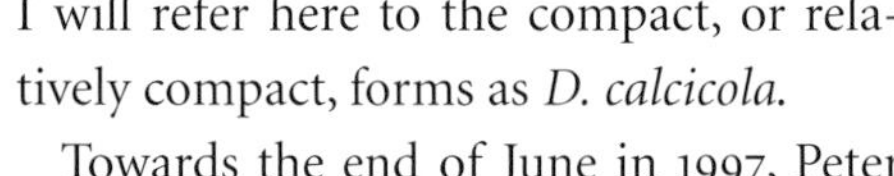

I will refer here to the compact, or relatively compact, forms as *D. calcicola*.

D. calcicola in the wild, Gang Ho Ba valley, Sichuan. (Photo: Peter Erskine)

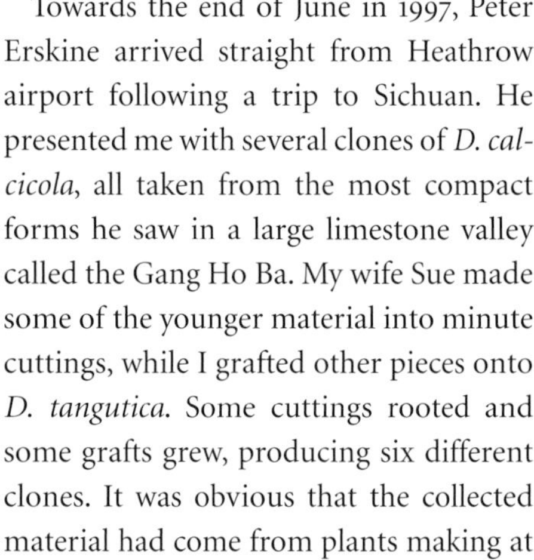

Towards the end of June in 1997, Peter Erskine arrived straight from Heathrow airport following a trip to Sichuan. He presented me with several clones of *D. calcicola*, all taken from the most compact forms he saw in a large limestone valley called the Gang Ho Ba. My wife Sue made some of the younger material into minute cuttings, while I grafted other pieces onto *D. tangutica*. Some cuttings rooted and some grafts grew, producing six different clones. It was obvious that the collected material had come from plants making at most 2.5 CM of growth each year; however, rooted cuttings and grafts started to grow strongly, making lax growth similar to my plants of *D. aurantiaca*. This continued despite growing the plants in a diluted alpine type of compost quite low in nutrients, so regular pinching back of growth was needed to produce anything resembling a bushy habit.

In the following years it was interesting to see that small new shoots were sprouting from the rather bare basal areas of plants on their own roots, and one plant was suckering from the root. It is to be hoped, therefore, that as plants age and reduce in vigour, they will develop the tight, bushy habit of those wonderful plants photographed in the wild. In the open, plants on their own roots have survived several winters with a minimum temperature recorded of –12°C (10°F). There is generally a considerable amount of unripened wood at the end of the current season's growth which does get damaged by the first sharp frosts of the winter. In an effort to improve the ripening process before winter I have sited plants to grow over tufa rock in the hope that the reflected heat will help.

It seems that many "daphnephiles" are keen to grow this species in character, so it may be helpful to know more about its natural habitat. I am grateful to Professor D. Rankin, of the University of Edinburgh's Chemistry Department, for the following information, gained in his research into the relationship between plants and soil in Yunnan: where *D. calcicola* grows in the Gang Ho Ba valley the virtually white soil is very fine limestone silt (not dolomite) with very small amounts of organic material, mainly as surface litter. The subsoil has a pH of 8.4 (the maximum possible with limestone). A pH of 6.6 was recorded for the root zone of a daphne site, indicating that a small amount of organic material was present. Growing in the conditions described by Professor Rankin, it is possible that lack of one or more essential nutrients, or the high pH hindering their uptake, may be the reason for the very slow growth and resulting compact habit of the plants.

D. calcicola, developing seed.

Daphne calcicola is an evergreen shrub. Unlike most daphnes, the dull green leaves are in opposite pairs; they are variable in shape and size. Areas of young bark exposed to sun are reddish purple, particularly when grown in the open; this matures to light tan. The bright yellow flowers, borne in pairs, may be axillary or terminal and are produced as growth is made, which on cultivated plants, particularly under protection, may be for seven months. Clones appear to vary in the intensity of flower fragrance; I would describe the scent as pleasant but pungent, not sweet, rather like some air fresheners. The fruit has a very thin, greenish yellow pericarp and remains enclosed in the dead perianth tube until ripe. During the winter months the leaves of some clones change colour from green to greenish purple. Experience to date suggests clones in cultivation should be hardy to at least –12°C/10°F (Zone 8).

Propagation

None of my plants, whether under glass or in the open, sets seed on a regular basis. As far as I know, collections of seed made by The Alpine Garden Society in the 1990s failed to germinate, but Professor Rankin reports a good germination on the small amount of seed he managed to collect. Cuttings are very slow to root; soft material appears to react badly to hormone powders. The best results I have had were from tip cuttings taken in February from plants under polythene shelter. *Daphne tangutica* and *D. laureola* seem to be the best species for using as a rootstock; there may be partial incompatibility when *D. calcicola* is grafted on *D. mezereum* or *D. longilobata.*

Named clones

In 2000 I selected and named what I felt were the two best clones of the material received in 1997 from the Gang Ho Ba.

Daphne calcicola 'Gang Ho Ba'

Selected on the basis of having the largest leaves, oblong to ovate in shape and measuring 1–1.5 CM by 0.8 CM, and the largest flowers, with a perianth tube 1 CM long, the mouth of flower 1–1.2 CM in diameter, flower lobes 0.4–0.5 CM wide. Young leaves dull, glaucous green, mature leaves dark green. Young stems crimson-brown where exposed to sunlight, older bark is tan in colour. Difficult to grow in character; new growth needs constant pinching. Cuttings root more readily than those of 'Sichuan Gold' (see facing page).

D. calcicola 'Sichuan Gold'.

D. calcicola 'Sichuan Gold' three years after planting in the "daphnetum".

Daphne calcicola 'Sichuan Gold'

Selected because it seems the clone most likely to make a compact plant of bushy habit, and for its freedom of flowering. A plant I grow in a 25 CM pot under glass starts flowering in March, producing a main flush in April and July, but it has seldom been without flower from March to October over the last few years. Leaves are small, linear in shape, 1 × 0.4 CM. The flowers are much smaller than those of 'Gang Ho Ba'—perianth tube 1 CM long, mouth of flower 0.7–0.9 CM in diameter, flower lobes 0.3 CM wide. Young stems are purple-brown where exposed to sunlight. Older bark is tan.

Daphne bholua Buch. Ham. ex. D. Don

Introductions in the second half of the 20TH century have resulted in hardier forms of this Himalayan species becoming more widely available. Not surprisingly, the fact that its flowers with their superb fragrance are produced in the darkest days of winter has led to a surge in popularity, and several clones have been named. Introductions from areas of high altitude by Major Spring-Smyth and Sir Peter Smithers have been particularly significant in producing the most popular varieties.

In the wild *D. bholua* grows in woodland areas subject to monsoon rains. It flowers in the early part of the year for several months. Once the fruits ripen and fall, germination is rapid in order to coincide with the monsoon rains; these provide ideal growing conditions for the young seedlings to make sturdy young plants before the dry, cold winter. *Daphne bholua* is variable in habit, leaf and flower. In the wild plants reach 3–5 M, but in cultivation 2–3 M is more likely. They may be columnar or bushy in shape; high-altitude forms tend to be more deciduous than those from lower levels, but forms considered to be evergreen in mild areas may prove to be deciduous if subjected to lower temperatures.

The narrowly elliptic to oblanceolate leaves vary in size from 4 to 10 CM long, by 1–2.5 CM wide. Although there are reports of plants with variegated leaves in the wild, I am not aware that any are yet in cultivation. Flowers are generally produced in terminal clusters of 8–15, but vigorous growth, particularly of young, grafted plants, bears axillary inflorescences which open as the terminal ones fade, so prolonging the flowering season. No flowers are produced on the current season's growth. Flower colour varies from white to rosy purple. The large, black fruits are seldom produced in the open in the United Kingdom, but are set quite readily on plants flowering under cover, especially if more than one clone is present.

Like most monsoon plants, *D. bholua* needs a steady supply of moisture during the growing season. It flourishes best in deep soil enriched with organic matter. The pH does not seem to matter, but shallow chalky soils or light sandy soils which will get very dry in summer are unsuitable. Choose a site protected from sun during the warmer times of the day, and out of strong winds—young growth is lax and can easily snap off at the point of origin with older wood. A combination of high wind and rain is most likely to cause serious damage.

Although some cultivars have a bushier habit than others, most healthy young plants of *D. bholua* produce long, lax, unbranched extension growth which can result in a plant of leggy appearance, prone to weather damage. Pruning rather than pinching out the growing point can encourage a sturdy, bushier plant; long shoots should be reduced by about half their length, no later than halfway through the growing season. Even with this intervention, support may be needed for young plants in windy areas.

It is normal for *D. bholua* to drop most of its older leaves shortly after flowering, as new growth commences. This does cause concern to people who have recently purchased and planted flowering specimens, but there is no need to worry about this natural cycle.

When grown in the United Kingdom's climate *D. bholua* is one of the species most likely to be surprised by the first sharp frost of winter, but hotter summers and a gradual progression to cold night temperatures would no doubt help to prevent this. Frost scorch to unripened terminal growth and some leaf drop are the type of damage caused. Fortunately, the inflorescences seem more resistant to low temperatures, and frosts which may damage open flowers leave the unopened buds unscathed, ready to develop during the next mild spell. The hardier cultivars should be tolerant of temperatures down to –17°C/0°F (Zone 7). In harsher climates several years of pleasure will be provided if a plant is container-grown outside for the summer and moved under cover for the colder months.

Propagation

Since the seed has a short period of viability it should be sown as soon after harvest as possible and given gentle heat. Germination should be complete in six to eight weeks. Seed-grown plants flower after three or four years. Cuttings from 'Alba' and 'Darjeeling' are the only clones I have had consistent success in rooting. The most successful cuttings are those taken in mid-July, when the basal growth is ripe and the terminal bud has just formed; however, they are quite slow to root. All clones seem to grow vigorously grafted onto *D. longilobata* or

D. mezereum. Daphne bholua seedlings could also be used as rootstocks. A good plant with one or two strong shoots can be produced in one growing season from January grafting, but it is difficult to produce a well-branched plant in less than two seasons, because pinching out the growing point of a single stem does not reliably stimulate branching.

Botanical variants and named clones

Daphne bholua 'Alba'

The origin of this clone is uncertain, and the Latin cultivar name is invalid. My original plant came from a Cornish nursery in the early 1980s. It may be the white-flowered clone grown in the gardens of Windsor Great Park from seed collected in the early 1960s by plant enthusiast Dr. Herklots. This was given the cultivar name of 'Sheopuri', after the mountains in Nepal where the fruiting plants grew. However, a plant of 'Sheopuri' which received an award in 1973 had flowers with uneven-sized perianth lobes, and the lobes of 'Alba' are even in size and shape. The leaves are distinct from other clones I have seen, being narrow, dark green and glossy. The habit is bushier than in other forms, with 4–12 blooms per inflorescence. The buds and perianth tube are palest pink with white perianth lobes, 0.8–1 CM by 0.5 CM. The flowering period is January to March.

Daphne bholua 'Darjeeling'

Probably the oldest clone in general cultivation, distributed in the late 1970s from the Royal Horticultural Society Gardens at Wisley. The habit is fairly

D. bholua 'Alba'.

D. bholua 'Darjeeling'.

bushy, with 5–12 blooms per inflorescence. Both the buds and flowers are pale pink, with narrow perianth lobes, 1–1.2 CM by 0.4–0.5 CM. The scented flowers are produced from November to January, making it a valuable addition to a daphne collection.

Daphne bholua var. *glacialis* (Smith & Cave) B. L. Burt

The plant introduced under the number TSS132B by Major Spring-Smyth in 1962 seems to be referable to this variety. Seed was collected on the Milke Dhanra ridge, Nepal, at around 3200 M. This clone has been given the cultivar name 'Gurkha', and should be most tolerant of low temperatures. It is deciduous when subjected to temperatures much below –10°C (14°F), but it has been wrongly stated that if a plant is not completely deciduous, it will not be true to name. The deciduous habit is less pronounced in vigorous young plants with unripened wood, and my stock plant growing in a polythene tunnel keeps leaves towards the apex of its stems unless subjected to low temperatures. The habit is upright, creating a columnar shape; the bark of mature wood is distinct in its bright tan colour. Mauve-purple buds open to flowers that are pale pink on the inside. Flowering period is January to March.

Daphne bholua 'Jacqueline Postill'

A form chosen by Alan Postill from a batch of seedlings raised from a plant of 'Gurkha' growing in the Hillier Arboretum and named after his wife. It was picked out because it was more evergreen than its siblings. This is the most widely available variety of this species and has proved a valuable addition to winter displays in many gardens. It appears to have inherited the hardiness of the seed parent, and is probably the hardiest evergreen form of this species in cultivation. The flowers are similar to those of 'Gurkha', with 12–15 blooms per inflorescence, and purplish-pink perianth lobes, 1–1.1 CM by 0.8 CM. Flowering period is January to March.

Daphne bholua 'Peter Smithers'

Since the early 1970s Sir Peter Smithers has successfully grown *D. bholua* in his Swiss garden of Vico Morcote. His plants were raised from seed he collected in the Daman Ridge area of Nepal. Seed from Sir Peter's plants was sent to Wakehurst Gardens, a subsidiary of the Royal Botanic Gardens, Kew, where a large number of seedlings were grown and planted in the Himalayan valley area. In 1990, Tony Schilling allowed me to take material for grafting from several of the

D. bholua 'Jacqueline Postill'.

D. bholua 'Peter Smithers'.

D. bholua SCH 2611 'Rupina La'.

D. blagayana.

plants; one in particular had very dark, rosy purple flower buds and lilac-pink perianth lobes, with up to 25 flowers per inflorescence. In 2000 this clone was shown to the Royal Horticultural Society Floral Committee B, who gave it an Award of Merit and named it after the donor of the seed to Wakehurst. Flowering period is January to March.

Daphne bholua 'Rupina La'

This very distinctive clone was collected by Tony Schilling in 1983 with the number SCH 2611 in the Gurkha Himalaya, Central Nepal. When I saw it in the winter garden at Wakehurst in 1990, there were lines of suckers shooting up from the main roots. The main stems were much thicker than in any other clone I have seen. The large leaves are 10–12.5 CM long by 2.5–3 CM wide and the bark is pubescent and pale greyish-brown. The dusky pink flowers are much larger than in any other form I have grown, with a diameter of 3.5–4 CM and a very pubescent perianth tube. The perianth lobes have jagged edges and may be curled inwards or outwards; they measure up to 1.5 CM by 0.4–0.6 CM. There are up to 25 blooms per inflorescence. It would be interesting to know if the chromosome number differs from normal, as unlike all other clones, it has never set any seed.

Grown without protection, this variety was deciduous at Wakehurst; however, the original plant was almost killed by cold weather, and I have yet to try growing a plant in the garden because of this. Grown with protection, plants retain some foliage. This first-rate plant is well worth trying to grow outdoors in mild areas, and spectacular enough to warrant space in a conservatory. The flowering period is January to March.

Daphne blagayana Freyer

This excellent species from southeastern Europe has been in cultivation since the second half of the 19TH century. In the wild it is generally found growing on limestone in alpine or sub-alpine areas, often in light woodland. The long, prostrate stems naturally become buried by leafmould over the years, enabling the plant to layer itself. Thus, given room, cultivated specimens may cover a wide area while not exceeding 30 CM in height. The evergreen foliage, dark glaucous green in colour, is clustered near the tip of the current season's growth, forming a rosette for the terminal inflorescence which is enclosed in conspicuous, pale green, caducous bracts. There are 20–30 flowers in each inflorescence, creamy white in colour with a superb fragrance similar to narcissus. Records suggest that there may be forms with pale pink flowers.

The normal flowering period is March and April, but due to the fluctuating temperatures of our maritime climate, the time of flowering may vary considerably from year to year; the inflorescence is well developed from early winter, so a mild spell of weather from the turn of the year onwards stimulates blossom; however, these early flowers seem vulnerable to frost damage, followed by fungal infection which may destroy the whole inflorescence. I have only known seed to be set on plants under glass; the translucent, greyish white pericarp remained enclosed in the dead perianth tube.

To keep an individual plant of *D. blagayana* looking good is not at all easy. Top-dressing its prostrate stems with a friable mixture such as leafmould or old potting compost does encourage self-layering and helps to hide bare stems. I suggest a better effect is achieved by interplanting with species which like similar conditions: dwarf ferns such as *Adiantum venustum* or *Adiantum aleuticum* 'Subpumilum'; *Cyclamen hederifolium*; *Hepatica* species and *Erica carnea* forms are just a few suggestions. It is most important to get the balance of light correct; shade that is too deep will result in weak growth and little or no blossom. Sunshine at the hottest part of the day, particularly combined with dryness at the roots, is resented.

Dieback of the stems needs to be watched for. This is generally caused when floral bracts or dead flowers fail to fall away and become infected by *Botrytis cinerea* (see p. 213). Since new growth arises from the base of the inflorescence, this type of infection can quickly kill small plants. The leaves, buds and flowers of this species are particularly vulnerable to attack by slugs and snails. *Daphne blagayana* can be considered hardy to at least –20°C/–4°F (Zone 6), and will probably survive lower temperatures when snow cover is present.

Propagation

Provided they can be kept free of fungal infection, soft tip cuttings root well. I favour semi-ripe tip cuttings taken towards the end of July. This species is made for layering. 'Brenda Anderson' (see below) grows well grafted on *D. longilobata.*

Named clones

Daphne blagayana 'Brenda Anderson'

Compact forms of *Daphne blagayana* have been recorded in the 20TH century, particularly a clone named 'Wells Variety', but none seemed to be in commerce until recently. A few years ago, plants started to appear under the name *D. blagayana* 'Nana', an invalid name. The origin of this form has been traced to a collection in 1975 by the late Brenda Anderson, a noted Scottish plantswoman, who found this plant in Bosnia on a large mountain southeast of Sarajevo called Durmitor. As 'Nana' is not a valid cultivar name, I have suggested that this excellent form be re-named 'Brenda Anderson'. After several years growing in my "daphnetum", where it is shaded from the midday sun by a large piece of tufa, I can vouch that this is a real improvement on the typical form in terms of habit, remaining relatively compact because annual extension growth is 3.5–6 CM compared with the 10–15 CM of the standard form. The inflorescence of 'Brenda Anderson' has 25–40 flowers compared to 20–30 for the standard form. The blooms are often open by mid-February, and seem less prone to frost damage. Unfortunately, the large number of flowers per inflorescence does encourage fungal infection in damp, mild conditions. I think this is a much better plant for the average rock garden than the typical *D. blagayana*, and it would also look good in a trough or similar container.

D. blagayana 'Brenda Anderson'.

D. caucasica.

D. altaica.

Daphne caucasica Pallas and *Daphne altaica* Pallas

Plants I have grown for a number of years under the names of *D. caucasica* and *D. altaica* are similar in many respects apart from vigour, the former being a taller plant. (And although I have never managed to obtain plants of *D. sophia* or *D. taurica*, a description of *D. caucasica* should also give a good idea of what these two species are like.)

As its name suggests, *D. caucasica* comes from the Caucasus Mountains and parts of Asia Minor, where it is generally found growing on the edge of deciduous woodland. Deciduous itself, it has an erect habit, and may reach 1.5–2 M in height. In the garden *D. altaica* has a bushier habit and has not exceeded 1.3 M. In the dormant season, another noticeable difference is the well-developed, pale green bud scales of *D. altaica*, compared to the smaller, brownish red ones of *D. caucasica*. The latter's pale green, narrow leaves measure 5–8 CM by 1–1.4 CM at their widest and have a willowy appearance; the leaves of *D. altaica* are broader and shorter.

In late April and May both species bear pure white flowers on short lateral shoots produced from the previous season's growth. They have a very characteristic, sweet scent which has been passed on to the hybrids that *D. caucasica* is parent to. A few terminal inflorescences are produced in late summer on the current season's growth. Although *D. caucasica* is known to set plentiful seed in cultivation, my clone seems reluctant to do so on a regular basis, but does have occasional fruits which slowly progress through shades of red to finish purple-black.

Daphne caucasica does not seem demanding in its requirements, but would no doubt resent hot, dry conditions, while deep shade will result in spindly growth and poor flower production. Care should be taken to encourage a strong, bushy habit in the first few seasons to reduce the chances of snow or wind damage. Young growth of *D. caucasica* is prone to attack from slugs and snails. Both this species and *D. altaica* are very hardy and should survive temperatures as low as –29 to –34°C/–20 to –30°F (Zone 4) (Ward 2002).

Propagation

Fresh-sown seed of *D. caucasica* germinates readily the following spring, and young plants are not difficult to grow in containers. A substantial plant can be produced in three years. Semi-ripe cuttings have not rooted for me, but softwood cuttings should root better under mist or fogging conditions. Plants grow well grafted on stocks of *Daphne longilobata* or *D. mezereum*; the grafts need careful hardening off because the soft growth is very vulnerable to dehydration.

Many plants grown in the United States under the name *D. caucasica* are in fact a hybrid between *D. caucasica* and *D. collina* which has been given the name *D.* ×*transatlantica* 'Jims Pride', and is described in the chapter on hybrids (see p. 149).

Daphne circassica Woronov ex. Pobed.

Seed of this interesting species from the Caucasus Mountains has only been available since the mid 1990s, but my experiences so far are promising. From my plants I estimate that *D. circassica* will make a well-shaped, bushy plant, 20–30 CM high and 30–60 CM wide. Naturally occurring in alpine areas, this species is evergreen, with dull, glaucous green leaves. The fragrant, rosy-purple flowers are freely produced in April to May, in terminal inflorescences on the previous season's growth. Good-quality flowers are also produced on new growth in succession as summer progresses. The flowers hold their colour well as they mature, even when the weather is sunny. The fleshy fruits are yellowish orange.

D. circassica.

To date, both plants on their own roots and ones grafted on *D. longilobata* have grown well planted in the open and in containers under polythene. I think that this plant will be a welcome addition to gardens, but it may be used to plenty of water from snowmelt during the growing season, so drought tolerance is doubtful.

Of the two plants I raised from wild-collected seed, kindly given to me by alpine plant expert Robert Rolfe, one was definitely superior in quantity and quality of flower; it is possible therefore that there are more distinct or better forms yet to be found in the wild. There are reports of hybrids in the wild between *D. circassica* and *D. glomerata*. I estimate that *D. circassica* will be hardy in temperatures down to –23°C/–10°F (Zone 6).

Propagation

Fresh-sown seed germinates well the following spring. Semi-ripe basal or tip cuttings root easily. Plants I have grafted on *D. mezereum* or *D. longilobata* have grown well.

D. cneorum in the wild, Monte Baldo, northern Italy. (Photo: Peter Erskine)

Daphne cneorum L.

Daphne cneorum has been cultivated since at least the mid-18TH century, and there are records of it being grown as a cut flower, which may explain the origin of its common name of "garland flower". Having been in cultivation for so long, it is not surprising that *D. cneorum* is one of the best known and most sought-after daphnes, particularly the cultivars 'Eximea' in the United Kingdom and 'Ruby Glow' in the United States. However, this species is regarded as difficult to container-raise for sale by nurserymen; fewer than 30 suppliers of 'Eximea' are listed in an up-to-date edition of the *RHS Plant Finder*, so plants may not be easy to obtain.

This species is distributed over a large area of Europe, from France, northern Spain and Italy north to Slovakia, Poland and Hungary. Wherever I have seen *D. cneorum* growing in the wild it has been a semi-prostrate, trailing plant, occasionally scrambling up its neighbours to reach 30–40 CM in height. Prostrate, relatively dwarf forms can be found above the treeline growing through alpine turf, while lower down, more vigorous forms ramble through low scrub consisting of plants such as erica, polygala, juniper and vaccinium. In these situations plants may layer themselves and spread over a wide area.

In cultivation, vigorous clones can reach 30 CM in height by 2 M in width, while dwarf clones may be 45–60 CM wide and virtually prostrate. The evergreen leaves are variable in size; measurements taken from plants growing in close proximity under the same conditions give figures of 1.7 CM long by 0.3 CM wide for the cultivar 'Velky Kosir' compared to 0.8 CM long by 0.2 CM wide for *D. cneorum* var. *pygmaea.* The leaves are generally oblanceolate in shape, but the apex may be obtuse or apiculate. Forms from northern Italy such as 'Benaco' and 'Leila Haines' have narrowly linear-oblong leaves averaging 1.5 CM by 0.2 CM; this could be an adaptation to dry summer conditions, so on their own roots these cultivars may be more suitable for hot, dry areas. Leaf colour is generally dark green, but 'Lac des Gloriettes' has foliage with a definite bluish shade. The bracts enclosing the inflorescence also vary in colour from green to orange-red.

The flowers are generally borne in dense terminal clusters, but strong growth made in the previous season can produce axillary inflorescences towards the apex of the stem; 'Benaco' and 'Velky Kosir' in particular tend to do this. There are 6–20 strongly fragrant flowers per inflorescence; they may vary in colour from very pale pink through bright rose pink to reddish pink, and occasionally white. The colour deepens as the flowers mature. The profusion of flower on a healthy plant virtually hides the foliage. Most clones do not repeat-flower, but strong-growing juvenile plants produce the odd inflorescence on the current season's growth, and 'Blackthorn Triumph' can be quite free-flowering on new summer shoots. There is considerable variation in the length of the calyx tube, the diameter of the flower mouth, and the width of the ovate perianth lobes; some of these comparisons are included in the descriptions of individual clones.

As the inflorescence develops from the terminal bud in early spring, the peduncle, which has several leaf-like bracts, elongates by up to 2 CM. (This is in marked contrast to my clone of *D. juliae* which has little or no elongation of the peduncle.) The various clones of *D. cneorum* provide an order of flowering which can be loosely placed into three groups—early: 'Benaco', 'Blackthorn Triumph', f. *alba*, 'Snow Carpet'; mid-season: 'Eximea', 'Lac des Gloriettes', 'Leila Haines', ex. Klaus Patzner; late: all the dwarf, prostrate forms which equate to var. *pygmaea.*

It is not unusual for plants under protection to set some seed, and there are reports of seed regularly set in areas which experience warmer weather than the

D. cneorum: the swelling pericarp splits the dead perianth tube.

United Kingdom. The fruit develops within the remains of the perianth tube, which is split as the pale yellow pericarp swells at the last stage of development.

Given sun and good drainage, the more vigorous clones of this species can be grown successfully in a variety of situations, but their ability to cover quite a wide area should be taken into account at planting. The more compact clones are ideal for the rock or scree garden, or in a trough. As plants develop the centre may become bare of foliage and flower, a situation where pruning back to within a few inches of the centre after the spring flush of flowers can be very successful. Alternatively, a mulch over the bare stems will encourage layering and regrowth. This problem can also be worked around well by using other plants to cover any bare growth; *D. cneorum* naturally rambles through its neighbours in the wild, and shows no objection to close company in the garden—an exception to the general rule for daphnes. A wide range of plants would be suitable for this; I have used *Lithodora diffusa* and *Genista sagittalis*, while various thymes or heathers might also work well.

Daphne cneorum is a hardy species, but the cold-tolerance of a given clone may well depend on its origin. It is unlikely that plants from near sea level in southwest France, for example, will be as hardy as those from high altitude or central Europe. Hardier clones should be capable of withstanding temperatures down to –29°C/–20°F (Zone 5).

Propagation

When I have collected and sown seed it has always germinated well the following spring. Cuttings, however, are the standard method of increase, although advice on the timing of these varies widely: recommendations range from using the previous season's growth in April to May, after removing soft growth and flower, through soft tip cuttings in May or June, to ripened wood at the end of the growing season. I have taken cuttings on the same day of the year two years in succession, and had an 80 percent take the first year yet a very poor take in the second. I favour taking semi-ripe tip cuttings in July; if these fail I can try again with riper material in September! As you can see, I am reluctant to make a firm recommendation. Once rooted, cuttings generally grow away well, but I would advise planting out from a small pot whenever possible, because trying to produce a good-sized pot-grown plant over two seasons often results in failure, generally due to root problems. All clones of *D. cneorum* grow well grafted on *D. mezereum* or *D. longilobata*, and I use this method for the dwarfer clones. The prostrate, pliable growth of *D. cneorum* makes it a good candidate for layering.

Botanical variants and named clones

Daphne cneorum forma *alba*

A plant of medium vigour, perhaps more inclined than some to develop a bare-stemmed centre. The cream buds open to pure white flowers. Mature size 15–20 CM high, 1–2 M across. One of the better clones for summer flowers on new growth.

Daphne cneorum var. *pygmaea* Stoker

The original plant collected in 1935 to be given this name was described as an "almost exact, though smaller replica of the type species". Unfortunately, there are numerous plants from widely differing locations which could fit this description. The Jura, the French Alps, the Pyrenees and the Dolomites all seem to have dwarf variants of the species. Plants that have been given to me under this name include:

Clone A This plant, from the late plantsman and author Jack Elliot, does not have totally prostrate stems; their habit is more arching. Leaf edges tend to be crinkled and it is inclined to drop its leaves in cold weather. It has mid-pink flowers. Mature size 7.5–10 CM high, 30–40 CM across.

Clone B I am inclined to believe that this plant, from Oakdene Nursery, is the nearest I have to the original; the stems hug the ground and the leaves are small, averaging 1 CM by 0.2 CM. The pale pink flowers number 6–10 per inflorescence. Mature size 2.5–5 CM high, 45–60 CM wide.

D. cneorum var. *pygmaea* clone B has a ground-hugging habit.

Daphne cneorum var. *pygmaea* 'Alba'

Connie Greenfield was a noted grower of alpine plants in the 1950s and '60s. This cultivar was introduced by her, but its origin is unknown. The name may not be valid and is inappropriate, because this plant's habit is unlike the pink-flowered forms of *D. cneorum* var. *pygmaea*. It is a slow-growing plant, but the stems are not totally prostrate. The leaves have an apiculate apex rather than the obtuse one of the pink-flowered clones. The short, compact growth results in a low, dense plant which smothers itself in flowers of pure white. Mature size 7.5–10 cm high, 45–60 cm wide.

Daphne cneorum 'Benaco'

This is a lovely introduction from northern Italy by Peter Erskine. It is a plant of medium vigour, fairly prostrate in habit, with bright green, narrow foliage and noticeably scarlet-tinted bracts protecting the overwintering inflorescences. Strong-growing plants produce axillary as well as terminal inflorescences. The flowers are bright rose pink, emerging from bright, reddish pink buds. On average there are 15 flowers per inflorescence and the diameter of the mouth of mature flowers is 1 cm. Plants can reach 15–22.5 cm high and 60–90 cm wide.

Daphne cneorum 'Blackthorn Triumph'

This is a seedling from *D. cneorum* var. *pygmaea* clone A, pollinated by clone B. It has the prostrate habit of the pollen parent, but the larger flowers, 1 cm in diameter, are a better colour than in either parent, and more numerous per inflorescence. An excellent plant for a trough, as are all the prostrate clones, since they grow over the edge and clothe the sides of the trough very effectively. Reliably produces a good show of bloom on new growth from midsummer onwards. Mature size 5–7.5 cm high, 45–60 cm wide.

Daphne cneorum 'Ewesley'

A fine introduction from the Spanish Pyrenees by the late Mr. E. J. Watson. The dwarf, prostrate habit is akin to that of *D. cneorum* var. *pygmaea* forms, but the flowers are reddish pink, definitely the deepest colour I have seen on a dwarf *D. cneorum* form. Estimated mature size is 2.5–5 cm high by 45–60 cm wide.

Daphne cneorum 'Eximea'

Since the mid-1930s this has been the standard and deservedly most popular cultivar in the United Kingdom and much of Europe. While the odd seed-

D. cneorum 'Benaco'.

D. cneorum 'Blackthorn Triumph' performs well in a trough.

D. cneorum 'Benaco'.

D. cneorum 'Eximea', 1 M wide after three seasons' growth.

raised plant may be masquerading under this name, it must be generally accepted that vegetative propagation has maintained most plants today as true to the original clone. Over the last 20 years this cultivar seems to have become more difficult to produce in the nursery trade, even when propagated by tissue culture, so one has to ask if this clone is getting "genetically tired"—or is most stock now carrying a virus, but not showing obvious symptoms?

There are reports of plants reaching 2 M or more in diameter, and 30–35 CM in height, or higher if allowed to scramble into a taller neighbour. A plant I have put in the "daphnetum" is making annual extension growth of 25–30 CM. The flowers buds are bright carmine red and the flowers open a deep pink.

Daphne cneorum 'Lac des Gloriettes'

In the early 1990s a stay at Gavarnie in the French Pyrenees included a memorable picnic lunch sitting on alpine turf near the Lac des Gloriettes. *Daphne cneorum* was running throughout the turf, its scent drifting on the air as we revelled in the mountain scenery. One plant we looked at had much more glaucous leaves than its neighbours, which we felt offset the bright pink flowers very well. In cultivation this plant has a tight, prostrate habit, and the perianth lobes are broader with a more rounded apex than most of the dwarf forms. Mature size 5–10 CM high, 45–60 CM wide.

D. cneorum 'Leila Haines'.

Daphne cneorum 'Leila Haines'

In the early 1970s a party of alpine enthusiasts visiting northern Italy was being led by Ernst Hauser when he found this plant, and named it after a member of the group from British Columbia. Hauser believed it to be a natural hybrid between *D. cneorum* and *D. striata*; however, information from Swedish daphne enthusiast Severin Schlyter indicates that Tage Lundell treated the plant as *D. cneorum*, and more recently, careful examination by Chris Brickell confirms that there is no trace of *D. striata* in this plant. 'Leila Haines' was used by Schlyter as the seed parent for his hybrid with *D. arbuscula* (see *D. ×schlyteri*, p. 138). This cultivar has a fairly compact, bushy habit, with narrow leaves which have an apiculate apex. Like 'Benaco', which comes from the same area, it can produce axillary inflorescences, and the flower colour is bright rose pink. This may be a plant which is more resistant to drought conditions than those forms with broader leaves. Mature size 7.5–10 CM high, 60–75 CM wide.

Daphne cneorum 'Peggy Fell'

This clone has been distributed by David Mowle, and I have sold plants of it as ex. D. Mowle. It was collected as a seedling in 1977 when Peggy Fell visited the French Pyrenees. 'Peggy Fell' has the totally prostrate growth associated with *D. cneorum* var. *pygmaea* clone B, but the freely produced flowers are larger and a deeper pink.

Daphne cneorum 'Puszta'

A selection from Hungary which matches *D. cneorum* 'Eximea' for vigour and flower, but the buds lack the bright carmine colour. Mature size 25–30 cm high, 1–2 m wide.

Daphne cneorum 'Ruby Glow'

I have never grown this cultivar, which is widely available in North America. It is a vigorous plant with reddish-pink flowers. I suspect that it would match the description for 'Velky Kosir' (see below).

D. cneorum 'Snow Carpet'.

D. cneorum 'Velky Kosir'.

Daphne cneorum 'Snow Carpet'

An interesting selection from northern Italy, introduced by Austrian plantsman Fritz Kummert, with narrow leaves that seem typical of that area; however, they are light green and unusually shiny. There are 16–22 flowers per inflorescence, which makes for a fine display. The inner perianth lobes differ considerably from the outer ones; the former are 0.2 cm wide with an acute apex, while the latter are 0.3 cm wide with a rounded apex. Mature size 7.5–10 cm high, 60–90 cm wide.

Daphne cneorum 'Velky Kosir'

A selection from eastern Moravia in the Czech Republic by a Mr. Obdrzalek of Prague, which was originally sold as *D. cneorum* 'Rubrum'—an invalid cultivar name. The foliage is distinctive in turning a reddish purple tone in cold weather, and the leaves have a narrow edging of the same colour in summer. The habit is vigorous and bushy. Axillary as well as terminal inflorescences are produced on strong growth. The dark crimson buds produce reddish pink flowers which, at 1.5–1.6 CM in diameter, are larger than those of the other forms grown here. Mature size 25–30 CM high, 0.9–1.2 M wide.

Variegated cultivars

Daphne cneorum 'Argentea', with a pale cream edge to the leaf but flowers sparse in number, and *D. cneorum* 'Variegata', with a yellow leaf edge and pale pink flowers, are two variegated selections I do not rate highly. Their leaves are too small to make an impact, and neither flowers as well as plain-leaved forms. They can be expected to make plants 25–30 CM high by 60–90 CM wide.

Daphne 'Stasek', which I received as a variegated form of *D. cneorum*, is described under *D.* ×*napolitana* in the chapter on hybrids, page 134.

Unnamed clones

I have been given other forms of *D. cneorum* which lack names, yet are distinct and of interest, as well as helping to emphasize the variation in this species.

An introduction from near Pontresina by D. Bryan is dwarf in habit, but not prostrate. Measurements of 0.8–1 CM long by 0.4 CM wide make the leaves relatively short and broad, and the mature bark is very dark brown, which is unusual since *D. cneorum* bark is normally greyish-brown. The flowers are 0.8–1 CM in diameter, with rounded perianth lobes, 0.2 CM wide.

Some years ago I was given a small plant growing on its own roots labelled *D. cneorum*, collected by Klaus Patzner in the Dolomites. The plant survived, but did not impress; however, a couple of years ago it showed signs of failing, so I made a few grafts, one of which I planted out in a raised bed. Even allowing for the vigour of a young grafted plant, I still think its display in 2004 was outstanding. The flowers are of better quality than those of any other dwarf form, 1–1.2 CM in diameter, with broad 0.3–0.4 CM lobes which have an acute apex. With his permission I shall name this form after Herr Patzner.

Daphne collina Dickson ex. J. E. Smith

Daphne collina of gardens is a taxonomic mystery, since no plant which resembles it closely has been found in the wild. In their 1976 monograph Brickell and Mathew provide a great deal of conflicting information on the history of the

D. collina of gardens.

D. collina of gardens: flowers show little of the top whorl of anthers.

D. collina (?) collected in southern Italy.

D. collina (?) collected in southern Italy. Note clearly visible anthers and obovate leaves. Compare with *D. collina*, above.

species, which they accurately describe as a "tangled skein". Visits to the type locality in southern Italy in 1962 by the late Hugo Latymer and in 2001 by Chris Brickell and Peter Erskine only resulted in the discovery of plants similar to *D. sericea*, although their leaves were markedly obovate compared to the oblanceolate or narrowly elliptic ones of *D. sericea*. The key point here is that in Chris Brickell's opinion the plants found in southern Italy resemble a plate of *D. collina* which accompanied Smith's original description in 1792, published in *Spicilegium Botanicaum*, but in my opinion they are very different from *D. collina* of gardens. Flora Europa may thus be justified in uniting *D. collina* and *D. sericea*, but gardeners should not confuse these plants from the wild with the plant widely cultivated in the gardens of many countries. A new name for *D. collina* of gardens may be justified, and would certainly help to avoid confusion.

Even without the use of a hand lens, numerous differences between *D. collina* of gardens and the wild forms collected in 2001 are apparent. The former is a compact, bushy evergreen, broader than tall, with elliptic to oblanceolate leaves 2–3.5 CM long by 0.8–1 CM wide, their upper surface glossy with no obvious lateral veins. The inflorescence is always terminal, with a narrow perianth tube 1–1.2 CM long by 0.2 CM wide; the perianth lobes are a bright rosy purple, not fading or changing colour as they mature. The upper whorl of anthers is inserted in the mouth of the perianth tube. In contrast, plants raised from material collected by Brickell and Erskine from Marina di Albetese and the Abruzzi Mountains have an upright, straggly habit, taller than wide. The evergreen leaves are broadly obovate, 2–3.5 CM long by 1.2–2 CM wide, the upper surface dark, matt green with obvious lateral veins. The inflorescence may be terminal or axillary, the perianth tube 0.8–1 CM long by 0.3–0.4 CM wide, with broad lobes of dull rosy purple, maturing to muddy purple. The anthers are clearly visible in the mouth of the perianth tube. If the latter description is compared with *D. sericea* (see p. 101), it can be seen that these wild plants are closer to that species than to *D. collina* of gardens.

Records show that plants have been grown under the name of *D. collina* for 250 years, but since the form grown today does not correspond with the original plate it seems possible that at some stage in the last two and a half centuries either a mutation was selected and propagated, or a seedling which may have been a hybrid assumed the name. Seed is occasionally set on plants of *D. collina* of gardens grown under protection here, but the resulting plants have almost always proved to be hybrids with adjacent species; however, a single seed produced in 2000 flowered for the first time in 2004, and seems identical in leaf and blossom to its parent.

Daphne collina of gardens has stood the test of time as a first-class dwarf evergreen shrub. In a sunny, well-drained situation it makes a dome-shaped plant which over time may reach 45–60 CM high by 1 M across, or more if it layers itself. The terminal inflorescences contain up to 15 rosy purple, intensely fragrant flowers. The main flush of bloom in April to May is followed by further blossom on new growth through the summer. The fruit remains enclosed in the dead calyx tube until ripe, its pericarp a dull orange and not very fleshy. When grown in the open, I have found this species susceptible to attack by the leaf spot fungus *Marssonina daphnes* (see p. 212). The wetter the climate, the greater this problem is likely to be. This flaw has been passed on to its hybrids.

D. collina of gardens: the fruit develops within the dead perianth tube.

Despite its claimed origin of southern Italy, *D. collina* of gardens is surprisingly hardy; apart from some browning of unripened foliage, plants are known to have survived temperatures down to –17°C/0°F (Zone 7).

Propagation

Rooting semi-ripe tip cuttings taken in June to July, or later ripewood cuttings, is not a problem, but in recent years potting up and establishing the rooted cuttings without losing the terminal buds has proved difficult for me and, as far as I know, other growers in the United Kingdom too. Why this should be is a mystery, but once the terminal bud is lost, cuttings seldom make lateral shoots and fail to establish. Peter Erskine reports that no such problem is encountered by growers in Slovakia, so it would be interesting to obtain material from this source to see if we can propagate it more easily here. Plants grafted on *D. mezereum* or *D. longilobata* grow in character if initial vigorous growth is pinched to encourage a bushy habit.

Daphne domini J. Halda

This small, evergreen shrub has been widely confused by myself and others with *D. kosaninii* Stoj., a species which, according to J. Halda, grows at higher altitudes of the Pirin Mountains in southwest Bulgaria, also the habitat of *D. domini* (J. Halda and Z. Zvolanek 1982).

D. domini: the flowers do not open fully.

Daphne domini may not be in the top rank of daphnes, but the fact that it inhabits dry, rocky, calcareous areas indicates that it is tolerant of drought, which makes it useful for growing in similarly inhospitable sites. It makes a small, rounded, well-branched bush, 20–30 CM in height and width. The lanceolate leaves are leathery, with a bright green glossy upper surface; they are clustered towards the apex of the stems, which have reddish-brown bark. The flowers are produced in terminal inflorescences in April to May; the pale pink blooms do not open properly, so self-fertilization must occur, as the flowers are followed by a large crop of orange fruits in June and July which are as attractive as the flowers.

This species appreciates the extra warmth and controlled moisture supply I can give under glass or polythene, but I have grown it successfully in a sunny, well drained spot in the open. I would estimate that it should be hardy to –17°C/0°F (Zone 7).

Propagation

Sown fresh, the freely set seed germinates readily the following spring. The top growth of seedlings is slow compared to their prolific production of fine roots, an adaptation to the dry habitat from which the plant comes. Seed-raised plants are best planted out at an early stage since they do not grow especially well in containers.

Daphne gemmata E. Pritz

It has yet to be resolved whether this species from Sichuan, China, should be placed in the genus *Wikstroemia* or *Daphne*; since the Flora of China includes it under *Daphne*, I include it here.

Daphne gemmata is a relatively new introduction to this country, so we are still on a learning curve with it. It is described as a deciduous shrub, but if it is not subjected to temperatures below freezing, it may well remain partially evergreen. Leaf fall is certainly not induced by short days: plants growing in a tunnel here were still in full leaf in mid-December, while the *D. mezereum* beside them had lost its leaves. Low temperatures produced a crimson flush in the immature leaves at the apex of the new growth.

D. gemmata: flowers generally have five perianth lobes. (Photo: Doug Joyce)

The branches are thin but not lax, and pale green in colour for several months, maturing to grey-brown. The habit is open, and young plants need their growth pinching to promote branching. Ultimate height is given as 1 M. Leaf shape and size on the clones I have seen is variable, ranging from ovate, 3–4 CM by 1.8–2 CM, to oblanceolate, 4–5.5 CM by 1.5 CM. The young leaves are pale green, maturing to dark green with a matt finish. Flowers are produced throughout the growing season in terminal inflorescences of 5–10 blooms. It is characteristic of this species that the long, 1–1.4 CM perianth tube, greenish yellow in colour, is curved and slightly inflated. The majority of the scentless flowers have five perianth lobes, but the clone I have does produce some with four on those flowers towards the centre of the inflorescence. The bright yellow buds mature to primrose yellow flowers. The width of the perianth lobes seems quite variable between the few clones I have seen, ranging from 0.4 to 0.5 CM long by 0.2–0.4 CM wide. The diameter of the mouth of a mature flower is 0.9–1 CM. I have yet to see any of the red fruits, which are given as ellipsoid in shape.

In my limited experience, *D. gemmata* has proved easy to grow in a container in a glasshouse shaded in the summer. I think it will grow in sun or semi-shade in the United Kingdom, but may need some shade in areas nearer the equator. Despite the lack of scent, the long flowering period of this species does give it garden value. I suspect it will be intolerant of drought and, given the low altitude of its habitat, unlikely to survive temperatures below –10°C/14°F (Zone 8).

Propagation

When available, seed should be a reliable means of increase. Soft and semi-ripe tip cuttings root with ease throughout the growing season. Although a union between stock and scion develops, I have not persuaded grafts of *D. gemmata* to grow on *D. longilobata* or *D. tangutica*, but Kath Dryden—expert grower of so many plants for more years than she cares to remember—reports success using the latter as a stock.

Daphne genkwa Sieb. & Zucc.

A species from China and Korea that is unique for the genus in colour, and unusual in having no scent that I can detect. It was introduced to the west in the late 19TH century, but unfortunately seldom grows well for long in maritime climates. It has been cultivated in Japan as a cut flower and for garden decoration for a long time, and flourishes in its native habitats. Reports from 19TH-century and modern-day plant hunters indicate that these range from rocky, limestone hillsides to banks between paddy fields. The common factors are probably strong sunlight, good drainage, but a moisture supply available to deep roots.

A root of *D. genkwa* exposed to the light soon developed adventitious shoots.

Daphne genkwa suckers readily from the root, and so can form thickets where growing well. Certainly, healthy plants in cultivation can make up to 90 CM of growth in a season, so it would be possible to grow plants as a stool, pruning hard to within a few centimetres of the ground immediately after flowering—or as the plant comes into flower if material is required for floral decoration. The thin branches are furnished with deciduous leaves which may be opposite or alternate, and vary from narrowly lanceolate to ovate. The flowers are carried in every leaf axil of the previous season's growth in short-stalked inflorescences of 2–7 flowers. In cultivation the flowers are in various shades of lilac-blue, but white forms are relatively common in the wild. The fruits have a greyish white pericarp, but seed is seldom set on my plants even when different clones are grown together under protection. In contrast, Fritz Kummert, who gardens near Vienna, Austria, reports that a single clone which flourishes in his garden regularly sets good quantities of seed.

There is no doubt that the hot summers and evenly cold winters of a continental climate are what *D. genkwa* requires for successful cultivation. In areas of North America where these conditions occur, it is considered a straightforward species to grow when given a suitable site. The hot summers are what is needed to ripen growth, and a cold season without the interruption of mild spells keeps the plant dormant, in which state it can withstand temperatures as low as –29 to –34°C/–20 to –30°F (Zone 4). As soon as dormancy is broken, and sap starts to rise in the plant, it becomes vulnerable to cold damage. I have had a plant just coming into flower killed by a frost of –5°C (23°F). In maritime climates which have fluctuating winter temperatures, it is therefore important to site *D. genkwa* where it will receive maximum summer heat, but protection from spring frosts. I have grown a plant near to a south-facing wall for several years; in such a position it is important to avoid dryness at the roots during the growing season. In recent years the availability of horticultural fleece has made it possible to protect a special plant like this from late spring frosts.

D. genkwa provides a unique flower colour for the genus.
(Photo: John Fielding)

Propagation

Seed is not readily available at present, but will hopefully be offered from China before long. Soft tip cuttings root easily, but must be grown on steadily until dormancy sets in to avoid winter losses; supplementary winter lighting would be beneficial. Semi-ripe cuttings taken in July to August seem to overwinter best if left in their trays until growth starts in the spring. Root cuttings are

D. genkwa: a procumbent form growing in New York Botanic Garden. (Photo: John Bieber)

recommended for propagating *D. genkwa*; roots left in the benching when a container-grown plant was moved here did produce shoots and grew satisfactorily when potted up. Roots of *D. genkwa* accidentally exposed to the light have readily produced adventitious shoots, so it would be worth trying root cuttings, placed horizontally in trays and not totally covered (see also Root cuttings, p. 180). Using *D. mezereum* as a rootstock for grafting does not produce such good plants as grafts on *D. longilobata*. Grafting in early August has given better results than in January or February.

Botanical variants

A distinct form of *D. genkwa* with a prostrate or procumbent habit has been grown for many years by the New York Botanic Garden. Although the original plant died, cuttings were rooted to maintain the clone. It would be interesting to graft material of this on to the stem of an upright form to create a plant with a weeping habit.

Daphne genkwa, Hackenberry form

A selection raised from wild-collected seed obtained from Beijing Botanic Garden by Don Hackenberry has a particularly vigorous, upright habit. I believe plants raised from seed of this Hackenberry form have been sold under the name, in which case Hackenberry group might be more appropriate unless all the plants produced from seed are virtually identical.

D. genkwa, Hackenberry form growing in John Bieber's New York garden. (Photo: John Bieber)

Daphne giraldii Nitsche

This species raises questions for me; in particular, is more than one species grown under this name? In their 1976 monograph Brickell and Mathew credit this species from western China with being most attractive and one of the easiest to grow, and wonder why it has been neglected by gardeners. Attractive it certainly is and, once established, plants have grown well, but I have found seedlings difficult to grow on in pots

D. giraldii

D. giraldii in fruit.

beyond a few true leaves; a point which may explain why this species is not more widely available. Given the difficulty I have experienced in raising plants from seed, I am surprised that *D. giraldii* is recommended as a rootstock for grafting. A possible explanation arose in 1998 when I was given some seedlings under the name of *D. giraldii*. Once I had grown them on, the plants showed a marked difference from the species as I knew it, with more vigorous growth and an open habit, while the stems and leaves were narrower, giving a willowy appearance. The flowers and fruits were also smaller.

I managed to trace the origin of this atypical plant to a collection made in 1986 by Mr. P. Cox of Glendoick Garden, under the number 2565, from Jiuzhaigou in northwest Sichuan. It is interesting to note that in a visit to the same area in 2001, Dr. Christopher Grey-Wilson records seeing several specimens of the "greenish yellow flowered *D. giraldii*, which made a gawky bush"; a description which again does not fit well with *D. giraldii* as I know it. Seed-raised plants from Mr. Cox's collection have been distributed in the United Kingdom as *D. giraldii*; it certainly seems a much easier plant to grow from seed than the typical form of the species. Further study by a botanist is necessary to determine whether this recent collection is a variation within *D. giraldii*, or a different species. What I can say is that as an ornamental shrub it is inferior to *D. giraldii* as originally introduced, though it may have value as a rootstock. Further confusion may arise from the fact that plants I have raised from seed offered in J. Halda's seed lists as *D.* aff. *flaviflora* and *D.* aff. *feddei* are both identical to the typical form of *D. giraldii* I grow.

Daphne giraldii has been grown in the United Kingdom since the early part of the 20TH century. Plants I have grown for many years were seed-raised from a very large old plant growing on sandy soil in the New Forest. The habit is erect and sturdy, up to 1 M in height, and generally less in width, but old plants produce basal shoots and may be 1.3–1.6 M across. The bark is bright reddish brown, developing conspicuous pale striations with maturity. The foliage is deciduous, leaves narrowly oblanceolate in shape, 3–6 CM long, 0.5–1 CM wide. The inflorescence is terminal, without bracts, borne at the end of short axillary growths arising from the upright main stems. The golden yellow flowers are fragrant, in clusters of 4–8. Flowering period in the open is May/June. Plenty of seed is set, the ovoid fruits being orange-red in colour.

Young seedlings planted in a raised bed in a polythene tunnel have grown well in spite of annual attack by red spider mite. One-year-old seedlings planted in my "daphnetum" have established, but growth is slow. My lack of success in growing young plants in pots prompts me to recommend planting out seedlings as soon as possible. *Daphne giraldii* should be given a sunny site, but be provided with ample summer moisture. In its natural habitat it would receive plenty of summer rain, but be dry in winter. With its deciduous habit *D. giraldii* should tolerate temperatures to −29°C/−20°F (Zone 5).

Propagation

Plants under polythene set copious quantities of seed. Sown fresh, this germinates well the following spring. Potted up at cotyledon stage, seedlings establish and grow well for a few months, but by their first winter many show signs of root loss, and few survive in pots for a second season. I have not attempted cuttings, but grafts grow well on *D. longilobata.*

Daphne glomerata Lam.

I hesitated to include this species from northeast Turkey and the Caucasus Mountains in this book. Firstly, it has a justifiable reputation of being difficult to grow in this country; secondly, I find the smell of the flowers unpleasant. But those who have seen *D. glomerata* growing in the wild enthuse about it, bringing back wonderful, enticing photographs, so I am including it in the hope that gardeners in other climates may be more successful in growing it, and maybe some clones will be introduced into cultivation with a nicer smell!

D. glomerata in the wild, Zigana Pass, Turkey.
(Photo: Robert Rolfe)

D. glomerata, Truso Gorge, Georgia.
(Photo: Chris Brickell)

Daphne glomerata grows naturally in alpine turf or areas of light shade, such as that cast by *Rhododendron luteum* or pine trees. In most areas it would be covered by snow for much of the winter, which I believe to be an important point for its successful cultivation. It is semi-prostrate in habit, freely suckering to create broad clumps up to 30 CM in height. The glossy leaves are probably evergreen when covered with a protecting blanket of snow, but plants in my garden tend to drop some of their leaves if there is an autumn spell of damp, muggy weather, or after the first sharp frosts of winter. To my relief, they make good new growth the following spring. In late spring the terminal inflorescences can carry 30 or more creamy white flowers. The perianth tube of some forms is tinged deep pink, particularly as flowers mature. The fruits have a fleshy, red pericarp.

Records of successful cultivation and companion plants in nature indicate that *D. glomerata* is happy in a damp, humus-rich soil of neutral or acid pH. However, two plants on their own roots are growing well in the alkaline pea shingle of my "daphnetum" bed, where they are shaded from sun at the hottest time of the day. Areas which experience cool summer temperatures and regular rainfall will provide the best conditions for *D. glomerata*. Unfortunately, these conditions suit slugs and snails, who find this species much to their liking. Snow cover could well be a critical factor in determining hardiness, and plants of high altitude origin should be best adapted to survive lower temperatures. Suggested hardiness would be to minimum temperatures of –17°C/0°F (Zone 7).

Propagation

Even when seed is sown soon after harvesting, germination may be erratic. It is interesting to record the results from 20 seeds from the Caucasus, given to me by Peter Erskine with their pericarp removed: collection date 9/7/98, sown 20/7/98; four germinated April 1999, twelve germinated April 2000, one germinated April 2001. Tip cuttings of the current season's growth, taken before the wood ripens, root well. Plants grow well grafted on *D. longilobata*, while *D. pontica* or *D. albowiana* would be good rootstocks to try because they are closely related species. However, if obtainable, plants grown from seed or cuttings, which will retain the species' suckering habit, are preferable to grafted plants for garden use.

Botanical variants

Daphne glomerata var. *nivalis*

The clone of *D. glomerata* I have most experience with was given to me under this name. It is meant to be a high-altitude form of particularly low growth, with a greater number of flowers per inflorescence than the typical form. To date it has proved equally difficult to please for long enough to make a good-sized plant in a container, but a plant is growing well in the "daphnetum" alongside ones I raised from seed collected in the Caucasus.

Daphne gnidioides Jaub. & Spach

Eyebrows may be raised at my inclusion of this species as a garden-worthy plant, but I feel it has not been given the credit it deserves, and those who garden in mild coastal areas or a hot and dry situation may want to try growing it. *Daphne gnidioides* should not be confused with *D. gnidium*, a straggly shrub native to southwest Europe; its natural distribution is southern and western Turkey and eastern Greece. For several years I have grown plants from seed collected in Crete by John Fielding and Nicholas Turland, and more recently in Turkey by Brian Mathew. The Cretan forms seem to have a stouter, more branched habit than those from Turkey; the latter may become straggly with age. Ultimate height is given by Brickell and Mathew (1976) at 2 M, which Chris Brickell confirms is true for plants seen in Turkey, but John Fielding confirms my opinion that the Cretan form would be nearer to 1.3 M, and is more densely branched than its Turkish relative. The evergreen, pale green, lanceolate leaves of the Cretan forms have a characteristic twist when mature, while to date, my Turkish plants have distinctly more glaucous leaves without a twist.

D. gnidioides. This form originates from Crete.

The cream flowers are borne in terminal inflorescences of 3–5 at the end of extension growth and on short axillary growths; the pale green perianth tube measures 0.5 CM long by 0.2 CM wide. The perianth lobes are almost round, giving a flower diameter of 0.8–0.9 CM. Although Brickell and Mathew (1976) give the flowering period as May, none of my Cretan plants flowers until late summer, when the blossom, and especially its pleasant almond fragrance, is welcome. When seed is set on my plants it is enclosed in a pericarp which is fleshy and orange-red in colour, but no doubt in the hot dry conditions of its native habitat the pericarp would soon become coriaceous and brown.

Daphne gnidioides is unlikely to be very hardy, but the evergreen, salt-resistant foliage would make it useful for planting near the sea. It requires a sunny, well-drained situation and can be considered a drought-tolerant species. I estimate that temperatures below –10°C/14°F (Zone 8) would cause damage. I suggest that the Cretan form may be hardier than the Turkish, and definitely seems to have a better habit.

Propagation

Seed is set regularly and germinates well the following spring. I have not attempted cuttings, but soft material might root. Plants grafted on *D. mezereum* have grown well.

Daphne jasminea Sibth. & Sm.

This species is native to Greece, where it inhabits limestone cliffs. In cultivation it exists in two distinct forms, one of which is of botanical rather than garden value. This "poor relation" is known as the upright form, because it produces vigorous, upright growth, 60–90 CM in height. Even though the upright clone I grow does have attractive blue leaves, the yellowish cream, scentless flowers will not appeal to many people. Material of this form from Crete which I grew for a while lacked this glaucous foliage, making it even less attractive. The form which has proved popular with alpine enthusiasts in the United Kingdom for cultivation—with glasshouse protection for the winter—is generally called the Delphi form, since it is common on cliffs in that area.

D. jasminea, Delphi form growing under glass. Flower colour is more intense in the open.

The Delphi form of *D. jasminea* produces tightly packed, well-branched growth. A 20-year-old plant in my glasshouse, growing in a tall clay pot, has rooted into the bench grit, and its habit is to grow downwards, a trait perhaps influenced by the fact that it normally grows on cliffs. Despite providing an annual supply of cuttings, it now measures 90 CM across, with a depth, rather than height, of 70 CM. In the open, plants are likely to make specimens 20–30 CM in height by 60–90 CM wide. The stems of *D. jasminea* are extremely brittle; great care is needed when moving container-grown plants, and in areas where it can be grown outdoors, avoid planting where chance contact with people or animals is likely.

The small, oblong to obovate leaves are bluish green in colour. Grown with winter protection the plant is evergreen, but outdoors a sudden drop in winter temperatures may cause leaf drop. Under glass the first flowers of the season are produced in terminal pairs from mid-April, but this early display is only a warm-up for what is to follow; a flush of vegetative growth which will carry a steady succession of axillary flowers from mid-June onwards. At peak flowering time, July in my case, plants are spectacular. Growing under shaded glass does reduce the colour of the flower buds and perianth tube to pale pink, whereas in the open they are rosy purple. When the flowers open, the white perianth lobes form a marked contrast with the pink of the perianth tube.

The flowers of *D. jasminea* are described as fragrant, but I have found it difficult to detect any scent in either of the two Delphi form plants I have grown. At best, a slight sweetness in the late evening is all I can discern. Individually, forms of *D. jasminea* appear to be self-sterile, but when I grew two different clones together, plenty of seed was produced. The fruit remains encased in the dead perianth tube until almost ripe, when the fleshy pericarp, yellowish green in colour, will usually split the dead covering material.

For successful cultivation in the open *D. jasminea* must be given a sunny, well-drained position where growth can be fully ripened before frosts occur. The top growth is particularly vulnerable to fungal infection in mild, wet conditions, so try to position plants where there is plenty of air movement. Plants may well be more comfortable under snow protection in cold areas than exposed to the conditions they experience in our English climate in winter. I have had difficulty establishing plants in the open; unripened growth, damaged by frost, gets infected with *Botrytis*, and sudden frosts have caused total leaf drop from which plants are slow to recover in the spring. Protection from winter wet is one of the key factors to success in growing *D. jasminea*, and my plants have grown well in clay pots under glass, whether on their own roots or grafted, for many years. An ideal regime would be to provide protection for the winter months, but bring pots outside for the summer to reduce the chance of attack by red spider mite, which can be a problem under cover in hot weather. In the summer months, *D. jasminea* consumes a surprising amount of water; my large plants may need watering twice daily. The flowers let you know when the plant is short of water by bending at the perianth tube; thirsty plants soon recover when given water, and I am sure *D. jasminea* would be drought-tolerant when well established in the ground in a hot, dry climate (however, reduced growth would limit the quantity of flower produced in such conditions).

Unless a very sheltered site is available, or the atmosphere has very low humidity, I think *D. jasminea* would be difficult to grow outside where winter temperatures fall below –12°C/10°F (Zone 8).

Propagation

Seed is seldom available, but what seed I have collected has germinated well the following spring. Cuttings are the standard propagation method; stock plants need to be in a good state of nutrition to produce soft shoots long enough to make into tip or basal cuttings 2.5–3.7 CM long. Softwood cuttings which are just starting to ripen at their base, taken in May or June, root easily, but do not make a lot of root compared to other small daphne species. What root is made is very fine and easily broken, so I leave the rooted cuttings in their tray until the following spring, by which time they have produced sturdy enough roots to ensure establishment when potted. Plants grafted on *D. mezereum* have grown in character for many years.

Daphne jezoensis Maxim. ex. Regel

The difference between *D. jezoensis*, *D. kamtschatica* and *D. koreana* I leave to the botanists, but my understanding is that *D. jezoensis* is the most desirable of the three. Native to northern Japan, where it grows in sub-alpine woodland, its fragrant winter flowers make this a much sought after shrub.

Whether grafted or on its own roots, *D. jezoensis* is slow-growing, seldom making more than 5–7.5 CM of extension growth in a season. It is not naturally bushy, producing a few well-spaced limbs furnished with short axillary growths. Mature plants may be 45–60 CM in height and width.

Daphne jezoensis has the curious habit of dropping its leaves in summer, although young plants, particularly if grafted, will retain their foliage on unripe growth. New leaves are produced from late summer to early autumn, the timing no doubt governed by a combination of day length, moisture availability and temperature; they are accompanied by flower buds which are not enclosed by bracts. No extension growth occurs at this time, and there is little further development of the flower buds until early spring, when they produce deep yellow flowers with a delicate fragrance similar to that of freesias. Under cover a succession of flowers will open over eight to ten weeks, but in the open rain and frost tends to shorten the life of the flowers. Some descriptions declare *D. jezoensis* to be dioecious, which means that male and female reproductive parts are not borne on the same plant. This may be so, but Brickell and Mathew (1976) state that flowers they examined were hermaphrodite, possessing male and female parts in the same flower, and my stock plants, together with all plants I

D. jezoensis.

D. jezoensis with fertile stamens (left). *D. kamtschatica* (?) with rudimentary stamens (right).

have raised from seed, have also proved to be hermaphrodite. I do have a plant which I have grown outside in a woodland area for many years which has smaller, paler yellow, scentless flowers that only possess rudimentary stamens, incapable of producing any pollen. This plant came from Japan as *D. jezoensis*, so it may be an example of a dioecious plant, or perhaps *D. kamtschatica*.

Under protection some seed is set every year. The quantity can be increased with hand-pollination between different clones. The fruits are elliptical, with a thick, fleshy red pericarp, relatively large for so small a shrub.

The natural habitat of *D. jezoensis* is woodland, so planting in strong sun should be avoided. The soil or compost should be humus-rich; a neutral or slightly acid pH may be preferable to an alkaline one, but I have yet to notice symptoms of chlorosis on my outdoor plants. Extension growth commences once flowering is over, so it is important to give any feed required at this point. The fragrant winter flowers and slow growth rate make this species an ideal candidate for container cultivation in the open during the growing season. Plants can then be brought into a protected environment to appreciate the scent and beauty of the flowers during winter.

Daphne jezoensis is prone to virus infection, or at least, plants have shown symptoms of virus several times since I have grown this species; this may be because it is more prone to aphid attack than most other species. The new foliage and, importantly, the flower buds are liable to attack from slugs and snails during mild winter periods. Northern Japan experiences cold winters, so *Daphne jezoensis* can be considered hardy to –20°C/–4°F (Zone 6), although flowers might be damaged by temperatures as low as this.

Propagation

Freshly sown seed germinates well the following spring. Seedlings do not branch naturally, so the apex must be pinched towards the end of the first growing season or early in the second, to avoid the "palm tree" look. Grafts can be made in August or January using *D. mezereum* or *D. longilobata* as stocks; *D. mezereum* would be preferable for colder areas. I have never tried taking cuttings, but soft tips might root under mist or fog. Several years ago the top-growth of one of my seed-grown plants died, whereupon suckers appeared from the roots—which suggests that root cuttings could be a successful propagation method.

Daphne juliae Kos.-Pol.

This species from the Voronezh district of Russia is obviously closely related to *D. cneorum*, if not a geographical form of that species. The clone that I grow has a sturdier, more upright habit of growth and flowers two weeks earlier than any *D. cneorum* clone. Without careful pruning it makes an open-centred plant 30–45 CM high and 45–60 CM across.

The leaves are similar to those of *D. cneorum*, averaging 1.7 CM by 0.4 CM in size. The inflorescence and the bracts enclosing it are larger than in any form of *D. cneorum* I grow. The former may consist of up to 25 blooms, which again exceeds most *D. cneorum* forms. When the flowers are fully developed, the well-spaced inflorescences have a more rounded shape than those of *D. cneorum*. The flower colour is deep

D. juliae. Note the rounded inflorescence compared to *D. cneorum* (see p. 44).

pink; the perianth lobes have a rather crumpled appearance when the flower first opens, but their shape evens with maturity. Unlike *D. cneorum*, the stem of the inflorescence—the peduncle—does not elongate as the flowers develop.

Unlike *D. cneorum*, *D. juliae* does not produce any flowers on new growth, which may explain why I have only seen seed set once; like *D. cneorum*, the fruit has a fleshy pericarp, yellowish green in colour.

The early-flowering habit of *D. juliae* makes it a worthwhile addition to a collection. In my garden, the strongly scented flowers open in early April. Unfortunately, I have not found it an easy plant to establish in the ground. Possibly it is used to a warm, dry blanket of snow in winter, making it vulnerable to the fluctuating temperatures of our winter climate. Both plants on their own roots and ones grafted on *D. longilobata* have grown well for me in an unheated polythene tunnel.

Daphne juliae should be hardy to at least –23°C/–10°F (Zone 6).

Propagation

Unlike *D. cneorum*, semi-ripe tip cuttings root without difficulty. Since this species is early into growth they can be taken in mid-June, and will root in time to get them potted up and established by autumn. Plants grafted on *D. mezereum* or *D. longilobata* grow well.

Daphne laureola L.

This species, commonly known as the spurge laurel, is native to Britain, much of Europe and North Africa. Records going back to the 16TH century indicate that early cultivation was mainly for medicinal purposes. Typically, *D. laureola* makes an evergreen bush up to 1.2 M in height and width. The glossy, dark green leaves have a leathery texture, and range from oblanceolate to obovate in shape. The green flowers are produced in February and March in axillary clusters at the apex of the previous season's growth; their colour and position under the leaves mean that they go largely unnoticed. There are records of the flowers smelling unpleasant, but on mild days the flowers of *D. laureola* 'Margaret Mathew' are pleasantly scented of honey. Flowers are often followed by generous crops of black, ovoid fruits.

In the British Isles, *D. laureola* is generally found growing in deciduous woodland on calcareous soils. It will certainly tolerate quite deep shade, and so has a use in gardens providing structure in awkward, shaded areas. However, plants of the native form of this species I have seen growing in shade have become bare of foliage at the base and present a leggy appearance, while plants I have seen in mountainous areas of Europe, often growing in open, sunny areas, were furnished with foliage to the ground, and their leaves were a much brighter green than in U.K. native woodland plants. The hardiness of *D. laureola* forms may vary according to the area from which they originated, but most should tolerate temperatures as low as –23°C/–10°F (Zone 6).

Propagation

Fresh-sown seed germinates well the following spring. Selected clones can be propagated from cuttings taken in July or August; soft tip cuttings root easily, while those from riper material may not produce roots until the following spring.

Botanical variants and named clones

Daphne laureola var. *latifolia* (Cosson) Meissn.

I have no experience of this variety from southern Spain and Morocco, which has much broader leaves and can grow up to 2 M in height. Fritz Kummert, however, is enthusiastic about plants he saw in the Sierra Grazalema, Cadiz, Spain.

Daphne laureola subsp. *philippi* (Gren.) Rouy

This is a compact, low-growing, high altitude form from the Pyrenees. Plants in the French Pyrenees around Gavarnie seem very variable in height and vigour, ranging from comparatively prostrate, slow-growing forms around 30 CM high to bushes 60–90 CM in height and 1–1.5 M across. A low-growing form I collected has remained in character in cultivation and makes a useful, dwarf evergreen for a semi-shaded or cool area.

Daphne laureola subsp. *philippi* (?) 'Kingsley Green'

A fine introduction from the French Pyrenees by Susan and Michael Ayling, possibly a little tall to be classified as subsp. *philippi*. Against a south-facing wall in the Aylings' Hampshire garden, this plant makes a bold statement all year round. Measuring 1.2 M in height and 1.5 M across, it is well furnished with large, bright green leaves to ground level. The oblanceolate leaves are large, measuring 8–10 CM long by 2.5–3 CM wide at their broadest point. I counted 30 leaves on 9 CM of stem. Flowers are freely produced in late winter, generally followed by generous crops of seed.

D. laureola subsp. *philippi*, approximately 20 x 90 CM; French Pyrenees.

D. laureola subsp. *philippi* (?) 'Kingsley Green'.

Daphne laureola 'Margaret Mathew'

This cultivar was introduced from Sicily by the late Hugo Latymer, and named by Kath Dryden after Brian Mathew's wife. It makes a well-branched plant, generally wider than it is tall—1.2 M wide by 90 CM tall on average—and remains well furnished with foliage to ground level whether grown in sun or semi-shade. The first honey-scented flowers often open in December. It is a useful plant for providing winter structure in the garden, and a good companion for species of sarcococca and skimmia.

D. laureola 'Margaret Mathew' remains furnished with foliage to the base in maturity.

Daphne longilobata (Lecomte) Turril

In the United Kingdom at least, there has been considerable confusion between this species from Tibet and China and *D. acutiloba*. While one- and two-year-old seedlings are similar, once plants start to mature they are quite distinct. To help sort out any confusion, I have made a comparison of some of the main differences between the two species (see table, overleaf).

I would not rate most forms of *D. longilobata* as garden-worthy, but amongst plants I have raised from seed and grown in a polythene tunnel to provide

A comparison of the main distinguishing features of *D. acutiloba* and *D. longilobata*

	D. acutiloba	*D. longilobata*
Habit	Firm, bushy, 0.7 to 1 M	Thin open growth, 1.2 to 1.5 M
Bark colour	Dark brown to grey-brown	Tan to grey
Leaves of young plants	Obovate to lanceolate 10 × 1.8 CM	Lanceolate to oblanceolate 10.5 × 1.8 CM
Leaves of mature plants	Lanceolate to oblanceolate 7.5 × 1.8 CM	Lanceolate to oblanceolate 5 × 0.9 CM
Flowering time	April to May plus occasional summer blooms	May to September
Inflorescence	6 to 10 flowers enclosed in caducous bracts	4 to 6 flowers, no bracts
Flower	Pink-flushed bud opening pure white	Greenish white, purple base to perianth tube
Scent	Excellent daytime scent	Striking evening scent to some clones
Fruit size	1 to 1.2 CM by 0.7 to 0.8 CM	0.9 to 1 CM by 0.6 to 0.7 CM

further seed for rootstocks, two have strongly scented flowers from early evening onwards, presumably to aid pollination by moths. Why they are not all scented is difficult to fathom. The perfume is very exotic, rather like gardenia. Correctly sited, a plant with this scent would be an asset to anyone who enjoys the various fragrances of a garden on a summer evening.

Mature plants have an open, loose habit, with thin spindly growth making a bush 1.2–1.5 M in height and width. The foliage is evergreen; the narrow leaves are lanceolate to oblanceolate in shape. Under cover the first flush of flowers appears in May, borne on old wood at the end of main stems or at the apex of short axillary growths. Four to six flowers form inflorescences that are not enclosed by bracts. By July flowers are produced on the new season's growth in succession until September. The flowers have cream perianth lobes, with a

D. acutiloba CD&R 626 'Fragrant Cloud'. Compare with *D. longilobata*, right.

D. longilobata. Compare with *D. acutiloba*, left.

greenish cream perianth tube which has a purple flush at the base. Good crops of reddish orange fruits follow both flushes of flower, often weighing the thin branches down. While *D. longilobata* tolerates shade, growing it in low light levels will encourage its tendency to thin, weak growth. Records show that it is tolerant of a wide range of soil conditions.

As I have no experience of growing *D. longilobata* in the open in low temperatures, I can only repeat that it is reputed to be less than hardy. The thin, lax growth would make plants very vulnerable to snow damage. For me, the species is useful to provide rootstocks, but it should not be used for this purpose in areas where the ground is frozen for long periods. I suggest that it would tolerate temperatures down to –12°C/10°F (Zone 8).

D. longilobata in fruit.

Propagation

Seed is the obvious and straightforward way to propagate this species, while clones selected for scent or foliage could easily be grafted.

Named clones

Daphne longilobata 'Peter Moore'

This form was selected and named by Peter Moore while he was propagator at Hillier Nurseries. It makes a bush 0.9–1.2 M in height and width. The leaves have a greyish green central zone, with irregular cream edges, providing a striking background for the fruits. The variegation is very stable.

D. longilobata 'Peter Moore'.

Daphne longituba C. Y. Chang

Thanks to Kath Dryden, I have grown this species from Guangxi, China for several years. I have not yet tried to grow it outside, but early indications are that it will not be hardy in the United Kingdom.

Daphne longituba is an evergreen shrub that I estimate could grow to a height and width of 1.5–2 M. Plants branch well naturally, and growth is strong enough to create a bushy, upright habit. The alternate leaves are broadly elliptic or ovate, 4–8 CM by 2.5–3 CM, dark green, and with noticeably wavy margins. The inflorescence of 3–10 blooms is terminal, at the apex of branches or on short side growths, enclosed in light green, caducous bracts. The pure white flowers have a long perianth tube, 1–1.4 CM by 0.2 CM, and relatively short, pointed lobes, 0.3–0.4 CM long by 0.2 CM wide. The flowers of the clone I grow have a curious scent; newly opened ones remind me of gardenia, but this tends to deteriorate to tomcat as the

D. longituba.

flowers mature! Under glass the plants start to flower in early November, continuing until February. The fleshy fruits have a pale orange pericarp.

In mild climates the autumn and winter blooming of this species would be useful. It will certainly benefit from the shelter of trees or other shrubs, and will tolerate a degree of shade. I think temperatures below –10°C/14°F (Zone 8) would be damaging.

Daphne ludlowii Long & Rae

A species with quiet charm, known only from the type locality in central Bhutan. The plant I grew was introduced in 1990 by Keith Rushforth under the collector's number KR 1177; it was found growing in mixed picea, tsuga and rhododendron forest at an altitude of 3450 M. Sadly my plant has succumbed to virus infection.

D. ludlowii.

Daphne ludlowii is an evergreen, suckering shrub with stems 60–90 CM in height. The lateral branches are slender and well spaced. The leaves are of leathery texture, dark, glossy green with a retuse apex and revolute margins, oblong to lanceolate, 3–4 CM by 0.8–1 CM. The terminal inflorescence of 10–25 flowers is contained by caducous bracts. The terminal clusters of flowers are creamy yellow, and contrary to other descriptions, have a pleasant, sweet, clove-like fragrance. Flowering period is from early April to May. My clone did not set seed, but the fruit is described as a red, fleshy drupe.

I grew *D. ludlowii* successfully for several years on its own roots in a humus-rich raised bed in a netting shade tunnel with no winter protection. Temperatures down to –12°C (10°F) caused little damage. Once the flowers started to develop from their protective bracts they were vulnerable to late spring frost damage. Given its provenance, *D. ludlowii* is likely to grow best in a humid atmosphere, and a cool, shady site. I suggest temperatures below –12°C/10°F (Zone 8) would be damaging.

D. mezereum.

Propagation

Tip cuttings of semi-ripe wood root easily, and plants grafted on *D. longilobata* grow satisfactorily. The suckering habit of this species suggests that root cuttings would be successful, and no doubt branches could be layered.

Daphne macrantha Ludlow

I wish I could write from experience about this species, known only from its type locality in southeast Tibet, because it sounds special. Hopefully plants may be introduced to cultivation before too long. *Daphne macrantha* is described as a semi-evergreen shrub up to 30 CM in height, with dull green leaves which have deeply indented veins. The flowers sound exciting!—large (2.5–3.5 CM in diameter), creamy yellow and very fragrant.

Daphne mezereum L.

This is the species most likely to spring to the mind of most people at the mention of daphnes. When the leafless stems are covered with heavily scented flowers in February and March, plants on sale prove irresistible to many gardeners. Native to central Asia and much of Europe (possibly including England), records of cultivation go back to the 16TH century. A good proportion of early cultivation was for medicinal use in spite of its poisonous properties.

In nature *D. mezereum* is usually found growing in woodland, but it is an adaptable species, and certainly tolerant of sun in northern latitudes. It generally makes a well-branched, deciduous shrub about 1.2 M in height and width, but I have seen a plant approaching 2 M high, and grown a form collected above the treeline in the Kamnik Alps, Slovenia, which never exceeded 45 CM in height. The flowers are borne in lateral clusters of 2–4 on the previous season's growth before the pale green, deciduous leaves appear. They are capable of scenting a wide area on a warm spring day; I find the scent similar to hyacinths. The flowers are followed by a generous crop of fruits, bright red if the flowers are pink, yellow if the flowers are white. In the open, fruits are soon taken by blackbirds for their fleshy pericarp, or by greenfinches and mice for the seed. However, in a tunnel I have seen fruits still in situ in December.

There are records of *D. mezereum* growing well on both acid and alkaline soils, but it is generally considered to prefer a moisture-retentive alkaline soil. Since flowers are only produced on the previous season's growth it is important to provide a deep fertile soil or feed regularly to achieve a good display of flowers the following spring. While it is a shade-tolerant species, it should not be sited where competition from tree roots denies it moisture and nutrients.

Young seed-raised plants, two or three years old, have the best chance of establishing well after planting. If you are purchasing a plant, particularly in the United Kingdom, make sure it has been container-grown, because plants are often imported bare-rooted when dormant, having been raised in open ground, then containerized and offered for sale in bloom within a few weeks. These plants seldom establish when planted. *Daphne mezereum* is a hardy shrub; while open flowers may be damaged by low temperatures, the plant should tolerate temperatures down to –23 to –29°C/–10 to –20°F (Zone 5).

Propagation

Seed is the easiest method of propagation. Fresh-sown seed germinates reliably the following spring. Seedling growth is relatively slow during the first season, 7.5–15 CM on average, so it is generally best to pot on seedlings for another season before planting out. During the second year many seedlings will branch naturally, but if they do not, they should be pruned back to encourage a well-branched habit.

Growing a number of young plants from seed allows for selection for flower quality, as a large proportion of seedlings flower on growth they make in their second season. Apart from the instance mentioned below, I have always found that seed from red fruits produces pink-flowered plants and that of yellow fruits produces white-flowered plants. Any selected forms of *D. mezereum* would obviously grow well grafted on seed-grown rootstocks of the same species. There are records of successful propagation by root cuttings, and thick roots exposed to light have several times produced adventitious shoots on the nursery. Laying root cuttings horizontally and not fully covering them would be a worthwhile experiment.

Botanical variants and named clones

Although there are records of plants of *D. mezereum* thriving for more than 20 years, this species seems more susceptible to virus infection than most, perhaps because it is one of the species most likely to be attacked by aphids, which are vectors of virus. This probably accounts for the fact that several variants described in the 19th century, such as both pink and white double-flowered forms, an autumn-flowering variety, and several forms selected and named for flower colour or size, no longer seem to be in cultivation. Clones with variegated foliage also appear occasionally, but do not stand the test of time.

D. mezereum f. alba.

Daphne mezereum forma *alba* (Weston) Schelle

The white-flowered form was given this name in 1903. A particularly good selection from the garden of E. A. Bowles was distributed in the middle of the 20th century under the names 'Bowles Variety' or 'Bowles White'. It had a vigorous, upright habit and pure white flowers. Over many years of propagation by seed, these characters now seem much diluted, at least in the plants I have seen.

It is generally accepted that the pink- and white-flowered forms of *D. mezereum* breed true to colour when grown from seed; for many years that held true for me. During the course of making our garden in the late 1980s, we used all spent compost from seed trays and pots to improve our heavy clay soil. Among the many stray seedlings that appeared was a *D. mezereum* which was left to grow. The flower colour was the normal pink, and the fruits standard red. Seed from this plant was grown to produce rootstocks, but a few multi-stemmed plants were potted on to grow into plants to sell. I was very surprised to find that a proportion of these plants produced white flowers. The parent plant was the only *D. mezereum* in the garden, so seed produced was from self-pollination. For a number of years this parent continued to set good crops of seed which, if grown to flowering, were mainly pink-flowered but with a few in white. Fruits on the white-flowered plants were always yellow, and plants from these fruits were all white-flowered. In the autumn 2002 edition of the Daphne Society Newsletter, a similar case of white-flowered plants arising from a pink-flowered parent is recorded by a grower on Vancouver Island, British Columbia.

Daphne mezereum 'Variegata'

Records of variegated forms go back to the 19TH century when a plant with yellow and grey-green leaves was named.

Amongst the many *D. mezereum* seedlings I have raised to use as rootstocks, occasional plants produced some first true leaves which had sections of cream variegation. Invariably, further growth on these plants only produced plain green leaves.

Daphne mezereum 'Kingsley Purple'

A recent introduction from the French Pyrenees by Susan and Michael Ayling, which may provide the answer to the puzzle of where the leaf colour of *D.* ×*houtteana* 'Louis Van Houtte' comes from (see p. 124), since *D. laureola* grew in the same area. If planted where it receives at least half a day's sunshine, the leaves of this form turn purple as they mature; this coloration is particularly noticeable on the undersurface of the leaf. When self-pollinated, the offspring remain true to type.

D. mezereum 'Kingsley Purple'. (Photo: Michael Ayling)

Dwarf forms

Plants growing above the treeline in mountainous areas are often of much smaller stature than lowland forms, and are sometimes referred to as var. *alpina*, a name which has not been validated. Seed from a plant of this type which I brought back from the Kamnik Alps produced plants which maintained their dwarf character in cultivation; even when grafted on *D. mezereum*, plants did not exceed 45 CM. Since little growth was made, not many flowers were produced, so I rate this as a form with botanical interest only.

I have recently received material of a free-flowering alpine form from Mike and Polly Stone, proprietors of Askival Nursery. The seed of this was collected near Presolana, in northern Italy. The plant they grow is now 1.2 M across, but only 45 CM high.

Daphne odora Thunb.

This is the first daphne I ever put my nose to. After all these years, I still look forward to the first flowers opening each spring to renew my acquaintance with a scent that I rate unbeatable. Due to the wonderful fragrance of the flowers, this Chinese species has been cultivated in its native land for thousands of years, and reached this country towards the end of the 18TH century. In the 19TH century it was an important addition to the range of plants grown in the conservatories and stove houses of wealthy Victorians. Although there are records of western plant hunters finding *D. odora* in the wild towards the end of the 19th and early 20TH century, I am not aware that anyone has found it in more recent times. It seems possible, therefore, that *D. odora* as grown today is in fact the result of mutation which occurred sometime during the centuries of its cultivation in China. Its abnormal chromosome count would support this possibility. The long history of cultivation of this species has resulted in many selections being named, especially in Japan, where forms with variegated foliage are particularly sought after.

In cultivation, *D. odora* makes a rather gawky bush, around 1.2 M in height and width. Young plants are reluctant to make lateral growths to create a bushy plant. Pinching out the growing point of a strong-growing leader to make it bush out tends to result in only a single shoot growing from the topmost axillary bud; pruning back into more mature wood may be required to encourage lateral shoots. The evergreen leaves tend to cluster towards the tips of the shoots, so careful training is needed to avoid a poorly shaped plant which shows a lot of bare stem at the base; regular harvesting of flowering growth to take indoors may help to produce a better shaped plant!

Mature plants produce all their flowers in terminal inflorescences, but strong-growing young specimens often follow terminal blossom with flowers on short axillary growths. The flower buds are rosy purple, and when open the perianth lobes are palest lilac on the inside. The delicious scent has a strong citrus element. I have yet to see fruits, but they are recorded as being fleshy and red. *Daphne odora* is particularly susceptible to infection by a number of different viruses (see p. 217). Symptoms are usually a yellow mottling of the foliage (particularly if the plant is growing in full sun), poor growth and excessive leaf drop.

Since *D. odora* in one or other of its many forms is probably the most widely cultivated daphne species, it should be possible to obtain plants in most parts of the world where it can be grown successfully. If you are lucky enough to live where winter temperatures allow *D. odora* to be grown outside, try to plant it near the house or by a main path so that savouring the wonderful perfume is made easy. In areas too cold for outdoor cultivation, *D. odora* can be grown successfully in a container for a number of years, and a succession of plants produced from the easily rooted cuttings.

This species is perhaps less tolerant of alkaline conditions than most daphnes; occasional applications of chelated iron, incorporating generous quantities of organic matter into the soil, and regular feeding and mulching can overcome or prevent the tell-tale signs of poor growth and yellowing leaves (not to be confused with a virus infection).

The hardiness of the various clones of *D. odora* does seem to vary; during several cold winters in the 1980s, I had *D. odora* 'Aureomarginata' growing alongside a plain-leaved clone from New Zealand called *D. odora* 'Leucanthe'. Temperatures down to –15°C (5°F) killed the latter, while the former was undamaged apart from some leaf browning. I would suggest that hardier clones of *D. odora* could be planted in sheltered sites in Zone 7 (–12 to –17°C/10 to 0°F), but extra protection with fleece or burlap might be required when temperatures are below freezing for long periods. Plants in containers would be liable to fatal damage if their roots were frozen for long.

Propagation

My stock plants are grown under the protection of unheated polythene providing soft tip cuttings by early June and semi-ripe material by early July. Tip, basal or heel cuttings taken from lateral growth root in six to eight weeks in a closed polythene frame. I have found that some of the softer cuttings are liable to be damaged by my standard rooting powder, but untreated cuttings root well enough to make hormone treatment unnecessary. Cuttings taken in early September from riper wood, either as tips or as heels, take longer to root but give as good a result; these would be the best type of cutting to take for rooting in a cold frame. The early cuttings can be potted by September, and a proportion will make reasonable plants by the end of the next growing season. Later cuttings are grown in a 9 CM pot for one season, then potted on to produce a strong plant with several branches after two seasons.

Some of the highly variegated clones lack enough chlorophyll to grow strongly on their own roots; these I graft on *D. longilobata*, which produces a branched plant in one growing season.

Botanical variants and named clones

After such a long period in cultivation, it is not surprising that many selections for flowers and leaf have been named, particularly in the Far East, but this species' susceptibility to virus has resulted in some of these dying out. Selected forms have often reached the west from more than one source; in such cases there may be confusion over nomenclature. The following list contains cultivars which should be available in Europe and the United States of America.

Plain-leaved cultivars

Daphne odora forma *alba* (Hemsley) Hara

This name applies to all plain-leaved plants with white or cream flowers. I once grew a plant with this name which produced so little flower and so much fasciated growth that it went on the bonfire.

Daphne odora forma *alba* 'Sakiwaka'

A green-leaved cultivar from Japan with white flowers which I am told does not produce fasciated growth. How freely the flowers are produced remains to be seen.

Daphne odora 'Leucanthe'

I believe this cultivar originated in New Zealand. It has been widely sold in the United Kingdom since the 1980s. Unfortunately this is not a valid cultivar name, and creates confusion with *D. odora* var. *leucantha*, which is a synonym of *D. odora* forma *alba*—I originally bought plants assuming that they would have white flowers. It is a plain-leaved, vigorous clone, with noticeably bright crimson buds and large flowers, but not the hardiest of *D. odora* forms.

Daphne odora 'Zuiko Nishiki'

Material of this Japanese cultivar was kindly given to me by John Bieber, president of the U.S. Daphne Society, who believes it is not among the hardier clones of this species. To date, I have not managed to confirm this. The flowers in bud are deep pink rather than rosy purple and, with an average diameter of 2.5 CM, slightly larger than those of other cultivars.

Variegated cultivars

There are numerous forms of *D. odora* selected for their variegated foliage, some of which are described below. The colour of the sections of leaf lacking chlorophyll usually varies within a cultivar according to leaf age, nutrition and light intensity—areas which are yellow in young leaves may be cream or greenish-cream in old ones; a high level of nutrition can result in a larger area of green in a leaf; strong sunlight induces a smaller portion of green leaf, while shade may give a green flush to cream or yellow areas. Due to the varying growth rates of plain and variegated tissue within an individual leaf, young leaves often distort, but develop a more regular shape as they mature.

Daphne odora 'Aureomarginata'

This variety has a narrow, yellowish-cream edge to the leaves and is by far the most widely cultivated form in the United Kingdom; it also seems to be the hardiest clone in cultivation. Several laboratories in the U.K. and in New Zealand are producing this cultivar in large quantities by means of tissue culture, which does help to reduce the incidence of virus in young nursery stock, so reasonable quantities of healthy plants are available. The flower buds are rosy purple and mature flowers average 2 CM in diameter. This clone should be chosen for its relative hardiness and freely produced blossom, because the narrow band of variegation is not significant in the garden.

D. odora 'Aureomarginata'.

Daphne odora 'Forde Abbey'

A selection made by Alan Lewis when he ran Forde Abbey Nursery. The marginal area of the leaf is a clear, pale yellow, 0.3–0.6 CM wide. The central area is irregular in shape, and is partially dark green, the rest grey-green. Flowers are not freely produced. Sports similar to this occur relatively often on 'Aureomarginata', but some are unstable, and all I have seen are rather weak growers, unlikely to exceed more than 1 M in height and width. *Daphne odora* 'Bakers Gold' was a similar plant on offer in the 1980s, but is seldom seen now.

Daphne odora 'Geisha Girl'

The leaf has a thin, irregular dark green edge about 0.1–0.2 CM wide. Within this is a large area which can vary from pale yellow to pale green. There is an irregular central zone of pale and dark grey-green. The leaves have enough chlorophyll to support a reasonable growth rate, so plants should reach 1–1.2 M in height and width. Flowers are freely produced as plants mature. This cultivar regularly sports to produce a form I have named 'Limelight' (see below).

Daphne odora 'Limelight'

I have given this sport of 'Geisha Girl' a cultivar name because I think its even variegation is most attractive. In good light the foliage is a clear pale yellow with a dark green irregular edge, 0.1–0.2 CM wide. Mature or shaded leaves have a wider green edge, up to 0.6 CM, while the rest of the leaf area is lime green. 'Limelight' has a good growth rate and should make a plant 1–1.2 M in height and width. This form occasionally throws a sport back to 'Geisha Girl'.

Daphne odora 'Mae Jima'

This is an outstanding selection from Japan; it is the best variegated form of this species I have seen, and could hold its own with any variegated evergreen even without the bonus of the scented flowers. The major portion of the leaf is a shiny, dark green, providing enough chlorophyll for the plant to grow well; the broad, bright yellow margin, up to 0.6 CM wide, forms a striking contrast. Plants should reach 1–1.2 M in height and width. Flowers are freely produced as plants mature; the buds are bright rosy purple, the flower diameter of mature blooms averages 2.2 CM. Provided it proves equally hardy, this cultivar should replace 'Aureomarginata' as the most popular form of this species.

D. odora 'Forde Abbey'.

D. odora 'Geisha Girl'.

D. odora 'Limelight'.

D. odora 'Mae Jima'.

Daphne odora 'Rebecca'

A promising new variegated cultivar which came from a sport on 'Aureomarginata'. It was a lucky find by nurseryman Steve Watson, who spotted the plant on a market stall. The leaves have a margin of cream variegation which is much wider than that of 'Aureomarginata', and to date this variegation has proved stable. Mr Watson reports that cuttings root easily and plants have plenty of vigour. Community Plant Variety Rights have been applied for for this cultivar, which should be on sale in the United Kingdom from 2006.

Daphne odora 'Walberton'

In the mid-1960s Mr. David Tristram propagated a sport which arose on a plant of 'Aureomarginata' growing in his garden in Ireland. The resulting plants carry more flowers per inflorescence than 'Aureomarginata'. On moving to England to set up Walberton Nursery, Mr. Tristram increased production of this cultivar, particularly in response to demand created by display plants in the RHS Gardens at Wisley.

Daphne oleoides Schreb.

This species has a wide distribution throughout Mediterranean countries and the Caucasus, and may be found growing from near sea level to at least 3000 metres; it is therefore variable in form and hardiness. Several closely related species and botanical varieties have been described, but until detailed field studies are made it is impossible to arrive at any satisfactory classification of the group. Some forms seem to be quite upright in habit, and soon develop bare stems at their base, while others are more bushy and spreading. The average plant should be 30–60 cm in height and slightly more in width. The evergreen foliage, which is generally grey-green but may be plain green, is tough and leathery, helping the plant to withstand summer drought. The leaf is obovate to elliptical in shape, 1–4.5 cm long by 0.3–1.2 cm wide, although a form growing in Peter Erskine's garden, of unknown origin, has narrow, lanceolate leaves up to 3.2 cm long by 0.6 cm wide. The flowers are produced in terminal inflorescences from May to June. I have only grown white- or cream-coloured forms, but there are records of pale pink flowers. The narrow perianth lobes, up to 0.7 cm long, give the flower a star-like appearance. Although I do detect a sweet fragrance in the evening from one of the forms I grow, scent is not a strong point of this species. The flowers are generally followed by a good crop of orange fruits, even on single plants, which are well set off against the grey-green foliage.

D. oleoides.

Daphne oleoides is a useful plant for a hot, dry site if it can be established, but I have not found this easy to do. Apart from a 10-year-old plant in the corner of a deep trough, I have failed more often than not. Plants seem to have a death wish in pots, at least in my compost, but seed-raised plants which I planted in my "daphnetum" soon after producing their first true leaves have established well, so this may be one way to get plants started. Grafted plants are easier to grow in containers, but would probably be less tolerant of hot dry conditions than plants on their own roots. There are conflicting reports on the hardiness of this species, which may be due to the widely differing habitats from which plants have been introduced. Introductions from cold areas should be hardy to –17°C/0°F (Zone 7).

Propagation

Seed is readily set, and germinates well the following spring if sown fresh. My few attempts at cuttings were not successful. I have grafted wild-collected material given to me at various times in the summer which has grown well on *D. mezereum* rootstocks.

Botanical variants and named clones

Daphne aff. *oleoides* 'Palermo'

In 2002 I was given material of a daphne which Michael Kammerlander has grown for many years in the botanic garden at Würzburg, Germany. He raised these plants from seed sent to him in 1973 from Palermo botanic garden, Sicily. Presumably this seed came from plants native to Sicily, although there are no records to confirm this. Mr. Kammerlander reports that this plant breeds true from seed, and so can be given a cultivar name. The botanical status remains to be confirmed, but if 'Palermo' is a form of *D. oleoides*, it is certainly the best I have seen.

D. aff. *oleoides* 'Palermo'. (Photo: Michael Kammerlander)

Even allowing for the fact that my plants are grafted, growth is strong, up to 10 CM in a season, compared with the 3–4 CM normal for this species, and Mr. Kammerlander's oldest plants are now up to 45 CM tall and 1.5 M in diameter. The stems are thick and the bark dark brown, rather than tan or grey-brown as normal. The obovate leaves are dark green, 2.5–3 CM long by 1 CM wide. The silky-haired perianth tube is pale green and the lobes creamy white, but low temperatures induce a rosy purple coloration to the perianth tube and the edge of the lobes. The perianth lobes are shorter and broader than other *D. oleoides* at 0.5 CM long by 0.3–0.4 CM wide, with an acute apex; they are not reflexed. As well as terminal clusters of flower there are axillary inflorescences near the apex of the stem. A generous quantity of flower is produced in spring, followed by occasional flowers in late summer. The flowers are sweetly fragrant at all times. The fruits are typical of *D. oleoides.*

I have no experience of the plant's hardiness, but given Mr. Kammerlander's success in Germany it can be considered hardy to –17°C/0°F (Zone 7). This plant promises to be a useful addition to gardens.

D. petraea in the wild, Cima Tuflungo, northern Italy. (Photo: Peter Erskine)

Daphne petraea Leybold

Many writers before me have sung the praises of this species. Although I get tremendous pleasure from the beautiful flowers and wonderful scents of other daphne species, for me *D. petraea* is the gem, providing a complete package of form, foliage, flower and scent.

Daphne petraea is native to a very small area of northern Italy, west of Lake Garda. Seeing the inhospitable nature of the limestone cliffs it inhabits has increased my admiration for this wonderful species, and I make no apologies for writing in some length about the forms I am lucky enough to grow, many of them thanks to the efforts of Peter Erskine.

Different forms of this dwarf, much-branched evergreen shrub show subtle variations in habit when grown in cultivation. Upright growth may be vigorous enough to produce a flattened, dome-shaped plant, 15 CM or more in height, while slower-growing forms produce a tight bun 10–15 CM in height and width; others make an even mat of growth 5–7.5 CM high by 20–30 CM wide. I have seen venerable plants in the wild 60 CM or more across, which must be of a great age. A 20-year-old plant in cultivation has reached 30 CM in diameter. In the wild *D. petraea* can often be seen growing in fissures in cliffs or in narrow gaps between large pieces of rock, at any angle from vertical to horizontal. Colonization of these areas is aided by the production of stolons (horizontal stems) which may travel some distance before making a rosette of foliage and putting down roots. This characteristic has been passed on to hybrids with another cliff-dwelling species, *D. jasminea*: both *D.* ×*whiteorum* 'Beauworth' and 'Kilmeston' occasionally produce stoloniferous growth. Natural vigour also varies, from 'Michele', which may make 2.5–5 CM of growth in a season, to 'Lydora', at less than 1.2 CM.

The glossy, dark green leaves cluster towards the tips of the short branches. Size and shape is variable, ranging from narrow, linear, 1.7 CM by 0.2 CM in 'Flamingo' to short, oblanceolate, 0.7 CM by 0.15 CM in 'Lydora'. The upper surface of the leaves is protected from dehydration by a thick, waxy layer, the cuticle; a sudden sharp frost in early winter may result in the cuticle being separated from the cells beneath to give the leaves a pale green appearance. This is most likely to happen on strong but unripened growth of young plants, particularly if they are grafted. Leaves damaged in this way usually drop off by late spring.

Vigorous young plants, especially those which are grafted, produce axillary inflorescences; but as plants mature, the inflorescence is terminal, enclosed by narrow, persistent bracts which tend to hold dead flowers in place, so increasing the risk of dieback problems. The sweetly scented flowers number 3–5 per inflorescence, and range in colour from white through pink to red. Unlike most daphnes, the flowers turn paler rather than darker as they mature (see photo on p. 95). The perianth lobes are variable in size and shape; those of cultivars such as 'Grandiflora' may be 0.6 CM wide, broadly ovate and overlapping, compared to those of 'Tremalzo'—0.4 CM wide, narrowly ovate and not overlapping. The diameter of the mouth of the flower ranges from 'Flamingo' at 1.5 CM through 'Grandiflora', 1 CM, to 'Lydora' at 0.7 CM. Some cultivars have a distinct pale "eye" at the mouth of the perianth tube, while 'Punchinello' has two pale inner lobes and two dark outer ones.

The flower colour of a clone can vary from year to year or season to season. The best quality flowers with the most intense colour are produced in spring on old wood; annual variation in temperature and nutrition are two factors I believe to influence this. Flowers produced on new growth are generally smaller and always less intensely coloured.

In cultivation the foliage of a healthy *D. petraea* is hidden by the quantity of flower produced in April and May, and more flowers are borne on new growth through the summer, particularly on vigorous young plants. In the wild, flower production may not be so generous, and plants can be seen without any flower.

Biennial flowering may be the reason, and dry summer conditions will affect the formation of flower buds for the following spring.

Growing a number of different clones in the same bed reveals a difference of more than two weeks between the earliest and latest to flower. Under unheated cover the former are flowering by the first week of April. Individual flowers last from ten to fourteen days depending largely on the prevailing temperatures.

I find seed is rarely set by the spring flowers of *D. petraea*, but summer flowers frequently produce seed. This is probably due to the increased activity of moths, which have a proboscis long enough to pollinate flowers, and bumblebees, which bite into the perianth tube (see p. 211). In the wild the flowering period of May to June would ensure pollinating insects were present; a lasting memory of my visit to the home of *D. petraea* was the number of butterflies. The seed frequently remains encased in the dead perianth tube, though occasionally the greenish yellow pericarp swells enough to split it.

Since *D. petraea* is a popular show plant for members of the Alpine Garden Society, it is generally grown in containers in the United Kingdom and given some form of winter protection, from wet rather than cold. I am pretty certain that plants do not like the constant winter moisture on their foliage that our maritime climate provides. In a more continental climate plants may well be grown easily in the open. That is not to say that *D. petraea* cannot be grown outside in England, but quantity and quality of flower, which is what we all want, is easier to obtain with winter protection.

I have found that both plants on their own roots and those grafted on *D. mezereum* or *D. longilobata* have grown well in raised beds in a polythene tunnel. Growing *D. petraea* in pots is more of a challenge, but if you get things right plants grow and flower happily for many years.

There is little to choose between plants grown on their own roots and grafted plants other than initial vigour. A plant on its own roots may take six years to reach the size of a three-year-old graft, but by ten years there is little difference in size and flower production. Using *D. longilobata* as a stock tends to make plants flower a few days earlier than they do on their own roots or on *D. mezereum* stocks. Plants in pots which are given winter cover will generally be happier and easier to look after if they are moved outside after flowering. Where high summer temperatures are the norm, this would be essential. By late summer the terminal inflorescences which will provide the spectacular spring display are well developed; if pot-grown plants are allowed to get too dry through the winter, a large proportion of these flowers abort.

D. petraea clones grafted on *D. longilobata* four years after planting in the "daphnetum".

To grow well outside in my climate, *D. petraea* needs a site which provides plenty of light and air circulation to allow foliage and overwintering flower buds to dry quickly after rain or dew. The dwarf habit makes it ideal for a trough or a choice pocket in the rock garden, or for planting in tufa. To date, grafted plants have established and flowered better in my "daphnetum" than ones on their own roots, but grafted plants are not suitable for planting in tufa or for wedging in narrow cracks between pieces of stone. If you intend to plant in tufa, try to drill the hole right through to soil beyond or underneath, so that deeply searching roots can obtain a better supply of nutrients once the plant has established in the tufa pocket. Failure to do this may result in plants which remain healthy, but grow little and flower less. Burying two pieces of tufa or limestone rock with a gap of 2.5–5 CM between them creates an ideal site for *D. petraea* to grow on its own roots.

As a cliff-dweller in the wild, *D. petraea* is unlikely to benefit a great deal from a blanket of snow to protect it from low temperatures. The small leaves of leathery texture are ideally adapted to freezing temperatures and wind chill. I doubt if plants would be harmed by temperatures down to –23°C/–10°F (Zone 6).

Propagation

When I have sown freshly harvested seed of *D. petraea*, a proportion has germinated reliably the following spring. Seedlings should be moved on quickly as they soon make a long, fine root. Seed-raised plants flower after three or four seasons. Semi-ripe basal cuttings, taken towards the end of June from plants under glass, generally root well. It is often only a single root which grows from the base of the cutting, so great care should be taken when transferring to pots, an operation I leave until the following spring. From a commercial point of view, grafting is the standard method of propagation. There is little to choose between *D. mezereum* and *D. longilobata* as a rootstock, except that the cambium of the former, when exposed by the transverse cut (see also p. 171), tends to produce adventitious shoots which are difficult to remove without damaging the scion, while use of the latter may reduce overall hardiness. It is important not to use rootstocks which are old and pot-bound, since the small scion cannot provide the carbohydrates necessary to promote active root growth—a situation which can result in slow establishment or failure.

Botanical variants and named clones

Daphne petraea 'Cima Tombea'

A delightful introduction by Peter and Penny Watt, rescued many years ago from a rock fall. Like other very slow-growing cultivars, it makes a distinct dome shape. The pale pink perianth lobes are broad and overlapping and there is a pale "eye" to the mouth of the perianth tube. I have sold this plant for a number of years as "Watts form".

Daphne petraea 'Corna Blacca'

A selection by Harry Jans with well shaped, overlapping perianth lobes. Flowers red or deep pink. One of the best clones to grow in the open.

Daphne petraea, double-flowered form

This clone has a justifiable reputation for its flowers not opening from the promising-looking buds. Dryness at the roots during the winter or invasion of the inflorescence by red spider mite are two likely causes. When the flowers do open they are fully double and dusky pink in colour.

D. petraea 'Corna Blacca'.

D. petraea 'Garnet': the earliest flowers to open are now fading.

D. petraea 'Flamingo'.

D. petraea 'Grandiflora'.

Daphne petraea 'Flamingo'

I think this is one of the best introductions that Peter Erskine made in 1999. It is very distinct in its long narrow leaves (1.7 × 0.2 cm), the pale pink flowers (1.5 cm in diameter), and the unusually long perianth tube—2 cm compared to 1.2 cm in 'Grandiflora'. This clone has a more open habit than most; the inflorescences are well spaced, allowing the large flowers plenty of room to develop and be displayed against the deep green foliage. The latest form to flower.

Daphne petraea 'Garnet'

This clone forms a vigorous mat of growth and grows well in the open. It is one of the earliest to flower. The year I named it the flowers were reddish pink, but to my chagrin, for the last two springs they have been relatively pale.

Daphne petraea 'Grandiflora'

A clone which has been widely grown since it was collected in 1914, and has won many prizes on the show bench. The large flowers, 1 CM in diameter, have particularly broad, overlapping perianth lobes. Flowers of the spring flush are a deep, intense pink, 5–7 blooms per inflorescence.

Daphne petraea 'Idro'

A selection by German daphne enthusiast Hans Bauer, with deep reddish pink flowers on a low mat of foliage.

Daphne petraea 'Lydora'

A marvellous 1997 introduction by Peter Erskine, who named it after his two granddaughters, Lydia and Flora. Very neat, with a slow-growing habit which forms a perfect dome. Small crimson flowers with a pale eye, 5–7 blooms per inflorescence.

Daphne petraea 'Michele'

An excellent clone selected by Margaret and Henry Taylor, inveterate plant explorers with an enviable reputation for spotting the best forms of a species. 'Michele' is certainly the most vigorous cultivar when a young plant. Pale pink flowers are produced freely during the summer after the main spring flush.

Daphne petraea 'Persebee'

Another excellent introduction by Peter Erskine. Young grafted plants of this vigorous clone may make very long growth, which is ideal for cuttings but should otherwise be pinched to encourage branching. Both plants on their own roots and grafted on *D. longilobata* are performing well in my "daphnetum". The medium-sized flowers are deep pink.

Daphne petraea 'Punchinello'

Distinct in having flowers with the two inner lobes palest pink, the two outer lobes deep pink. Narrow leaves with an acute apex. Introduced by Peter Erskine under the number 97/CB1.

Daphne petraea 'Tremalzo'

A beautiful white-flowered clone introduced by Ernst Hauser. Growth is slow, which creates a dome-shaped plant. The lobes of the perianth are narrow, so

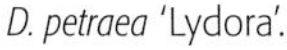

D. petraea 'Lydora'.

D. petraea 'Punchinello'.

D. petraea 'Tremalzo'.

they do not overlap. They seem to have a crystalline texture when the sun shines on them.

Unnamed clones worthy of mention

CDB 11554 Low, spreading habit. Pale pink flowers with a long perianth tube.

PE 87/C Earliest to flower. Very bright pink flowers.

PE 87/E Open habit. Pink flowers with a pale "eye". Late-flowering.

PE 87/F Low, prostrate habit. Bright pink flowers.

Daphne pontica L. and *Daphne albowiana* Woron. ex. Pobed.

Apart from fruit colour and leaf size, *D. pontica* and *D. albowiana* are very similar. The latter species has at times been treated as a subspecies of the former, named *D. pontica* subsp. *haematocarpa*. *Daphne pontica* is native to northern Turkey, through the Pontic Mountains to the Caucasus Mountains, while *D. albowiana* inhabits sub-alpine regions of the southern Caucasus.

Daphne pontica makes a bush about 1 M in height, and will gradually sucker to reach 1 to 1.5 M in width. The evergreen leaves are a deep, glossy green. The

D. albowiana.
(Photo: John Fielding)

D. albowiana in fruit.

flowers are produced in multiple pairs at the base of the current season's growth; they are a soft yellowish green in colour, with long, narrow, reflexed perianth lobes. Some clones have a delicate fragrance, particularly in mild spells and in the early evening. Seed is set freely; the fruit has a fleshy pericarp which ripens to blue-black in *D. pontica*, bright red in *D. albowiana.*

These species grow best in humus-rich ground which does not get too dry in summer, sited in a position where they are shaded from the sun at the hottest part of the day. Deep shade must be avoided, as it results in plants with a gawky habit and few flowers. The glossy evergreen foliage provides useful winter structure for shady borders or open woodland. The pale flowers, produced in April to May, are in pleasant contrast to the dark foliage. These species associate well with evergreen shrubs such as sarcococcas and skimmia.

The hardiness of *D. pontica* may vary according to the area stock originated from, but like all evergreens, it is vulnerable in protracted spells below freezing, particularly when coupled with wind chill. *Daphne albowiana* has a smaller, thicker leaf and, since it is native to colder areas, may well be hardier. Probable minimum temperatures these species will survive are, for *D. pontica*, –17°C/0°F (Zone 7), and for *D. albowiana*, –23°C/–10°F (Zone 6).

Propagation

Seed germinates readily the following spring if sown fresh. Fairly soft or semi-ripe tip cuttings can be rooted without problems. *Daphne pontica* 'Variegata' needs to be grafted; as well as *D. pontica* seedlings, *D. longilobata* is a suitable rootstock.

Named clones

Daphne pontica 'Variegata'

This clone has very attractive foliage, but lack of chlorophyll in the leaves makes growth very slow. Old plants may reach 60–90 CM, and show a lot of bare stem because the leaves cluster at the apex of growth. The bulk of the leaf is cream with a narrow green margin and an irregular central zone of grey-green; the foliage is prone to scorch in strong sun. The flowers are more yellow than those of green-leaved forms.

D. pontica 'Variegata'.

Daphne retusa Hemsl.

Without doubt *D. retusa* is closely related to or conspecific with *D. tangutica*. Both are native to western China and Tibet. However, since *D. retusa* is such a popular and distinct plant, it seems best for gardeners to treat them separately until further studies of plants in the field allow a more definite decision to be made.

Anyone wanting a dwarf, hardy, evergreen shrub which covers itself with intensely fragrant flowers in late spring should have *D. retusa* at the top of their list. The habit is upright and sturdy, but the slow growth rate and plentiful lateral growths result in a dense evergreen dome up to 60 CM in height and 45–60 CM in width. Given too much shade the plant will have a more open habit and less pleasing shape. The tough, leathery leaves have a shiny, dark green surface and vary in size and shape; on vigorous young growth the leaves can measure from 3 × 2 CM to 5 × 2 CM and are generally oblanceolate in shape; on more mature plants, the leaves average 3 × 1 CM and are more elliptic. The leaves are generally retuse, with a small notch in the apex, but this may also be true of mature leaves of *D. tangutica*; however, the leaf edges of *D. retusa* are much more revolute (curling downwards) than those of *D. tangutica*.

The terminal inflorescence contains 5–10 flowers. The exterior of the bud and the flower is deep rosy purple, the inside pale lilac to white. The scent is strong, reminiscent of lilac. With a mouth averaging 2.5 CM across, the flowers of *D. retusa* are larger than those of any form of *D. tangutica* I have seen. While the

D. retusa.

main flush of flower is produced in April and May on the previous season's wood, a few summer flowers with less intense external colour are borne on the current season's growth.

A few seeds are set every year. The round, orange-red fruits are relatively large, at 0.8–1 CM in diameter.

Daphne retusa grows in open wooded areas in its natural habitat, so it appreciates a humus-rich soil. While it may not object to full sun in northern latitudes, strong sun further south may be detrimental, and dry summer conditions will definitely not suit.

In the United Kingdom the hardiness of *D. retusa* is not questioned, but there are some reports of cold damage from Europe. Like all evergreens it may be damaged by long periods where daytime temperatures stay below freezing. It should certainly be hardy in temperatures down to –17 to –23°C/0 to –10°F (Zone 6).

Propagation

Freshly sown seed germinates readily. Seed-raised plants of the form I grow remain identical in all characteristics to their parent; I have yet to see any variation, despite the fact that *D. tangutica* is in flower at the same time in the same tunnel, which in theory should result in cross-pollination. I prefer to take basal cuttings quite late in the season, late August to early September. Records show that soft cuttings are also successful. I have never tried grafting, but do not doubt it would be successful, using *D. longilobata* or *D. tangutica* as a rootstock.

Botanical variants

Daphne aff. *retusa* KR 6411

This interesting introduction by arborist and woody plant expert Keith Rushforth was collected in Tibet in 1999. His field notes describe it as a low shrub up to 30 CM high occurring in low scrub. The habit is totally different to the known upright, congested form of *D. retusa*, since the limbs seem lax enough to bend almost to the horizontal. The leaves favour *D. tangutica* in size and shape, but they are retuse and the flowers are equal in size to *D. retusa*, though the external coloration is deep pink rather than rosy purple.

Daphne sericea Vahl.

This species is distributed from southern Italy eastwards to Turkey. I have grown a form from Turkey for many years which is self-fertile and breeds true from seed, and several very distinct clones from Crete which must be propagated vegetatively to retain their characters.

Turkish plants have a sturdy, upright habit which produces a plant 1.2–1.5 M in height, somewhat less in width, while the Cretan forms are bushier and more compact, reaching 1–1.2 M in height and width. The evergreen foliage is variable in size and shape, ranging from oblanceolate, 3.5 CM long by 1 CM for Turkish plants, to plants from the Omalos Plateau, Crete, with leaves narrowly oblanceolate, 3 CM long by 0.7 CM wide for JF119/0095, and ovate to obovate, 2–3 CM long by 1–1.2 CM wide for B&M 19043. The upper leaf surface is always dark green, but may be matt or glossy with varying amounts of fine hairs; the lateral veins are generally not clearly visible. The sweetly fragrant flowers are freely produced in axillary and terminal inflorescences. In the wild most plants flower in spring or early summer, but odd plants can be found in autumn and winter with plenty of open flowers. Flower colour ranges from dark purplish pink to pale pink or almost white, but the colour tends to have a muddy tinge, and the Cretan forms in particular change to a yellowish buff as they age; a colour which does not go well with the pink of the younger flowers. The 5–15 flowers per inflorescence have a broad perianth tube 0.8–1.1 CM long by 0.3–0.4 CM wide, and broad perianth lobes 0.5–0.6 CM long by 0.4 CM wide. The flowers of the Turkish form are of finer quality, with auriculate, overlapping lobes which hold their colour well. Seed sets routinely on all forms; the orange fruits of Turkish plants have a much fleshier pericarp than those of Cretan ones, which may be coriaceous in dry conditions, occasionally remaining encased in the dead perianth tube.

The flowers of *D. sericea* change from pink to buff as they age. Note the prominent anthers.

This Turkish form of *D. sericea* has large flowers which do not mature to buff.

Daphne sericea is not a difficult species to grow if given an open, sunny site with good drainage. Since plants can easily be raised from seed it would be worthwhile selecting for flower colour, period of flower production, and neat habit. Areas which experience long, dry summers without too cold a winter would find this a useful, drought-tolerant, evergreen shrub.

My account of *D. collina* (see p. 52) contains descriptions of plants from its type locality in southern Italy which match an early plate of *D. collina* in the RHS's Lindley Library, but in my opinion closely resemble plants of *D. sericea* and are totally distinct from *D. collina* as grown in gardens today.

The hardiness of plants is almost certain to vary according to their origin. I suspect that the less hardy forms will not survive long periods below –10°C/14°F (Zone 8), while plants from an area such as the Omalos Plateau on Crete may well tolerate temperatures down to –17°C/0°F (Zone 7).

Propagation

Seed germinates well in the spring after sowing. Seedlings grow rapidly and need to be pinched to encourage branching. Grafting has been successful on *D. mezereum* rootstocks. I have not tried cuttings, but semi-ripe or ripewood cuttings would no doubt be an alternative method of increase.

Daphne striata Tratt.

Native to the mountains of central Europe, this species has seldom settled down into cultivation in the United Kingdom. I have included it in this book to encourage people to try to grow it, as good forms are worthy of cultivation and it does fill a gap in the daphne flowering schedule.

Daphne striata is closely related to *D. cneorum* and has at times been confused with it. (AGS Bulletin Vol. 53 1985 page 141 shows a photograph of *D. striata* labelled *D. cneorum.*) The main differences are that *D. striata* is glabrous, the leaves are longer and the growth is more branched and less lax. Like *D. cneorum, D. striata* often grows in company with other small shrubby species such as *Rhododendron ferrugineum* and *Salix arbuscula*; in such a situation it may scramble through the growth of its neighbours, making a plant 30–60 CM high by 1 M or more across. Free-standing plants may grow to 30 CM high and up to 60 CM wide, but material I have grown from a plant collected by Peter Erskine above the Val Gardena in the Dolomites is much more compact in habit, which suggests that, like *D. cneorum,* dwarf forms of *D. striata* can be found. Plants are generally found growing above the treeline, and so would have a short growing season followed by a covering of snow in winter. Melting snow would provide a steady supply of water for most of the growing season, while the summer thunderstorms common in some mountainous areas of Europe would add to this. Records state that this daphne species is particularly intolerant of dryness at the roots.

There seems some confusion as to whether *D. striata* is evergreen or deciduous; I go for the middle road and say that it is semi-evergreen. Most of the foliage on my plants under unheated polythene drops off in the winter, but a few leaves are retained at the apex of the current season's growth. The flowers are in terminal inflorescences produced at the end of short lengths of new growth, from late May to late June on my plants under polythene. This makes *D. striata* later to flower than the majority of daphnes. My grafted plants produce a second flush of bloom in early autumn, but I doubt if this would occur on plants growing in the open. The flowers are sweetly scented and vary in colour from white to various shades of pink which are often muddy, so selection for flower quality is important. The flowers have a characteristically long (1.5 CM), narrow, hairless perianth tube with lengthwise lines of darker colour giving a striated effect, hence the species name. The fruits are ovoid in shape, larger than those of *D. cneorum*, dull orange when ripe and with a short stalk.

I have found *D. striata* difficult to grow on its own roots in a container for more than a year or so after rooting a cutting or germinating seed. I think that there would be more chance of success with youngsters planted out in their final growing position towards the end of their first growing season. This method has worked for me, planting out in a raised bed. Plants grafted on *D. longilobata* have grown well for several years in a raised bed as well as in containers under polythene. *Daphne striata* on its own roots should be hardy to –17 to –23°C /0 to –10°F (Zone 6).

Propagation

Seed sown soon after harvesting germinates readily the following spring. A reasonable percentage of semi-ripe basal cuttings taken in mid-July make root. Plants grafted on *D. mezereum* and *D. longilobata* have grown well.

Named clones

Daphne striata 'Wolfgang Reich'

As I mentioned earlier, most forms of *D. striata* I have seen in flower had rather insipid pink or muddy rose flowers. In the early 1990s, Wolfgang Reich from Alfeld, Germany, kindly brought me a plant whose bright rose-purple flowers are by far the best I have seen. Although he cannot remember where this plant came from, Wolfgang has given me permission to name it after him.

Daphne tangutica Maxim.

This species is native to western China, Tibet and possibly Taiwan. It is easily cultivated, and deservedly popular throughout the United Kingdom. Most of the plants grown today arise from collections made in the early part of the 20TH century, but I am uncertain as to whether the two different forms I have grown for many years would trace back that far. It is noteworthy that seed-raised plants from these two forms remain true and distinct.

D. striata 'Wolfgang Reich'.

D. striata 'Wolfgang Reich' has a long, glabrous perianth tube.

D. tangutica, Form A has more colourful flowers and a bushy habit.

D. tangutica, Form B has broader leaves and an open habit.

I call the form that I have grown for nearly 40 years *D. tangutica*, Form A. This is similar to a more vigorous form of *D. retusa* as far as habit goes, in time making a dense bush of 1–1.3 M in height and width. The deep green leaves are narrower than those of *D. retusa*—3–4 CM by 1–1.2 CM, with an acute apex. The strongly fragrant flowers have a rosy purple exterior and a white or pale lilac interior. They are smaller than those of *D. retusa*, at 1.4–1.5 CM in diameter.

I received *D. tangutica*, Form B as a cutting from a keen gardener in the late 1980s; it is slightly more vigorous than Form A, with a much more open habit which can leave bare stems at the base. It makes a bush 1.3–1.5 M in height and width in five or six years. The leaves are larger than those of Form A, 4.5 CM by

1.2–1.5 CM, more elliptic in shape and dull green; older leaves in particular may have a retuse (notched) apex. Flowers have a pink exterior and white or lilac interior and measure 1.5–1.7 CM in diameter.

After their main late spring flush of bloom, both forms reliably produce flowers on new growth at intervals through the summer, provided that they do not get dry at the root. Seed is set in good quantity, but the large, elliptic, orange-red fruits are soon taken by birds. There are reports from recent travellers to western China that white-flowered forms of *D. tangutica* have been seen, but I am not aware that they are in cultivation. Collectors' herbarium notes confirm that flower colour can range from white through pink to deep purple.

Cultural requirements are the same as those for *D. retusa*; a humus-rich soil which does not get too dry in summer. Avoid strong sun in southern latitudes; conversely, too much shade in northern climes results in weak growth prone to snow damage.

Apart from some frost damage to the tips of unripened growth, I have never seen cold damage to *D. tangutica*; it should be hardy down to –23°C/–10°F (Zone 6).

Propagation

Seed sown soon after harvesting germinates well the following spring. Seedlings are easy to grow on; I remove the growing point mid-way through the first season of growth to encourage branching. Semi-ripe tip or basal cuttings of both forms root well, but are slower than seedlings to make a good plant.

Daphne velenovskyi J. Halda

This species was named in 1981. It is native to the Pirin mountains of Bulgaria, notably Mt. Vichren (Halda and Zvolanek 1982). *Daphne velenovskyi* is closely related to *D. cneorum* and *D. striata*, and at first sight closely resembles the former. Growth is slow and habit compact, mature plants being 5–10 CM in height by 30–40 CM in width. This description is based on the single clone that I grow.

The evergreen foliage has a distinct glaucous hue and the leaves are shorter and broader than in most forms of *D. cneorum*—0.8–1.5 CM long by 0.4–0.5 CM wide. The inflorescences are always terminal, consisting of 10–15 strongly scented flowers which are bright rose pink on my plant, but paler pink and white forms are reported. The extension growth of the peduncle before the

D. velenovskyi.

flowers open is less than 1 CM compared to 2 CM or more for *D. cneorum* forms. The perianth tube is shorter than that of *D. cneorum*, and, although stated as glabrous, my plant does have fine, downy hairs. Unlike any form of *D. cneorum* I grow, the overwintering inflorescence is surrounded by a distinct ruff of small leaves. Plants grown under protection have set seed; the pericarp is fleshy, greenish yellow in colour and not enclosed in the dead perianth tube. *Daphne velenovskyi* seems far happier in a polythene tunnel than in the open. I think it prefers the extra warmth in summer and protection from excessive moisture in winter. I am sure it would grow well outside in a more continental climate.

Daphne velenovskyi is a hardy species which should withstand temperatures down to –29°C/–20°F (Zone 5).

Propagation

Semi-ripe tip cuttings root fairly easily, but grow very slowly. Plants grafted on *D. longilobata* or *D. mezereum* grow well, and the resulting plants seem to grow in character and are easier to manage than ones on their own roots.

Mature plants of *D.* 'Rosy Wave' (left), *D.* ×*burkwoodii* 'G.K. Argles' (centre) and *D.* ×*burkwoodii* 'Lavenirii'(right), growing on a west-facing bank.

3 *Daphne* Hybrids

As in the previous chapter on the daphne species, I shall only include in this chapter those hybrids that I consider worth a space in my garden, or those that, while not giving their best here in Hampshire, may perform well in areas with warmer, drier climates. In most cases, details on cultivation are kept to a minimum, since referring to the requirements of their parents should suffice.

The Latin epithets that are applied to hybrids described in this chapter have been published together with descriptions of the plants to which they relate. In addition, type specimens have been deposited in a herbarium where they are available for examination. In some cases, precedence is claimed for a different epithet, but it has not been possible to check these, either because type specimens are not available, or because the specimens supplied do not seem correct. (The Foreword contains a discussion of some of these issues.)

A hybrid plant is the result of a cross between parents that differ in genetic makeup. Daphne hybrids are generally a cross between two different species, although 'Rosy Wave' is an example of a cross between a hybrid, *D.* ×*burkwoodii*, and a species, *D. collina* of gardens. A cross between two species generally produces a plant with hybrid vigour—with a stronger constitution than either parent. This makes it easier to propagate and grow, and often results in more flowers, particularly on new summer growth.

Not all hybrids are worthwhile plants, even when they have two gardenworthy parents: repeated crosses between *D. bholua* and *D. mezereum* have always produced disappointing results. It is unfortunate that an inferior hybrid of *D. bholua* and *D. mezereum* was given the name 'Louis Mountbatten'. It is inevitable that if you create a hybrid, or one arises as a spontaneous cross in your garden, you will have a soft spot for the resulting plant, so by all means propagate and distribute it to friends. However, remember that it is important to establish its value as a unique, garden-worthy plant, or an improvement on existing hybrids, before giving it a name.

Over the last 20 years I have managed to raise a number of hybrids, some of which I considered worth propagating, others not. In some cases, I have simply sown seed that set on a plant, and other times I have deliberately tried to hybridize two species. In the latter case I use two different methods to attempt a cross. In the first, the plant intended as the "seed parent" has the top part of a flower removed by cutting through the perianth tube with a small pair of scissors. This allows access to the stigma using a fine paintbrush carrying pollen from a flower of the second plant—the "pollen parent"—of the intended cross. I have never bothered to remove the lower whorl of stamens from the flower of the seed-bearing parent, because if seed is set, a plant raised from it will soon show whether it is the result of a cross or self-fertilization.

The second method requires at least one of the parents to be pot-grown, but is far less fiddly and generally successful. Wait until the two plants you wish to cross have flowers open, preferably on new summer growth, and then isolate them from other daphnes, but ensure that moths and bees can have easy access. Then let nature do the rest!

My efforts do not always work; *D. tangutica* and *D. retusa* seem very reluctant to "walk out" with another species, and I have never seen a seed on *D. odora*, which does have an odd chromosome number.

When the exact parentage of a hybrid is known, I have given details, with the species that is the seed parent written first.

Daphne ×*burkwoodii* Turrill

Probably the most popular and widely distributed daphne hybrid, this is a medium-sized shrub, relatively easily propagated and grown in most temperate regions. This cross first arose as a spontaneous hybrid in France in about 1920, and was named *D. lavenirii*. Since the name was never validly published, the later valid name of burkwoodii applies, and lavenirii has become a cultivar name. In 1931 a deliberate cross between *D. cneorum* and *D. caucasica* by the brothers Albert and Arthur Burkwood resulted in two named cultivars; *D.* ×*burkwoodii* 'Albert Burkwood' (the type specimen) and *D.* ×*burkwoodii* 'Somerset'.

D. ×*burkwoodii* forms make well-branched bushes, 0.9–1.5 m in height and width. The extent to which they are evergreen or deciduous depends largely on winter temperatures; the lower these are, the more deciduous the plants will be. However, vigorous young plants tend to be more evergreen than mature specimens, and hot, dry conditions encourage autumn leaf drop. Loss of foliage after a dry summer or during a cold winter is not at all detrimental to a plant's performance the following spring.

The leaves are variable in size and shape, basically linear-oblanceolate, apiculate or obtuse at the apex, measuring 2.5–3.7 CM by 0.7–1.2 CM. Young plants are especially floriferous: strong growth of the previous season may bear closely clustered inflorescences along its top third, but with maturity the inflorescence is generally terminal. The flowers have a strong, sweet fragrance, and are in umbels of 10–15. The buds are pink or rosy purple; the inside of the perianth lobe is white when the flowers first open, aging to pink. Provided that adequate moisture is available, the new growth of healthy plants will produce flowers throughout the summer, in terminal inflorescences. Seed is set occasionally; the colour of the fleshy pericarp is similar to that of *D. caucasica*, at first orange-red, then turning blackish purple.

D. ×burkwoodii forms are easily grown in any sunny, well-drained situation. Young plants should not be allowed to make excessive extension growth without it being pinched to encourage branching. Failure to do this may result in a wineglass-shaped bush which will be prone to wind and snow damage. Provided they have a healthy root system, poorly shaped plants respond well to being cut back in late spring. Since both parents of *D. ×burkwoodii* are hardy, cultivars should tolerate temperatures of –29 to –34°C/–20 to –30°F (Zone 4).

Propagation

Records show that cuttings taken at virtually any stage have rooted, from soft tip cuttings under mist to hardwood cuttings taken in October. I favour taking semi-ripe tip cuttings in July; I find the major problem is keeping the soft growth which they make in the cutting frame free of *Botrytis* infection. Rooting cuttings is straightforward, but while I used to produce *D. ×burkwoodii* 'Somerset' in wholesale quantities in the 1980s without problems, nowadays young plants seem to lack vigour and are more prone to root disease. Maybe, after 80 years of vegetative propagation, this clone is getting tired? Plants I have bought which were propagated from tissue culture seem equally reluctant to grow well.

Variegated cultivars whose leaves still contain plenty of chlorophyll-bearing green grow perfectly well on their own roots, but I prefer to graft 'Briggs

Moonlight' and 'Golden Treasure', which grow more slowly on their own roots. *Daphne longilobata* and *D. mezereum* are suitable stocks.

Named clones

Daphne ×burkwoodii 'Albert Burkwood'

Parentage: *D. cneorum × D. caucasica*

Lower growing than 'Somerset', making about 1 m in height. The flower buds are distinctly darker than those of its sibling, and the leaves are narrower, with an apiculate apex. This cultivar has the best balance of height and spread, and so is a good choice where space is limited, or for a windy site.

Daphne ×burkwoodii 'Briggs Moonlight'

The result of a sport on a plant of 'Carol Mackie', this cultivar was introduced by the well-known Washington State nursery. 'Briggs Moonlight' can be spectacular, but needs more care and attention than other forms. Most of the leaf area is bright cream, with a few small green flecks and a narrow green edge. Inevitably, growth is slow, so a fertile soil and regular feeding may be necessary. Strong sun during the hottest part of the day may cause leaf scorch in southern latitudes, but it must not be planted in deep shade. This is primarily a plant for foliage effect; the pale pink flowers are not freely produced. The habit is upright, and mature plants should reach 75 × 60 cm in height and spread.

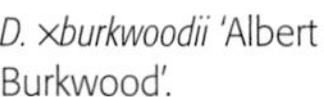

D. ×burkwoodii 'Albert Burkwood'.

D. ×burkwoodii 'Briggs Moonlight'.

D. ×burkwoodii 'Carol Mackie'.

D. ×burkwoodii 'G.K. Argles'.

Daphne ×burkwoodii 'Carol Mackie'

A first-rate plant which originated as a sport in the New Jersey garden of Carol Mackie in 1962. The leaves are edged with a distinct band which is gold on young leaves, maturing to cream. This cultivar grows and flowers well, but does not get too tall, a mature plant being 1 M high by 1.3–1.5 M across.

Daphne ×burkwoodii 'G.K. Argles'

A distinctive variegated form which makes vigorous, upright growth to 1.5 M or more. The broad leaves have a deep gold margin about 0.1 CM wide. Introduced by the Devon nursery of E. B. Champernownes. Although the habit does not match my plant of 'Lavenirii', the broad leaves and the pink mouth to the perianth tube suggest it may be a sport from that cultivar.

Daphne ×burkwoodii 'Gold Sport'

A recent mutation on a plant of 'G.K. Argles', but with a gold leaf margin which, at 0.2 CM, is twice as wide. It was selected by Tony Slater of Woodland Barn Nurseries. Reversion back to 'G.K. Argles' does occur occasionally. Young plants are vigorous, and this cultivar shows promise of making an attractive bush to brighten the garden. Suggested size of a mature plant: 0.9–1.2 M in height and width.

Daphne ×burkwoodii 'Golden Treasure'

A sport from 'Somerset' which was developed by Richard Hyman in the 1990s. Like 'Briggs Moonlight', the centre of the leaf is variegated, with a narrow green

D. ×burkwoodii 'Golden Treasure'.

D. ×burkwoodii 'Golden Treasure' makes a pleasing contrast with *D.* 'Rosy Wave' (left) and *D. ×eschmannii* 'Jacob Eschmann' (centre right).

margin, but the colour is bright yellow rather than cream. In shade this yellow area becomes lime green due to the formation of some chlorophyll; this allows all the lower leaves of the plant to photosynthesize, which results in strong growth and a reasonable display of flowers. Another good point about 'Golden Treasure' is that it does not scorch in sun here, although it may do so in more southern latitudes. Suggested size of a mature plant is 80–90 CM in height and width. After 3 years in my "daphnetum" (see p. 10), a plant of this cultivar is making an impressive display.

D. ×burkwoodii 'Lavenirii'.

D. ×burkwoodii 'Somerset'.

Daphne ×*burkwoodii* 'Lavenirii'

I have grown a plant under this name for about 15 years, and since it is distinct from the two Burkwood plants and answers the description given by Brickell and Mathew (1976), I think it is true to name. The habit is more open and spreading than in 'Somerset', but the stems are sturdier and the leaves broader than those of 'Albert Burkwood', with a slightly glaucous tint. The flower buds and perianth tube are darker in colour than the Burkwood varieties, and the area at the mouth of the perianth tube becomes noticeably darker than the rest of the flower as it matures.

Daphne ×*burkwoodii* 'Somerset'

Parentage: *D. cneorum* × *D. caucasica*

The best-known and most widely grown clone, this is a plant which should give 15 to 20 years of pleasure in most gardens. It fits the general description given for this hybrid on page 110.

Daphne ×*burkwoodii* 'Somerset Variegated'

This plant has a narrow cream margin to the leaves; unfortunately, I do not think this is wide enough to be conspicuous, so it does not compare well with other variegated cultivars. Siting a plant in full sun may help to bring out the variegation. A strong grower—plants will reach 1.2–1.5 M in height and width.

Daphne ×*eschmannii* 'Jacob Eschmann' C. D. Brickell & A. R. White

A spontaneous hybrid between *D. cneorum* and *D. blagayana*, raised by Swiss nurseryman Jacob Eschmann in the early 1960s. The single cultivar has been named after him. 'Jacob Eschmann' displays considerable vigour; if left unpruned, annual extension growth of 30–45 CM soon produces a lax, open-centred plant, 60–90 CM in height by 1–1.5 M in width. A more compact plant can be created by careful pinching of growth to encourage branching. The foliage is semi-evergreen, only the leaves towards the tips of the current season's growth being retained. The leaves are narrowly obovate in shape and measure 2.5–3.5 CM by 1–1.8 CM. The flowers are the strong point of this hybrid; 12–15 blooms are carried in terminal inflorescences at the apex of the stem and on short axillary growths. Each flower is of a good size, 1.5–1.8 CM in diameter, a

D. ×*eschmannii* 'Jacob Eschmann'. The inflorescences on short axillary growths form a large cluster of blossom.

clear purplish pink colour and strongly fragrant. The main flush of flower in April and May is followed by occasional blossom on new growth during the summer.

'Jacob Eschmann' has proved easy to cultivate in a sunny, well-drained site, but attention to pruning along the lines mentioned above is important to avoid an untidy plant. The alternative is the neighbourly system of cultivation suggested for both parents, allowing the plant to ramble through small shrubs, or planting perennials and bulbs to screen bare areas of branch. I should like to try underplanting 'Jacob Eschmann' with *D. cneorum* 'Eximea' to provide two layers of flower.

Given the origin, hardiness should not be a problem; temperatures to –23°C/–10°F (Zone 6) should be tolerated.

Propagation

Soft or semi-ripe tip cuttings root well. Plants grafted onto *D. longilobata* or *D. mezereum* have grown successfully.

Daphne 'Forarch'

D. 'Forarch'.

Parentage: *D. arbuscula* × *D. jasminea*

The result of a chance liaison at my nursery, this hybrid flowered for the first time in 2003. I am certain of the parentage because the seedling grew in a pot of *D. arbuscula*, and *D. jasminea* was the only other daphne in close proximity. Apart from this, the characteristics of 'Forarch' show a strong influence from *D. jasminea.* To date, plants show a compact, bushy habit, and should mature to 30–45 CM in height and width. The young bark is dark reddish brown, maturing to dark brown with grey striations. The evergreen leaves cluster towards the apex of the stems; they are glossy green, oblong to obovate, 1–1.2 CM by 0.3–0.4 CM, with 0.3–0.4 CM stalks and mucronate tips.

The inflorescence, generally terminal but occasionally axillary, consists of 2–5 flowers. The buds and perianth tube are rosy purple. The narrow, reflexed perianth lobes have a pale pink interior and a dark pink exterior and vary in size; the inner lobe measures 1.4 × 0.3 CM and the outer one, 1 × 0.6 CM. I have given flower colour for a plant growing in the open; under glass or polythene the colours are much paler. The sweetly fragrant flowers are produced from April to October on plants growing outside or under cover. The hardiness of this promising hybrid has yet to be assessed, though early indications are that it will be hardier than its pollen parent—my plant in the "daphnetum" has survived one mild winter unscathed. If it does not prove cold-tolerant, the long flowering period will still make it a worthwhile addition to a collection, to be grown with protection in cold climates.

Propagation

Soft and semi-ripe tip cuttings root easily. I have grafted plants on *D. longilobata* which are growing well.

Daphne ×*hendersonii* Hodgkin ex. C. D. Brickell & B. Mathew

This hybrid between *D. petraea* and *D. cneorum* was first discovered in the wild in 1930, when W. Scott Henderson and Sir Arthur Hill were botanizing in an area west of Lake Garda, in northern Italy, where both *D. petraea* and *D. cneorum* grow in close proximity. Hill named the hybrid after Henderson, but it was not until 1976 that a formal Latin diagnosis was published (Brickell and Mathew 1976). Daphne enthusiasts had to wait until 1981 for *D.* ×*hendersonii* to be introduced to cultivation, by Chris Brickell. While he was botanizing on a steep slope he slipped and only managed to save himself from a nasty fall by grabbing the nearest plant. Once on a firm footing, examination of some broken pieces in his hand revealed that they were not *D. petraea* or *D. cneorum*, but a hybrid between them. This material was propagated and introduced under the collection number CDB 11660.

Subsequent visits by sharp-eyed enthusiasts to areas where both species grow in proximity have revealed several more natural hybrids, some of which have been named, and at least four hybrids have been created in cultivation. Since both parents are variable in character, it is not surprising that the hybrids have considerable differences which will be highlighted under the individual descriptions. All clones are dwarf, evergreen shrubs of semi-prostrate habit which make flattened domes 10–30 CM high by 45–60 CM wide. Although there is considerable variation in foliage and flower, only terminal inflorescences are produced, and the floral bracts are caducous (both characteristics of *D. cneorum*). All clones have very fragrant flowers. Unlike many daphne hybrids, only small quantities of blossom are produced on new summer growth. Order of flowering falls roughly into two groups, 'Aymon Correvon', 'Fritz Kummert', 'Ernst Hauser' and 'Kath Dryden' flowering 7–10 days earlier than 'Blackthorn Rose', 'Apple Blossom', 'Rosebud' and 'Marion White'. I have yet to see a seed set on any clone of *D.* ×*hendersonii*.

Considering the quality of the parent species, it is not surprising that all clones of *D.* ×*hendersonii* I have seen are attractive, garden-worthy plants. They are excellent for the rock garden, trough or large container, or can be grown successfully in pots under protection. They are the ideal choice for a gardener who wants a small daphne that is quicker-growing and has a stronger constitution than *D. petraea*. The standard daphne requirement of free drainage is critical, and plants are bound to appreciate an alkaline soil, but it is not essential.

All clones of *D.* ×*hendersonii* should survive temperatures to −23°C/−10°F (Zone 6).

Propagation

Semi-ripe tip or basal cuttings can be rooted without difficulty. All clones possess enough vigour on their own roots to make plants large enough for planting out within 15–18 months of rooting. Grafted plants do seem more amenable to long-term cultivation in pots. I have used *D. longilobata* and *D. mezereum* successfully as stocks, while Henry Taylor recommends using *D. retusa* as a stock for 'Rosebud'.

Named clones

Daphne ×*hendersonii* 'Apple Blossom'

Introduced by Margaret and Henry Taylor in 1991, this is a plant of fairly open habit up to 15 CM high and 45 CM wide. The glossy, dark green leaves curve distinctly downwards. The deep pink buds, 5–7 per inflorescence, open to pale pink, fading to almost white as they mature. The perianth lobes are usually notched at the apex. Not as easy to grow as some clones, particularly when on its own roots.

Daphne ×*hendersonii* 'Aymon Correvon'

A clone which originates from the famous nursery of Correvon et Cie, Geneva. Swiss nurseryman Jacob Eschmann maintained and distributed stock as a clone of *D.* ×*thauma* (*D. petraea* × *D. striata*) (see p. 147), and I initially catalogued it as such in 1997. Careful examination by Chris Brickell indicates that morphologically it clearly falls within the range of variation of *D.* ×*hendersonii*, and shows no sign of any characteristics attributable to *D. striata*. 'Aymon Correvon' has a compact, prostrate habit, making a plant 10–15 CM high by 45 CM wide. The bright, shell pink buds open to pale pink and mature to almost white. Very free-flowering once established, but young plants may be shy to flower.

D. ×*hendersonii* 'Aymon Correvon'.

D. ×hendersonii 'Blackthorn Rose'.

D. ×hendersonii 'Blackthorn Rose'.

Daphne ×hendersonii 'Blackthorn Rose'

This plant was raised from a cross made at Blackthorn Nursery in 1993 by pollinating *D. petraea* 'Tremalzo' with *D. cneorum* f. *alba*. 'Blackthorn Rose' has dark, glossy green leaves and a bushy, vigorous habit, making a plant 20–30 cm high by 45 cm wide when mature. The reddish purple buds open to deep pink flowers which, at 1.6–1.9 cm in diameter, are the largest of the named clones. The auriculate perianth lobes are particularly broad, with ruffled edges.

Daphne ×hendersonii 'Ernst Hauser'

Introduced from northern Italy by Harry Jans in 1991 and named after his guide, who is famed for his knowledge of the Lake Garda area, this is a vigorous clone whose upright, open habit soon makes a bush 30–35 cm high and 45–60 cm across. Strong growth of young plants should be pinched to encourage branching. The dark green foliage assumes a purplish bronze tone in winter. This is the earliest clone to flower. The buds are purple-red, opening pale pink and maturing to almost white; however, they retain a deep pink centre, as does the exterior of the perianth tube. The perianth lobes are often notched at the apex and the edges have a ruffled appearance. This clone repeat-flowers more than most.

Daphne ×hendersonii 'Fritz Kummert'

This hybrid was raised by Austrian plantsman Fritz Kummert, who crossed *D. petraea* with *D. cneorum* var. *pygmaea* to create this delightful clone, distinct

D. ×*hendersonii* 'Ernst Hauser'. Note bumblebee damage to perianth tubes (bottom left of picture) (see p. 211).

D. ×*hendersonii* 'Jeanette Brickell'.

D. ×*hendersonii* 'Fritz Kummert'.

D. ×*hendersonii* 'Kath Dryden'.

in its small matt leaves and virtually prostrate habit, 8–10 CM high and 45–60 CM wide. It is one of the first to flower; the bright reddish pink buds open to warm pink blooms with a pale centre. This is an ideal variety to plant in a trough and is particularly good grown in the open.

Daphne ×*hendersonii* 'Jeanette Brickell' CDB 11660

As mentioned earlier, this was the first clone to be introduced into cultivation. Since it was responsible for saving Chris Brickell from a potentially serious fall, he is very attached to this plant, and has quite rightly named it after his wife! The habit of 'Jeanette Brickell' is relatively flat, which produces a plant 6–10 CM high by 45–60 CM wide. The 3–5 flowers per inflorescence are bright pink in bud, opening to soft pink and not fading much with maturity. From my experience this is one of the best clones to grow in the open garden.

Daphne ×hendersonii 'Kath Dryden'

In 1997 I pollinated a bright pink, early-flowering clone of *D. petraea*, Erskine 87C, with *D. cneorum* 'Velky Kosir'. The result produced several seedlings which first flowered in 2000. All had particularly bright, deep red flowers. I selected the best and named it after Kath as a small token of my appreciation for giving me my first *D. petraea* 'Grandiflora' in 1981. Kath grows her namesake with a couple of its unnamed siblings for company.

'Kath Dryden' has an upright, fairly compact habit. Mature plants should be about 30 CM high by 45 CM wide. The densely packed leaves are dark green and slightly glossy. The bright rose-red buds open to deep rosy pink, with dark, red-purple marks by the auricles.

D. ×hendersonii 'Marion White'.

D. ×hendersonii 'Rosebud'.

Daphne ×hendersonii 'Marion White'

My initial attempt at creating a white-flowered *D. ×hendersonii* resulted in 'Blackthorn Rose' (see p. 120). In 1997, I repeated the cross, this time using *D. cneorum* f. *alba* as the seed parent, with pollen from *D. petraea* 'Tremalzo'. Two seedlings resulted. When they flowered in 2000, one was pink, the other white. The latter I have named after the person who inspired my love of plants: my mother, who died a few weeks before it flowered for the first time.

'Marion White' has a compact, bushy habit and should make a plant up to 30 CM high by 45–60 CM wide. The dark green, glossy leaves are oblanceolate in shape, and relatively broad at 1–1.2 CM by 0.3–0.4 CM. The perianth tube is pale green, and the flowers pure white. The auriculate perianth lobes have a crystalline appearance in sunshine, and are usually notched at the apex; they are 1.2–1.4 CM in diameter when fully expanded. It is freer-flowering on new growth than most other clones.

Daphne ×*hendersonii* 'Rosebud'

Introduced by Margaret and Henry Taylor in 1991, this is a compact, slow-growing plant which may reach 15–20 CM high by 45 CM wide. The leaves are a dark, matt green. The flowers are bright reddish purple in bud, a striking contrast to the interior of the perianth lobes, which are palest pink as the flowers open, and soon mature to white.

This cultivar is less easy than some to grow on its own roots. Grafting produces a good plant which is easier to manage.

Daphne ×*hendersonii* 'Solferino' NES 99-4

This is probably the best of several clones of *D.* ×*hendersonii* found in northern Italy in 1999 by Peter Erskine and Chris Brickell. It has a sturdy, upright habit which should make a plant 25–30 CM high and 45–60 CM wide. The glossy green leaves measure 1.2–1.5 CM by 0.3–0.4 CM. The inflorescence contains 7–9 flowers, which is more than in other clones. The bright pink buds open to soft pink; the inner perianth lobes are slightly paler than the outer ones. It was named by Peter Erskine in 2004 after the 19th-century battle of Solferino, an event which led to the founding of The Red Cross.

Daphne 'Hinton'

Parentage: *D. acutiloba* × *D. collina* of gardens

Plants raised from this cross I made in 1997 flowered in 2000. The nine plants were very similar in leaf and habit, but flower production and size of flower was variable. I have named the best-flowered form, which has grown well in my "daphnetum" for four years.

'Hinton' has an open habit of growth which I think will produce a small, evergreen bush, 30–40 CM in height by 60 CM across. The obovate leaves are shiny, dark green, measuring 3–4 CM by 1–1.5 CM. Young bark is bright reddish

tan maturing to brown with grey striation. The inflorescences are mainly terminal, but strong stems may have several axillary flower clusters near the apex of the stem. The 6–8 flowers are enclosed in brownish purple bracts; they are exceptionally fragrant and, at 2–2.5 CM in diameter, larger than in either parent, with broad, auriculate perianth lobes. The colour is dark rosy purple in bud, opening to a purple-pink. The margins of the inner perianth lobes are curled inward. Only a spring flush of blossom is produced. Early indications are that this hybrid is straightforward to grow in a sunny site. Plants should be hardy to at least –17°C/0°F (Zone 7).

D. 'Hinton'. I hope to see this plant given the hybrid epithet ×*goodsoniae*: Goodson was my mother's maiden name, and the epithet would pay tribute to her encouragement of my interest in plants, and to my grandfather, a gentle man who showed me great kindness when I was an unruly youngster.

Propagation

Semi-ripe tip or basal cuttings are straightforward to root. Plants grafted on *D. longilobata* have grown well.

Daphne ×*houtteana* 'Louis Van Houtte' Lindley & Paxton

There are no records to confirm the origin of this hybrid, which was named in 1850, but it is suggested that it was a garden hybrid, possibly from a Belgian nursery (Brickell and Mathew 1976), the result of a cross between *D. laureola* and *D. mezereum*. The hybrid epithet and the clonal name commemorate the man who first publicized this plant to the horticultural world. By the 1980s, many plants had succumbed to virus infection, and *D.* ×*houtteana* was a rare plant. Thanks to the foresight and enthusiasm of several Wiltshire garden owners, virus-free material was successfully tissue-cultured and distributed to the nursery trade.

Until recently, I wondered where the purple leaf coloration of *D.* ×*houtteana* came from, since as far as I knew, both parents would have had green leaves. The likely answer appeared in 2002 when I heard about *D. mezereum* 'Kingsley Purple' (see p. 81). If *D.* ×*houtteana* was of garden origin, it might be that the

D.×houtteana 'Louis Van Houtte' is an attractive evergreen if given some sun and the right background.
(Photo: Chris Brickell)

D.×houtteana 'Louis Van Houtte'. The flowers are largely hidden by the leaves.

parent *D. mezereum* was a purple-leaved form. Alternatively, since the parent of 'Kingsley Purple' was growing in an area where *D. laureola* was common, *D.* ×*houtteana* could have been a natural hybrid found in the French Pyrenees.

Daphne ×*houtteana* is similar in habit to *D. laureola*, with erect growth up to 1 M in height. Young stems are purple in colour, maturing to pale grey-brown. Young leaves are green, but mature to greenish purple on plants in shade, or to glossy purple in sun. Foliage is retained through the winter on young growth. Young plants are shy to flower, but as they mature, rosy purple flowers are produced in short-stalked clusters in the axils of the uppermost leaves, so they are mostly hidden from view. A slight fragrance is detectable in mild conditions. I have never seen fruits, nor are there any records of them.

D. ×*houtteana* is tolerant of a wide range of soil and conditions, but does need careful siting to show its potential. Too much shade results in a dingy, straggly plant. Enough sunlight must be provided to keep the plant compact and allow the foliage to develop strong purple hues. Plants I have grown are prone to producing fasciated shoots; these should be cut out as soon as they are noticed.

Given the hardiness of its parents, *D.* ×*houtteana* should be tolerant of temperatures to at least –23°C/–10°F (Zone 6).

Propagation

Semi-ripe cuttings taken in July root easily. Grafting on *D. mezereum* produces strong-growing plants, which need their growth pinching regularly to develop a well-shaped plant.

Daphne ×*hybrida* Colv. ex. Sweet

Dating back to 1820, this hybrid between *D. odora* and *D. collina* is of French origin, but no accurate records are available. I believe *D. odora* has a chromosome number different to all other species in which they have been counted, so this seems an unlikely hybrid, but the flower colour and the scent are correct for a liaison between the two parent species. Whether the form of *D. collina* was the same as that we grow in gardens today is open to question; it may well have been *D. sericea*. Inevitably, after all this time, virus infection accounts for *D.* ×*hybrida* being a rare plant in gardens.

The habit of *D.* ×*hybrida* tends to let it down. Young stems are lax and sag under their own weight, so they may ripen and set in a horizontal or even downward pointing position if not shortened. Careful pruning and pinching is essential to produce a sturdy young plant. Mature plants should attain around 1.2 M in height and 0.9–1.2 M in width. The glossy, bright green foliage is evergreen. A steady succession of flowers in terminal inflorescences is produced from October to April; the flowers are well shaped, rosy purple in colour and strongly scented, with the same delicious fragrance as *D. odora*. I have never seen a fruit, and there are no records of any.

D. ×*hybrida*.

Daphne ×*hybrida* has grown well for me in a south-facing bed, but has never been through a really hard winter. It should be sited in a warm situation to encourage ripening of young wood before winter frost can damage it. The winter-long flowering habit and superb fragrance of this hybrid make it a worthwhile subject for cultivation in a container which can be brought into a conservatory or garden room in winter, but placed in the open during the summer. It is also worth growing to provide cut material; two or three flowerheads in a winter posy will scent a room. Try to place plants which are to be grown in open ground in a situation which will make sniffing the flowers easy during the winter months.

It is doubtful whether *D.* ×*hybrida* would survive protracted temperatures below freezing. I think it would need protection below –12°C/10°F (Zone 8).

Propagation

I have found semi-ripe cuttings difficult to root, although it is recorded that they should be straightforward. It might be worth trying soft tip cuttings. Grafts grow well on *D. mezereum* and *D. longilobata.*

Daphne ×*jintyae* 'Pink Cascade' C. D. Brickell & A. R. White

Parentage: *D. petraea* 'Cima Tombea' × *D. rodriguezii.*

When naming this hybrid, Chris Brickell was keen to acknowledge the efforts that the late Hugo Latymer made to introduce the little-known species *D. rodriguezii* to cultivation; at Hugo's request, it is named after his wife Jinty. In the mid-1990s I sowed some seed from a plant of *D. petraea* 'Cima Tombea' growing in the glasshouse. The two seedlings which germinated were virtually identical and soon showed the unmistakable influence of *D. rodriguezii.* Since then I have grown these two plants in a raised bed in an unheated polythene tunnel, where they have thrived and shown no sign of cold damage. However, I would estimate that they have not experienced temperatures below –8°C (21°F).

D. ×*jintyae* 'Pink Cascade'.

D. ×*jintyae* makes an evergreen, much-branched bush up to 45 CM high by 60 CM across. The thin, twiggy stems have dark tan bark covered in small hairs. The slightly glossy leaves are reflexed and clothe the whole of the current season's growth; they are linear to slightly oblanceolate, with an obtuse apex, 0.6–1 CM by

0.2–0.3 CM at their widest. The inflorescence may be terminal or axillary, enclosed in a few crimson, caducous bracts containing 2–6 flowers. The perianth tube and outside of the lobes is densely hairy, rosy purple in colour, while the inside is dusky pink. The diameter of the flower is 0.5–0.7 CM. Although the sweetly scented flowers are small, the number produced in the axillary inflorescences on strong growth creates thick spikes of blossom in the spring. Occasional flowers are produced on new growth. Doubtfully hardy below –12°C/10°F (Zone 8), but almost certainly drought-tolerant, this hybrid should thrive in warm climates.

Propagation

Semi-ripe tip or basal cuttings root easily. I have never grafted plants, but no doubt *D. longilobata* or *D. mezereum* would be suitable stocks, although they would reduce the plants' drought tolerance.

Daphne 'Kilmeston Beauty'

Two seedlings germinated in spring 1992 from seed that a plant of *D. caucasica* had produced in the late spring of the previous year. The seed parent was under polythene, and I thought at first it might have been pollinated from a late flower on a plant of *D. bholua*. However, I have since discounted this, and I would guess *D. tangutica* was the pollen parent. If I am correct, it is the only incidence I know of *D. tangutica* crossing with another species. Grown on for several years, both seedlings were similar in all respects. I eventually selected and named the one I thought had a slightly more compact habit and superior flower production.

The habit of 'Kilmeston Beauty' is best described as a more robust, evergreen *D. ×burkwoodii*; it has a well-branched, bushy shape, 1.2–1.3 M in height and width. The tough, evergreen foliage consists of dark, glossy green leaves, linear-oblanceolate in shape, 4–4.5 CM by 1–1.2 CM, with a mucronate apex. The inflorescence may be terminal or axillary, and consists of 3–8 blooms which are 1.1–1.2 CM in diameter when mature. The perianth tube and the exterior of the perianth lobes is rosy purple; the interior of the lobes is white when the flowers first open, maturing to pink. The flowers have a strong, sweet scent. After the main spring flush, a steady succession of flowers is produced on new growth from July onwards.

'Kilmeston Beauty' has proved easy to cultivate in a sunny, well-drained site.

D. ×latymeri 'Spring Sonnet'.

D. 'Kilmeston Beauty'.

Mature specimens may suffer from instability if exposed to high winds. Young growth is lax, so it is essential to pinch strong extension growth of young plants to encourage branching. In my garden, these plants are true evergreens, but lower temperatures than they have yet received may cause leaf fall. Plants should survive temperatures down to –23°C/–10°F (Zone 6).

Propagation

Soft tip cuttings root easily. Semi-ripe or ripe cuttings are more reluctant to root. Grafts on *D. longilobata* or *D. mezereum* grow vigorously, and need careful training to produce well-shaped plants.

Daphne ×latymeri 'Spring Sonnet' C. D. Brickell & A. R. White

Parentage: *D. rodriguezii × D. sericea*

In the mid-1980s the late Hugo Latymer kindly brought me a small plant of *D. rodriguezii*, a species endemic to the Balearic Isles. As daphnes go, it did not rate highly; small leaves, a rigid, upright habit, and dingy flowers with an unpleasant scent! But over the years I have always kept a plant of *D. rodriguezii* in the glasshouse where, with the help of bumblebees (who obviously do not mind the smell), it has proved to be rather promiscuous, resulting in spontaneous hybrids with *D. caucasica*, *D. petraea* and *D. sericea*. In the mid-1990s I raised three seedlings from a plant of *D. rodriguezii* which was growing beside the Turkish form of *D. sericea*. They were all similar in appearance, and soon showed that they were the result of a liaison between the two species.

Chris Brickell has named my selected clone 'Spring Sonnet'. This evergreen hybrid has a dense, bushy habit. A six-year-old plant growing in a raised bed in a polythene tunnel here is 40 CM high and 75 CM wide, with the stems virtually hidden by foliage. The leaves have a very shiny, dark green upper surface and a pale, glaucous lower one; linear, with an obtuse or slightly retuse apex and revolute margins, they measure 1.8–2 CM by 0.3–0.5 CM, and clothe the whole length of the current season's growth. The inflorescence is terminal, with 5–8 sweetly scented flowers. The bud and exterior of the perianth tube is a dark rosy purple, the interior of the perianth lobes purplish pink. The lobes are auriculate, reflexed, with ruffled margins and a slightly notched apex. The spring display is followed by occasional flowers on new growth.

I have not tried growing 'Spring Sonnet' in the open until recently, assuming that *D. rodriguezii* would be tender in my climate and that a hybrid with the less than hardy Turkish form of *D. sericea* would be equally prone to frost damage. I think this is probably true, but for the last two relatively mild winters, a plant of 'Spring Sonnet' has survived without damage in my "daphnetum". The low, vigorous growth of this hybrid, which is bound to be drought-tolerant, coupled with the glossy foliage and fragrant flowers, are enough to make it worthy of trial in dry, warm climates. It is unlikely to be hardy below –10°C/14°F (Zone 8).

Propagation

Semi-ripe tip cuttings root easily and grow strongly. Plants grafted on both *D. longilobata* and *D. mezereum* have grown well.

Daphne ×*mantensiana* 'Manten' ex. Taylor & Vrugtman

Parentage: *D.* ×*burkwoodii* 'Somerset' × *D. retusa*

The history of this hybrid is well recorded: it was the result of a deliberate cross made in 1941 by British Columbian nurseryman Jack Manten. *D.* ×*mantensiana* 'Manten' is a small, evergreen shrub of upright habit, which eventually reaches 60–75 CM in height and spread. The dark green, glossy leaves are oblong to obovate, with a distinct notch at the apex. The strongly scented flowers are produced in terminal inflorescences of 10–15; they are rosy purple on the outside, pale pink within. The flowers produced in late spring on the previous season's wood open fully, but the perianth lobes of flowers on new growth do not reflex, giving the flowers a half-opened appearance.

This is an easily cultivated plant which, in addition to its spring flush, produces a steady succession of flower on new growth until autumn. Unfortunately, although it never sets seed, it is very reluctant to drop the dead flowers, so the complete dead inflorescence stays in place and is difficult to remove without a tug; infection of these dead flowers by *Botrytis* frequently results in dieback of branches. Manten himself acknowledges the problem of dieback—wrongly, in my opinion, attributing it to too rich a soil rather than the persistent dead flowers, although, of course, the better the soil, the more flowers are produced on new growth. This plant should be hardy to –23°C/–10°F (Zone 6).

Propagation

Both soft and semi-ripe tip cuttings are straightforward to root. Grafts grow well on both *D. longilobata* and *D. mezereum*.

Named clones

Daphne ×*mantensiana* 'Audrey Vockins'

This attractive cultivar arose in the late 1990s as a sport on a plant of 'Manten' in the Berkshire garden of Audrey Vockins. The leaves have a yellow margin, 0.1 CM wide, which adds to the appeal of the plant in the winter months. The vigour of 'Audrey Vockins' is equal to the plain green-leaved form, so plants should reach similar proportions.

D. ×*mantensiana* 'Audrey Vockins'.

Daphne ×*mauerbachii* 'Perfume of Spring' C. D. Brickell & A. R. White

Parentage: *D. caucasica* × *D. petraea*

Fritz Kummert created this hybrid in the early 1970s, his aim being to produce a plant similar to *D.* ×*burkwoodii*, but with a more compact habit. In this he was extremely successful, creating a hybrid which can be grown in a wide variety of situations.

D. ×mauerbachii 'Perfume of Spring'. (Photo: Chris Brickell)

'Perfume of Spring' makes a rounded bush up to 45 CM in height and 45–60 CM wide. The foliage is semi-evergreen, the leaves towards the apex of the current season's growth being retained unless there are spells of winter temperatures below –12°C (10°F). The leaves, mid-green with a leathery texture, are narrowly obovate to oblanceolate in shape. As well as terminal inflorescences at the apex of stems or on short spurs, any vigorous growth carries numerous axillary ones. These consist of 2–5 flowers with a purplish-pink perianth tube. The lobes have some pink external coloration and are creamy white inside. The flowers have the strong, sweet scent typical of *D. caucasica*. The main flush of blossom is produced from mid-April to mid-May, but vigorous young plants do produce some terminal flowers on new growth which lack the pink coloration.

Cultivation of this hybrid is straightforward; a scion grafted on *D. mezereum* is one of the few daphnes to have survived in my earliest attempt at a raised bed. Plants can be expected to tolerate temperatures down to –34°C/–30°F (Zone 4).

Propagation

Although I have not attempted propagation by cuttings, it should be possible to root soft tip cuttings. Scions grow well grafted on both *D. longilobata* and *D. mezereum*; the latter should always be first choice where hardiness is required. Young grafted plants frequently produce one or two strong shoots at awkward angles, which should be pinched to encourage branching and an even shape.

Daphne ×napolitana Loddiges

The recent addition of other named clones of *D. ×napolitana* creates a requirement for a cultivar name for the original type clone. This book provides the opportunity to do that, and I propose the name 'Enigma'.

The origin of 'Enigma', which dates back to the 1820s, has generated considerable speculation over the years. The hybrid name is presumably a misspelling of neapolitana, which indicates that it was found, or originated in, the

Naples area of southern Italy. Suggestions include a wild selection of *D. collina*; a hybrid between *D. collina* and *D. oleoides*; or a hybrid between *D. collina* and *D. cneorum*. Careful examination by Chris Brickell has failed to find any characteristics in 'Enigma' that could be attributed to *D. oleoides*, but he found enough similarity between it and my two hybrids between *D. collina* of gardens and *D. cneorum* to suggest that *D. sericea* or *D. collina* was one parent and *D. cneorum* the other. The axillary inflorescences and the purplish pink flowers of 'Enigma' are certainly characters which match the plants seen by Chris Brickell and Peter Erskine in southern Italy in 2001 (see *Daphne collina* of gardens, p. 52), while the cultivars 'Bramdean' and 'Meon' have much clearer pink flowers and only produce terminal inflorescences, characters which I think they inherit from *D. collina* of gardens.

'Enigma' makes a well-branched, compact evergreen shrub, up to 1 M in height and 1.2 M in width. The leathery, dark green leaves are narrowly obovate, 2–3 CM by 0.5–0.7 CM. Axillary as well as terminal inflorescences are often produced on vigorous young plants, but on mature plants they tend to be terminal, composed of 6–8 blooms. The fragrant flowers are small at 0.7–0.9 CM in diameter, purplish pink in colour and produced on new growth in summer as well as the main spring flush on the previous season's growth.

'Enigma' is a good choice for novice daphne growers; it is drought-tolerant, easily grown in a reasonably sunny, well-drained site, and should be hardy to –23°C/–10°F (Zone 6).

Propagation

Semi-ripe tip or basal cuttings can be rooted without problem, and soft tip cuttings would be an alternative. Plants grafted on *D. longilobata* or *D. mezereum* grow well for me.

Named clones

Daphne ×*napolitana* 'Bramdean'

Parentage: *D. collina* of gardens × *D. cneorum* var. *pygmaea*

This cross was made in 1988, and 'Bramdean' was selected from several seedlings which flowered in 1991. It makes a low, evergreen mound up to 25 CM in height by 60 CM across. The light green, glossy leaves are narrowly oblong to obovate, averaging 1.5 CM by 0.5 CM.

D. ×*napolitana* 'Bramdean'.

The inflorescence is always terminal and consists of 10 or more rose-pink fragrant flowers, 1–1.1 CM in diameter. The spring flush of bloom on the previous season's growth is followed by a steady succession of flowers on new growth from July onwards.

'Bramdean' can be grown successfully for several years in a container, but will always be happier in the open ground in a sunny position. Plants have never shown damage from cold, and should tolerate temperatures down to –23°C/ –10°F (Zone 6).

Daphne ×napolitana 'Meon'

Parentage: *D. cneorum* 'Eximea' × *D. collina* of gardens

Also made in 1988, this cross resulted in a single seedling which proved to be similar to 'Bramdean', but more robust in habit and with larger flowers. 'Meon' creates an evergreen, flattened dome shape, 30–40 CM in height and 60–90 CM across. The leaves are dark, glossy green, averaging 2 × 0.6 CM in size. The inflorescence is always terminal, and consists of 7–10 fragrant, pale rose pink flowers, 1.1–1.2 CM in diameter. Summer flowering on new growth is not as generous as with 'Bramdean'. 'Meon' has proved an easily grown plant which is large enough for a place at the front of a border, but not too large for the rock garden. Hardiness should be similar to that of 'Bramdean'.

D. ×napolitana (?) 'Stasek'.

Daphne ×napolitana (?) 'Stasek'

This plant came to me in the late 1990s from two different sources, as a variegated form of *D. cneorum* which originated in Romania. However, after growing it for a number of years, I find it so very similar to 'Bramdean' that my suspicion that it is more likely to be a hybrid has gradually increased to the point where I am going to stick my neck out and include it under *D. ×napolitana*.

The cultivar name, given by Harry Jans, acknowledges the nurseryman who gave him his plant. 'Stasek' makes a flattened dome, 20–25 CM high and 30–40 CM across, identical in shape to 'Bramdean'.

Unlike any form of *D. cneorum* I have seen, the centre of the plant remains bushy and well furnished with foliage, and is the tallest part of the plant. The evergreen leaves, oblong to obovate in shape and measuring 1.6–2.4 cm by 0.5–0.6 cm, are a glossy light green, with a very narrow, irregular cream margin. The inflorescence is terminal and consists of 5–14 lilac-pink, fragrant flowers, rosy purple in bud, measuring 0.9–1 cm in diameter. The perianth lobes are broad, with ruffled margins. The variegated foliage is scarcely noticeable in the garden, but 'Stasek' is one of the earliest of the spring-flowering varieties to bloom, and is exceptionally free-flowering on new growth from July until the first frosts. I rate this plant highly.

Daphne 'Pink Star'

D. 'Pink Star'.

Parentage: *D.* ×*burkwoodii* 'Somerset' × *D. cneorum* 'Eximea'

I made this cross in 1997 with the aim of creating a plant similar to 'Somerset', but with pinker flowers. Only one seedling survived to maturity and flowered in 2001.

'Pink Star' has an open habit but the stems are not lax. Plants should reach 30–45 cm high by 60–90 cm in width. The bark is pale grey. The glossy, evergreen leaves clothe the whole of the stem; they are linear to oblanceolate, obtuse or apiculate at the apex, 2.5–3.5 cm by 0.4–0.7 cm in size. The inflorescence is terminal on short apical and axillary growths, enclosed in red-flushed bracts. As in its seed parent, these axillary growths furnish much of the vigorous shoots to create broad spikes of blossom. The flowers are produced in a single spectacular flush in April to May. There are 6–8 strongly scented flowers per inflorescence, each with a dusky pink perianth tube and bud; the interior of the perianth lobes is pale pink, deepening in colour with maturity. The flowers are 1.3–1.4 cm in diameter.

To date, this hybrid shows promise as a medium-sized daphne. It is important to pinch strong young growth to form a well-shaped plant. 'Pink Star' should be hardy to at least −23 to −29°C/−10 to −20°F (Zone 5).

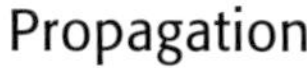

Propagation

I have rooted semi-ripe tip cuttings successfully, and grafts on *D. longilobata* have grown vigorously.

Daphne ×*rollsdorfii* C. D. Brickell & A. R. White

Parentage: *D. petraea* × *D. collina* of gardens

Two fine hybrids were created in 1979 by Fritz Kummert. The cultivar name 'Arnold Cihlarz' has been given to the above cross, which is used as the type clone.

'Arnold Cihlarz' is a dwarf evergreen shrub of bushy, upright habit 45–60 CM in height and width. The leaves are dark, glossy green, 1.5–2.5 CM by 0.5–0.8 CM, oblong to oblong-obovate in shape. The inflorescence is terminal and consists of 10–15 strongly fragrant flowers, which for the spring display are deep reddish purple; later flowers produced on the new season's growth are deep lilac-pink.

D. ×*rollsdorfii* 'Wilhelm Schacht'. (Photo: John Fielding)

Both 'Arnold Cihlarz' and 'Wilhelm Schacht' (see below) can be cultivated without problems in a sunny, well-drained site. Their compact habit makes them suitable for the smaller rock garden, or even a large trough. From my experience I would class them as drought-tolerant once well established. No sign of damage from cold temperatures has occurred, and both cultivars should tolerate temperatures down to −23°C/ −10°F (Zone 6).

Propagation

Semi-ripe tip or basal cuttings root easily and quickly, and young plants on their own roots grow strongly. There is certainly no need to graft, but both *D. longilobata* and *D. mezereum* have made suitable rootstocks.

Named clones

Daphne ×*rollsdorfii* 'Wilhelm Schacht'

This was the outcome of "reversing" the parentage—using *D. collina* of gardens as the seed parent—and the result is a plant similar to 'Arnold Cihlarz', but the habit is a little more vigorous and the flowers slightly larger.

Daphne 'Rosy Wave' and *D.* 'Richards Choice'

Parentage: *D.* ×*burkwoodii* 'Somerset' × *D. collina* of gardens

Peter and Brenda Stillwell grow a good selection of daphnes in their Hampshire garden, which is quite close to mine. In 1983 Peter noticed that a large plant of

D. 'Rosy Wave'
(*D.* 'Hinton', foreground).

D. ×*burkwoodii* 'Somerset' that had *D. collina* of gardens growing beside it had set seed. These were sown, and five germinated the following spring. Encouraged by this, Peter made deliberate crosses over the next few years. Each year some seed was set, and seedlings were distributed to friends and to the RHS Gardens at Wisley. One of the original seedlings was kept and named after the Silver Y moth, which Peter had noticed was active on the pair of daphne plants. 'Silver Y' has white flowers and makes a small bush, 60 × 60 CM, but the habit is rather straggly. I named the plant that I considered was the best hybrid that Peter gave to me after another moth, the Rosy Wave.

I think 'Rosy Wave' is similar, but superior to, *D.* ×*mantensiana* 'Manten' (see p. 130). The bushy, upright growth creates an evergreen shrub, 60–75 CM in height and spread. The oblanceolate leaves are mid-green, matt, with the lamina curved down toward the apex. The inflorescences of 5–8 flowers may be terminal, or on short axillary growths near the apex of strong stems. The strongly fragrant, rose pink flowers measure 1.4–1.8 CM across, and unlike 'Manten', the perianth lobes reflex whether the flowers are on old or new growth, which provides a better display. A steady succession of summer blossom is produced on new growth after the main spring flush on old wood. The dead flowers are easily shed, so dieback is not the problem it is with 'Manten'. 'Rosy Wave' is easily grown in a sunny situation; my original plant is 15 years old. It should be hardy to –23°C/–10°F (Zone 6).

Peter and Brenda Stillwell gave another of their seedlings to the late Richard Lee, who was head gardener at Rosemoor before Lady Anne Palmer donated her garden to the Royal Horticultural Society. The seedling thrived at Rosemoor, and the curator, Christopher Bailes, allowed Nick and Karan Junkers of PMA Plant Specialities to propagate and name it. They describe 'Richards Choice' as similar in habit to *D.* 'Rosy Wave', but with paler pink flowers. The only plant I have seen had a more open habit, and the pink of the flowers had a more lilac tone than its sibling. Dimensions of mature plants should be similar to 'Rosy Wave'.

Propagation

Soft or semi-ripe tip cuttings root without problems. Plants grafted on *D. longilobata* or *D. mezereum* grow well.

Unnamed clone of *D. ×schlyteri*, July display on new growth.

D. ×schlyteri 'Lovisa Maria'.

Daphne ×schlyteri C. D. Brickell & A. R. White

Parentage: *D. cneorum × D. arbuscula*

Swedish plantsman Severin Schlyter created this hybrid in 1973, but a correct name and description were not published until 2000. The type clone has been given the cultivar name 'Lovisa Maria' by Mr. Schlyter. In 1993 Fritz Kummert sent me material of a daphne under the name *D.* 'Leila Haines' × *arbuscula*, which I have sold under that name since 1995. Mr. Schlyter has confirmed that the seed parent he used for his cross was *D. cneorum* 'Leila Haines' and that he did supply material to Fritz Kummert. Thus, all plants named *D.* 'Leila Haines' × *arbuscula* are in fact *D.* × *schlyteri* 'Lovisa Maria'. Mr. Schlyter mentions that there were three other seedlings from his cross, and that material of these may be growing in various gardens in northern Europe. An unnamed daphne from Sweden which Piet Oudolf gave me is probably one of these, since it was clearly *D. cneorum* × *D. arbuscula*; I have sold plants as *D.* ×*schlyteri*, but without a cultivar name. It differs from 'Lovisa Maria' in being less prostrate in habit and has flowers of a brighter pink.

'Lovisa Maria' makes a compact, low-growing mat, 10–20 CM in height and 60–90 CM in width. The evergreen foliage consists of glossy, dark green leaves measuring 1.5–2.5 CM by 0.2–0.3 CM, narrowly oblanceolate in shape. The inflorescences are always terminal, made up of 5–8 blooms, bright rosy purple in bud and bright rose pink when open. The main spring flush of blossom is followed by further flowers on new growth through the summer.

This hybrid grows well for me in a raised bed under polythene and in the open. For those who find *D. arbuscula* difficult to please, it may prove an easier alternative. Plants should withstand temperatures down to –23°C/–10°F (Zone 6).

Propagation

Semi-ripe tip cuttings taken between mid-June and early July root very easily. Grafting or layering are possible alternatives.

Named clones

Daphne ×*schlyteri* 'Pink Panther'

This is a repeat of the original cross that occurred as a spontaneous hybrid between *D. cneorum* 'Leila Haines' and *D. arbuscula* in the alpine house of Dr. C. Lafong. A six-year-old pot-grown plant measured 12 CM in height by 25 CM across.

Daphne 'Spring Beauty'

Parentage: *D.* aff. *sureil* × *D. bholua* 'Peter Smithers'

Plants raised from this cross flowered for the first time in 2001. 'Spring Beauty' was selected as the best. There is doubt over the identity of the seed parent, but it should fit into the botanical complex of *D. papyracea*, *D. shillong* and *D. sureil*, all from the Himalaya and known as the paper daphnes, because their bark was used for making paper. My plant, which blooms at the same time as most of the

D. 'Spring Beauty'.

D. aff. *sureil*, beautiful but relatively tender.

D. bholua forms, has large, pure white flowers which are faintly scented. Unfortunately, this group of species is rated as tender.

As a young plant 'Spring Beauty' makes vigorous, upright growth which may need to be pinched to encourage branching. Plants can be expected to reach 3 M in height by 2 M across. The matt, mid-green leaves are oblanceolate, with undulate margins when young and generally have a retuse apex; they measure 7–10 CM by 1.5–2.5 CM. The young bark is grey-green, maturing to grey-brown. The inflorescence of 10–18 flowers may be terminal, terminal on short axillary growths, or axillary. It is enclosed by dark crimson bracts whose hairy margins give a silvery appearance. The dark crimson flower buds open to fragrant, lilac pink flowers, 2–2.2 CM in diameter. The open flowers are less crowded together in the inflorescence than those of *D. bholua*, which gives them a particularly elegant appearance.

To date, plants grafted on to *D. longilobata* have overwintered with no damage from temperatures down to –10°C/14°F (Zone 8), but I suspect a few more degrees of frost would cause damage. This is a beautiful daphne, which I hope will find favour in gardens with a mild climate.

Propagation

Cuttings have not been tried. Grafts on *D. longilobata* grow strongly.

D. 'Spring Herald'.

D. 'Spring Herald' has a bushier habit than *D. bholua*.

Daphne 'Spring Herald'

Parentage: *D. acutiloba* 'Fragrant Cloud' × *D. bholua* 'Jacqueline Postill'

Three seeds from a plant of *D. acutiloba* CD&R 626 'Fragrant Cloud' which grew beside *D. bholua* 'Jacqueline Postill' germinated in 1997. The plants favoured *D. bholua* in habit; one had pale pink flowers, the other two cream. They flowered later than *D. bholua* and had the spicy, citrus fragrance of 'Fragrant Cloud'. 'Spring Herald' was selected as the best.

'Spring Herald' is a tall evergreen shrub, 2.5–3 M in height and 2–2.5 M across. It is bushier in habit than *D. bholua* varieties. Plants grown on their own roots will sucker from the base and from the roots. The young bark is tan, maturing to greyish-brown. The leaves are matt, mid-green; narrowly elliptic to oblanceolate, they measure 5–10 CM by 1.4–2.5 CM. Flowers are produced from February to April under unheated cover, three to four weeks later in the open. The inflorescence may be terminal or axillary, and consists of 8–12 strongly fragrant flowers, 1.5–1.8 CM in diameter. The flower buds and perianth lobes are pink-flushed under cold conditions, but the general colour is cream. The axillary inflorescences do not develop until the flowers of the terminal clusters are virtually over, so there is a long period of flower—eight to ten weeks under cover.

Plants grafted on *D. mezereum* have grown well without winter damage in an open woodland situation. Although not quite as spectacular as *D. bholua* when in flower, this hybrid does have a later flowering period and exceptional fragrance. I think that it should prove slightly hardier than *D. bholua*, perhaps tolerating temperatures of –17 to –23°C/0 to –10°F (Zone 6).

Propagation

Semi-ripe tip cuttings taken in early July have rooted well, but to date they have not produced such robust young plants as those grafted on *D. longilobata* or *D. mezereum*.

Daphne ×*suendermannii* C. D. Brickell

Parentage: *D. arbuscula* × *D. petraea*

The original hybrid between these two species dates back to the 1920s. It is not clear whether a deliberate cross was made by the German nurseryman Franz Suendermann, but Chris Brickell has named this original plant to acknowledge Mr. Suendermann's work. Fritz Kummert reports that he saw a very old plant, possibly the original, when he visited the nursery in Germany, indicating that this hybrid is hardy and long-lived.

D. ×*suendermannii* 'Franz Suendermann'.

My original plant of 'Franz Suendermann' was given to me in the early 1990s by Jochen Herdramm (see also *D. arbuscula* f. *platyclada*, p. 27). This plant survives today in a pot plunged in sand in a polythene tunnel. It is a slow-growing evergreen with a low, almost prostrate habit. Mature plants may be 10–15 CM in height by 60 CM wide. The linear to linear-oblong leaves, with an acute apex, measure 1.3–1.8 CM by 0.2 CM and are clustered towards the apex of the stems; these have brownish grey bark maturing to grey. The terminal inflorescence contains 5–10 fragrant flowers; the perianth lobes are 0.7 CM long by 0.5 CM wide, with a flower diameter of 1.5 CM. Flowers are produced on new growth in the summer following the main spring flush on the old wood, but I would not describe this plant as free-flowering, particularly when compared to its parents—a criticism which could be applied to the two cultivars I have raised.

'Franz Suendermann' seems an easy plant to grow, whether in a container or in the ground. The slow growth rate also makes it suitable for a trough. Plants should be hardy to at least −23°C/−10°F (Zone 6).

Propagation

Semi-ripe basal cuttings of all three cultivars of this hybrid are straightforward to root, but growth is slow. Grafts on *D. mezereum* and *D. longilobata* grow more swiftly, and provided that early strong shoots are pinched, produce well furnished plants in character.

Named clones

Daphne ×*suendermannii* 'Blackthorn Gem'

Parentage: *D. petraea* 'Grandiflora' × *D. arbuscula* f. *grandiflora*

The result of a cross made in 1992, 'Blackthorn Gem' has a slow-growing, upright habit which should make a plant 20–30 CM in height and width. Although the dark green leaves tend to cluster towards the apex of the stems, the plants have a well-furnished appearance because new growth averages only 3–4 CM per season. The terminal inflorescence of 8–10 flowers is enclosed in persistent bracts which unfortunately do not allow the dead flowers to fall away. The flowers are similar in size and shape to those of 'Franz Suendermann', but are darker in colour; they are produced on old and new wood.

D. ×*suendermannii* 'Blackthorn Gem'.

Daphne ×suendermannii 'Chris Brickell'

Parentage: *D. arbuscula* f. *albiflora* × *D. petraea* 'Tremalzo'

This cross, made in 1996, was an attempt to create a white-flowered hybrid. Although unsuccessful, the flowers are particularly fine, and I am happy to name it after Chris in appreciation of his help with all the queries about daphnes I have raised with him over many years.

D. ×suendermannii 'Chris Brickell'.

'Chris Brickell' has slightly more vigour than the other two cultivars of this hybrid, creating a plant with a more open, upright habit which should reach 20–30 CM high and 45–60 CM wide. The glossy green leaves are mainly linear with a slight mucronate apex, measuring 2–2.4 CM by 0.2–0.3 CM. The terminal inflorescence holds 4–6 large, strongly fragrant flowers with auriculate perianth lobes, 0.7–0.8 CM long by 0.5–0.6 CM wide; their apex is notched. Allowing for the downy hairs that give the perianth tube a dusky appearance, all parts of the flowers are an even lilac-pink in colour; the interior of the perianth lobes has a crystalline texture in sunlight, inherited from 'Tremalzo'. Flowers are more freely produced on both old and new wood than by the other two cultivars.

Daphne ×susannae C. D. Brickell

Parentage: *D. collina* of gardens × *D. arbuscula*

Credit for the first recorded hybrid between these species goes to Swedish plantsman Severin Schlyter, who made the cross in Tage Lundell's garden in the late 1960s. Unfortunately, there are no records of this plant's distribution, but Mr. Schlyter would like to name this cultivar 'Tage Lundell'. Further hybrids have arisen in the United States and at Blackthorn Nursery. All are first-class garden plants which are free-flowering and grow strongly enough to make an attractive specimen in three or four years, while remaining compact enough for the smallest garden.

Plants of *D. ×susannae* are evergreen, with a dome-shaped habit, 30–40 CM tall and 60–90 CM across. The leaves may be matt or glossy. The inflorescence of 2–12 flowers is always terminal. A prolific flush of bloom on the previous season's growth in April to May is normally followed by generous quantities of flower on new growth from early July onwards. The flowers vary in colour from rosy purple to rose-pink and are strongly fragrant. The cultivars 'Anton Fahndrich' and 'Tichborne' flower 7–10 days before 'Cheriton' and 'Lawrence Crocker'.

D. ×susannae clones, planted in threes in the autumn of 1999, photographed spring 2004. Foreground 'Anton Fahndrich', mid-left 'Tichborne', mid-right 'Cheriton', back left 'Lawrence Crocker'.

Given a sunny, well-drained site, plants are not difficult to grow well, but attention to tidying away dead leaf material from the base of the plant, and inspection for the first signs of dieback, are especially important. With *D. arbuscula* as a parent, it is not surprising that the lowermost limbs, particularly of 'Cheriton', will layer themselves when conditions permit. It is possible that clones may vary slightly in hardiness, but temperatures down to –23°C/–10°F (Zone 6) should be tolerated.

Propagation

Semi-ripe tip or basal cuttings root easily and quickly; taken in mid-June, they can be potted in August to make a well-established young plant before winter. A substantial plant is made the following growing season. Grafts grow well on *D. longilobata* or *D. mezereum*. Layering would be successful, particularly to reproduce 'Cheriton'.

Named clones

Daphne ×susannae 'Anton Fahndrich'

The exact parentage and origin is not confirmed, but the Swiss nurseryman J. Eschmann distributed plants in the early 1980s. Harry Jans has suggested that this plant should be named after Anton Fahndrich, who gave propagation material to Eschmann.

'Anton Fahndrich' has larger, hairier leaves than other cultivars of this hybrid. The flowers are rosy pink, 1.3–1.4 CM in diameter, and it repeat-flowers well. Although they root easily, cuttings need careful cultivation to grow on, perhaps a trait inherited from *D. collina* of gardens. This may be the least suitable clone for damper climates.

D. ×susannae 'Cheriton'
(Photo: Pat Healing)

D. ×susannae 'Tichborne'.

Daphne ×susannae 'Cheriton'

Parentage: *D. arbuscula × D. collina* of gardens

Selected from seedlings germinated in 1988, this is the most vigorous cultivar. It has a more open habit which creates a plant 30–45 CM in height and 60–90 CM in width. The leaves are dark, glossy green. 'Cheriton' has the darkest coloured flowers of the named cultivars, deep rosy purple when they first open, and fading as they mature. Generous quantities of bloom are produced on new growth throughout the summer. In the United Kingdom the current *RHS Plant Finder* lists more suppliers of 'Cheriton' than *D. collina* of gardens, so those seeking the latter should certainly consider 'Cheriton' as a reliable substitute.

Daphne ×susannae 'Lawrence Crocker'

A spontaneous hybrid from the Oregon garden of Lawrence Crocker, who introduced it from his Siskiyou Rare Plant Nursery. This cultivar compares closely to 'Anton Fahndrich', but it is easier to grow on from cuttings. It is proving a popular plant of easy culture in the United States, and is growing well in my "daphnetum".

Daphne ×susannae 'Tage Lundell'

Brian Mathew has recently given me propagation material of this first recorded hybrid which he received from Severin Schlyter. At present, I am struggling to grow this cultivar, so I cannot make a firm comparison with the other clones. However, my initial impression is that this clone is distinct from 'Anton Fahndrich'.

Daphne ×*susannae* 'Tichborne'

Parentage: *D. collina* of gardens × *D. arbuscula*

Raised at the same time as 'Cheriton', this is the most compact cultivar, with neat, matt green leaves. It makes a tight dome, 20–25 CM high and 45 CM wide. The pale, rosy purple flowers are slightly larger than in other clones, at 1.4–1.5 CM in diameter. Apart from the odd bloom on young, vigorous plants, 'Tichborne' does not repeat-flower on summer growth; this makes it less liable to dieback from *Botrytis* infection of dead flowers, and results in a spectacular performance in April to May. I would recommend this clone for high rainfall areas.

Daphne ×*thauma* Farrer

D. ×*thauma.*

This plant is a natural hybrid between *D. petraea* and *D. striata*, introduced in 1911 by Reginald Farrer, who found it on the Cima Tombea mountain in northern Italy. As far as I know, the single clone in cultivation today is the original.

Daphne ×*thauma* has a slow-growing, densely branched habit, 15–20 CM high and 30–40 CM wide. It is generally evergreen, but I have known plants to suddenly drop most of their leaves towards the end of the summer, making a full recovery, however, by the following season. This is probably due to dryness at the roots, and indicates the influence of *D. striata*. The glossy green leaves are clustered at the apex of the branches. The inflorescence is terminal, and consists of 5–8 fragrant flowers with pale pink perianth lobes and a long, darker perianth tube reminiscent of *D. striata*.

Daphne ×*thauma* has a justified reputation for being shy to flower. I have found this particularly true of plants growing on their own roots. Well nourished grafted plants can produce a good show, particularly when grown under protection. Generally, a few blooms are produced in April and May on the previous season's wood; then, after making a flush of growth, the main display is on the new stems in June and July. *D.* ×*thauma* should tolerate temperatures to –23°C/–10°F (Zone 6).

Propagation

Semi-ripe tip or basal cuttings root without difficulty, but I recommend grafting for a reliable display of flowers; *D. longilobata* or *D. mezereum* both make suitable rootstocks.

Transatlantic chums: 'Eternal Fragrance' in front of 'Jims Pride'.

Daphne ×*transatlantica* C. D. Brickell & A. R. White

Parentage: *D. caucasica* × *D. collina* of gardens

In my opinion, time will prove these plants to be among the best of the daphne hybrids, ranking them with those plants regarded as essential to provide beauty and pleasure in our gardens. I base this on their ease of propagation and production by nurserymen, and cultivation by gardeners, together with their good habit and production of fragrant flowers for 6–8 months of the year. The exact origin of this hybrid is a mystery which may remain unsolved. Enquiries indicate that a nursery in the western United States was responsible for propagating and distributing it as *D. caucasica* from the early 1970s, so they must have raised a seedling of *D. caucasica* believing it to be the true species, when in fact it was a hybrid. The late Jim Cross, of Environmentals Nursery, Long Island, obtained propagation material from the Arnold Arboretum in 1977. Since then, a large number of plants have been propagated and sold in the United States as *D. caucasica*. Jim Cross obviously recognized the potential of *D.* ×*transatlantica*, so the type clone has been named 'Jims Pride' in his memory. Following examination of 'Eternal Fragrance', my own hybrid between the two parent species, Chris Brickell determined that 'Jims Pride' had enough similar characters to suggest the same parentage. The epithet of *transatlantica* was given in recognition of its origin in the United States as a result of a chance cross between a Caucasian and an Italian species.

D. ×*transatlantica* 'Jims Pride'.

'Jims Pride' is an open-branched, semi-evergreen shrub, 1–1.2 M in height and spread. The extent to which foliage is retained in the winter depends on how low temperatures fall. The mid-green leaves are narrowly obovate to narrowly elliptic, measuring 4–4.5 CM by 1.5–1.8 CM. Only a few terminal inflorescences are formed to overwinter; these produce a relatively sparse flush of bloom in April and May. However, from early April new growth is made, which by June is producing terminal inflorescences; a process which continues as long as growth can be made—I have seen flowers out at Christmas. The inflorescence contains up to 10 strongly fragrant flowers with reddish purple buds and perianth tube. The interior of the perianth lobes is white, maturing to palest pink. The colouring is more intense at times of the year when night temperatures are lower.

Although sold until 2000 as *D. caucasica*, the steady increase in popularity of 'Jims Pride' in the United States indicates that this is a plant which will tolerate a wide range of conditions (apart from summer drought). In areas with mild winters, plants will probably be in flower for most of the year. The one drawback to such prolific flower production is a susceptibility to dieback due to

D. ×transatlantica 'Beulah Cross'.

Botrytis infection, which may spread from dead flowers, or infect unripened growth damaged by frost. Since most of the blossom is produced on new growth through the summer, this cultivar can benefit from spring pruning if it gets leggy, or out of shape due to dieback problems. Plants should tolerate temperatures down to –29°C/–20°F (Zone 5).

Propagation

Cuttings taken at any stage from soft to ripe wood can all be rooted without problem. I favour using semi-ripe material in early July which roots in time to be potted in late summer. Plants have grown well grafted on *D. longilobata* and *D. mezereum*.

Named clones

Daphne ×transatlantica 'Beulah Cross'

This is a variegated sport of 'Jims Pride' which was selected and propagated by Jim Cross. His family asked for it to be named after his mother, Beulah Cross. The major part of the leaf is a soft grey-green in colour, with a narrow, irregular cream margin. There is enough chlorophyll in the leaves for plants to make vigorous growth and produce plenty of flowers throughout the summer. Plants should reach 0.75–1 M in height and spread.

D. ×transatlantica 'Eternal Fragrance'. These spring flowers show more colour than summer blossom.

Daphne ×transatlantica 'Eternal Fragrance' (Blafra)

Parentage: *D. caucasica* × *D. collina* of gardens

I made this cross in 1995 before I was familiar with 'Jims Pride'. Once the resulting seedling flowered, close examination by Chris Brickell revealed that the two plants were morphologically close enough to suggest that they had the same parent species.

'Eternal Fragrance' has a neat, bushy habit which creates a dome 60–75 CM in height. The dark green leaves are shorter and narrower than in 'Jims Pride' at 3.5–4.5 CM by 0.6–1 CM. The spring flush of flower is more generous than that of 'Jims Pride', because there are axillary as well as terminal inflorescences. The perianth lobes are broader and are not reflexed, giving the impression of a larger flower. 'Eternal Fragrance' matches 'Jims Pride' in scent and freedom of flower production, but there is more colour to the perianth tube. An uncommon feature of this hybrid is the ability to produce axillary flowers (in twos or threes) on new summer growth. This is fine for display, but a nuisance for propagators!

'Eternal Fragrance' was first offered for sale in the United Kingdom in 2005. It is protected from unlicensed propagation by European Union Plant Variety Rights and United States Patent. 'Eternal Fragrance' is the marketing name, while 'Blafra' is a code name which applies worldwide to all countries who are members of the International Union for the Protection of New Plant Varieties. The following quote from Bonnie and Scott Rose, who are trialling 'Eternal Fragrance', leads me to hope that it will give pleasure to many across the Atlantic: "*Daphne* 'Eternal Fragrance' is the best plant we have grown in the last decade. For the past four years in our cold, moody Pacific Northwest garden, this hybrid consistently blooms April to November. Last year our garden went down to 15°F for five straight days and it sailed through. We'll never be without it in our garden." This makes me feel like a proud father!

Daphne ×transatlantica 'Summer Ice'

A variegated sport of 'Jims Pride' selected and propagated by Dr. Robert Ticknor, a well-known grower of woody ornamentals in Oregon. The narrow cream leaf margins are similar to those of 'Beulah Cross', but the main leaf area is mid-green. Further sports on 'Summer Ice' which have greater areas of yellowish cream have been selected, and named 'Lemon Ice' and 'Marble Ice'. A decision on commercial production of these will depend on their stability. Reports from gardeners on the eastern side of the United States suggest that 'Summer Ice' is not as vigorous as 'Beulah Cross' and does not repeat-flower so well.

D. 'Valerie Hillier'.

Daphne 'Valerie Hillier'

Parentage: *D. longilobata × D. cneorum*

A hybrid created in the 1980s by Alan Postill, propagator at Hillier Nurseries, and named after John Hillier's wife, 'Valerie Hillier' has an open, lax habit of growth and makes a small shrub, 1–1.5 M in height and spread. The glossy green leaves are lanceolate to oblanceolate, measuring 3–4 CM by 0.6–0.7 CM. The bractless inflorescence is terminal, often on short axillary growths. After a few flowers in late spring on the previous season's wood, blooms are produced on new growth throughout the growing season. The inflorescence carries 4–10 fragrant flowers, reddish purple in bud. The interior of the perianth lobes is pale pink.

D. ×whiteorum 'Kilmeston'. The original plant.

D. ×whiteorum 'Kilmeston'.

'Valerie Hillier' has grown well in sun or semi-shade. The long period over which fragrant flowers are produced makes this a useful plant for the garden, but care is needed to build up a strong framework of growth on young plants to prevent wind or snow damage. Plants should tolerate temperatures down to –17°C/0°F (Zone 7).

Propagation

Soft tip cuttings root easily, but are slow to make a strong plant. Plants grafted onto *D. longilobata* and *D. mezereum* grow well, but careful pinching of young growth is important to produce a sturdy, well-branched plant.

Daphne ×whiteorum C. D. Brickell

Parentage: *D. petraea* 'Grandiflora' × *D. jasminea*

Daphne ×whiteorum 'Kilmeston', which is taken as the type form, was the first hybrid I gave a cultivar name. It was a spontaneous hybrid raised from seed which set on a plant of *D. petraea* 'Grandiflora' which grew in my glasshouse next to a plant of *D. jasminea* Delphi form (see p. 66). It flowered for the first time in 1989, and has since proved to be an attractive, free-flowering plant when cultivated under glass. In the United Kingdom climate a favoured site is necessary for successful cultivation in the open, but no doubt 'Kilmeston' would perform well in areas with warm summers and mild, dry winters.

'Kilmeston' is a dwarf, evergreen shrub, 20–30 CM in height by 45–60 CM wide. It has a much-branched, bushy habit, and may occasionally produce stolons, a character inherited from *D. petraea.* The dark grey-green, oblanceolate leaves, 0.8–1.8 CM by 0.2–0.3 CM, are purple-flushed when young, and the whole plant assumes a purplish tint with the onset of low winter temperatures. Under glass, flowers are produced in April on the previous season's growth, then following new shoot growth a more prolific period of flowering occurs from June to September. The terminal inflorescences on short axillary growths consist of 2–5 flowers, red-purple in bud, opening to deep purplish pink. The outer perianth lobes are noticeably broader than the inner pair.

'Kilmeston' thrives under cover in a pot or a raised bed, appreciating the warm summer temperatures and protection from excessive overhead moisture. Given adequate moisture and nutrients the flowers produced on new growth from mid-June onwards are superior to the spring display, a characteristic inherited from *D. jasminea.* Both low temperatures and excessive wet in winter are detrimental; plants are unlikely to survive below –12°C/10°F (Zone 8).

Propagation

Soft tip or basal cuttings root without difficulty. Semi-ripe or ripe wood is difficult to root. Plants grafted on *D. longilobata* or *D. mezereum* grow well.

D. ×*whiteorum* 'Beauworth'.

Named clones

Daphne ×*whiteorum* 'Beauworth'

Parentage: *D. jasminea* × *D. petraea* 'Grandiflora'

Whereas 'Kilmeston' is a fair mix of both parents, 'Beauworth' favours the pollen parent. It first flowered in 1992 and is similar in habit and size to 'Kilmeston'. The foliage is dark green rather than grey-green and does not take on a purple flush on young growth or with cold temperatures. The inflorescences are generally terminal, but strong shoots produce axillary flowers on the previous season's growth, creating a thick spike of flowers. The sweetly fragrant flowers are superior in size and shape to those of 'Kilmeston'. The reddish pink buds open to rose pink flowers,

1.1–1.2 CM in diameter with auriculate lobes, 0.6–0.7 CM by 4–5 CM. In contrast to 'Kilmeston', the main spring flush of flowers is the best display, but a steady succession of bloom is produced on new growth.

This plant has grown exceptionally well in a raised bed under polythene, but is also doing reasonably well in the open, where it is growing against the sunny side of a piece of tufa. Long periods of winter wet are probably more detrimental than cold. It should certainly be tolerant of temperatures to –12°C/10°F (Zone 8).

D. ×whiteorum 'Warnford'.

D. ×whiteorum 'Warnford', photographed in September.

Daphne ×*whiteorum* 'Warnford'

Parentage: *D. petraea* 'Grandiflora' × *D. jasminea*

This hybrid has the same parentage as 'Kilmeston' but it is very different, favouring *D. jasminea* in most respects. It first flowered in 1992. The slender stems are virtually prostrate, so a mature plant may be 10–15 CM in height by 90 CM across. The pale green leaves are basically evergreen, but a proportion are dropped if the temperatures fall below –10°C (14°F). A few flowers are produced on the old wood in early summer, but this plant does not perform well until July, when a fine display of flowers on new growth lasts well into autumn. The flower buds are a dark reddish purple—a pleasing contrast to the pure white, sweetly fragrant flowers. The bud colour is lacking when the plant is grown under cover, which detracts a great deal from their appearance, to the extent that I would not recommend this hybrid for indoor culture.

'Warnford' should tolerate temperatures to –17°C/0°F (Zone 7). Provided that it has sufficient moisture, I am sure it would perform well in hotter climates than that of the United Kingdom. Although it can be considered a drought-tolerant plant, lack of summer moisture may reduce the length of flowering. Extension growth of young plants should be pinched regularly to encourage branching.

Miscellaneous *Daphne* hybrids

Although they may not be garden-worthy, readers may be interested to know a few details of the following hybrids:

D. acutiloba* × *D. arbuscula I raised two similar seedlings from a 1997 cross at Blackthorn Nursery. Slow-growing and shy-flowering to date, but good flowers and an interesting leaf shape.

D. blagayana* × *D. arbuscula This was a cross made in 1997 at Blackthorn Nursery. One seedling, which flowered in 2001, had a good, prostrate habit and beautiful pure white flowers, but to date many inflorescences have failed to develop to maturity.

D. ×burkwoodii* 'Somerset' × *D. arbuscula I raised and flowered two seedlings from a spontaneous cross in the early 1990s. The habit and foliage resembled a dwarf *D. ×burkwoodii*. One had pink flowers, the other pure white. These hybrids showed promise, but I lost them both.

D. caucasica* × *D. rodriguezii I grew several seedlings which arose from a spontaneous cross at Blackthorn Nursery in the early 1990s which produced unexciting plants. None survive.

D. cneorum* × *D. jasminea I grew several dozen seedlings which arose from a spontaneous cross at Blackthorn Nursery in the late 1980s, some of which were sold. None were outstanding, and I doubt if any survive today.

D. gnidium* × *D. cneorum A spontaneous hybrid at Blackthorn Nursery in the early 1980s; one seedling was flowered. It had a weak, straggly habit. The panicles of 10–15 flowers were pretty; pale pink with a dark pink margin. The single plant died.

D. mezereum* × *D. bholua I have repeated this cross with no better result than Mr. Dummer had when he raised a plant at Hillier Nurseries in the mid-1970s and named it 'Louis Mountbatten'. This had an upright, deciduous habit with a few inflorescences of pink flowers which failed to open properly.

D. pseudosericea* × *D. cneorum A recent hybrid created by German enthusiast Hans Bauer, and given the name 'Zdenek Seibert'. It has a more open habit than *D.* ×*napolitana* hybrids. The fragrant flowers are deep pink.

***D.* ×*rossetii* (*D. laureola* subsp. *philippi* × *D. cneorum*)** Originally found in 1927 growing in the Pyrenees. An easily cultivated, low-growing evergreen, but very shy-flowering.

D. striata* × *D. arbuscula A spontaneous hybrid which I first flowered in 2004. It is intermediate between the two parents. Ease of cultivation and freedom of flowering have yet to be determined.

The author at the grafting bench. This contraption solves the problem of not having the three hands needed for the job.

4 Propagation

There are four standard methods of propagating daphnes: seed, cuttings, grafting and layering. To these must be added tissue culture which, although worth mentioning, is likely to be of more interest to commercial growers. My recommended methods for individual plants are given in their descriptions in Chapters 2 and 3—but certainly, as far as the propagation of daphnes is concerned, it is wrong to be dogmatic about anything. I have known of instances where apparently unsuitable cutting material has rooted, old seed has germinated and grafting at odd times of the season has worked. The following pages give recommendations for successful results, but do not be led into thinking that other methods will not work. My experience is based on commercial propagation, but the methods I use are not "hi-tech" and can serve as a guide for anyone.

While I hope that this book will enable gardeners to keep their daphnes healthy, propagating plants is an insurance against any sudden disaster, and spares make valuable swaps. The challenge posed by propagation by whatever method offers a thrill, and great satisfaction to reward success. Above all, do not give up if at first you are unsuccessful. That is advice I still follow today.

Hygiene

Basic hygiene is important when propagating because harmful bacteria, fungi and viruses that may infect and destroy cuttings or grafts are easily spread during this process. Use clean trays, containers, secateurs and knives, and above all disease-free plant material. Try to sterilize knives and wash hands between handling different plants. Readily available materials such as methylated spirit, diluted bleach or products used for sterilizing babies' bottles are suitable for this purpose.

Seed

Daphne fruits

Many *Daphne* species produce easily recognizable fruits in the form of drupes with a fleshy, coloured pericarp or outer layer. (Beware, as like any other fruits they are attractive to birds and animals. My fruiting plants have been set upon by blackbirds and thrushes, which are after the fleshy part of the berries, and greenfinches and mice which are after the seeds.) However, the fruits of some species, such as *D. arbuscula* and *D. petraea*, are not readily seen as they have a very thin fleshy or coriaceous pericarp and remain encased in the dead, brown perianth tube of the flower. The fruits of *D. cneorum* (see photograph, p. 46) and *D. jasminea* also remain hidden in the dead flower until ripe, when the pericarp, greenish yellow in colour, swells and splits the remains of the perianth tube. Therefore, if you are keen to get seed from a plant of these daphnes, watch out for any dead flower which does not readily detach from the plant, as it will probably contain a developing fruit. I have come across apomictic fruits in only one species, *D. tangutica*. An apomictic fruit looks perfect from the outside, but the black, shiny seed coat (testa) does not contain an embryo.

Treatment of dormant seed

The best germination results will always be obtained by sowing fresh seed within a few days of harvest. There can be problems with bought or gifted seed; if it has not been stored correctly, it may no longer be viable at all, but whatever the case it will be soundly dormant. A most interesting study was carried out by Anna Dourada, Tran Dang Hong and Richard Ellis (2000) into the germination of daphne seed. They found that the following procedure was effective in promoting the germination of dormant seed: the seed was soaked for 24 hours in a 3 percent solution of hydrogen peroxide, then for a further 24 hours in two thousand parts per million gibberellic acid (GA-3). This was followed by a 56-day moist pre-chill at 3–5°C (37–41°F), and then germination at 25°C (77°F). This treatment was more effective in treating dormancy than soaking in either chemical by itself. Further experiments placed daphnes into two groups: those in which seeds will germinate at a wide range of temperatures, for example *D. alpina*, *D. mezereum*, *D. oleoides* and *D. pontica*, and those in which seeds germinate at warm temperatures, that is, above 15°C (59°F): for example, *D. tangutica*, *D. longilobata* and *D. bholua*. By using the method described above they could be fairly certain of obtaining an acceptable germination rate from seed harvested some time before sowing. By contrast, if this seed was sown without any treatment and put into a cold frame, there would most probably be only sporadic germination in the spring of the following two or three years. Of course, the above treatment may seem a bit daunting for the average gardener—but if money has been spent on seed of a rare or desirable species, trying this method may be the key to successful germination.

It has been suggested the seed coat of some species, such as *D. mezereum*, may contain a germination inhibitor and so the fleshy pericarp must be removed and the seed skin cleaned to facilitate germination—and in addition, that seed harvested while the pericarp is still green will germinate sooner than that from a ripe, red fruit because the inhibitor will not have formed (Brickell and Mathew 1976). I can only record here that for many years now I have harvested considerable quantities of daphne seed when the fruits are ripe, sown them completely whole, and obtained good germination by the following spring. Harry Jans (2000) also obtains good germination without cleaning his daphne seed. I wonder whether leaving the fleshy pericarp on seed actually helps it to germinate better than if it is cleaned? As fungi and bacteria break down the pericarp, there may be compounds released which stimulate the seed. When you consider the way some seeds react to the gases created by burning, this may not be that far-fetched. Additionally, the decomposition of the pericarp will provide the germinating seedling with nutrients.

Seed sowing

I aim to keep the sowing of home-saved seed as simple as possible. I try to sow within a week of harvesting. The compost never varies; it consists of approximately two-thirds proprietary loam-free, peat-based seed compost, which has a fine texture and low nutrient content, and one-third seed-grade perlite. I use a standard seed tray or a two-litre plastic pot. After filling, the compost is drenched with a mix of fungicides which should protect against pathogens such as *Pythium* and *Rhizoctonia*. I grow quantities of *D. mezereum* and *D. longilobata* from seed to use as rootstocks for grafting; both have fruits with fleshy pericarps, and it would be a very messy and tedious job to clean them before sowing, so they are simply spread on the surface of the compost and covered with a layer of 5–6 MM grit. This is my standard treatment for other species with a fleshy pericarp, such as *D. caucasica* and *D. tangutica*. Seed which does not have a fleshy pericarp is covered with 2 MM grit which has a low proportion of "fines"—fine, dust-like particles. When choosing a material for covering seed, avoid anything with a high proportion of fines as it is liable to form a hard crust when dry, and more likely to encourage the establishment of moss and liverwort. Additionally, a covering material with a low proportion of fines helps to prevent evaporation of water from the surface of the seed compost, while a material with a high proportion of fines will increase drying-out of the compost by capillary action. All sown seed is placed in a cold frame, where it has a covering of 50 percent shade netting from June to October, and glass for the remaining time. Mouse traps are set and maintained always!

This method of seed sowing has worked well for me for many years now, never failing to give a commercially acceptable germination rate. *Daphne mezereum* seed is harvested and sown in early June. The proportion of seed which germinates by autumn varies from year to year, but the major portion germinates in March and April of the following spring. Seed of *D. longilobata* comes from plants grown in an unheated tunnel, and is harvested over a period of two to three months. Early seed from blossom on old wood may be sown by the end of July, and much of this will germinate by the autumn. Seed sown later remains dormant until the following spring. All of the other seed I sow on a regular basis, principally of *D. alpina*, *D. albowiana*, *D. giraldii*, *D. jezoensis*, *D. oleoides* and *D. tangutica*, delays its germination until spring.

I once received some seed of *D. genkwa* through the post which had not been protected by any packing material. The hard black seed coats of most of the seeds were cracked, and in some cases the embryo and cotyledons were bare. Nevertheless I felt I had to try sowing the precious seed, which I placed in a warm propagation frame. You can imagine my surprise and joy when, within a few weeks, a good proportion of the seed germinated. In spite of this, if you send seed through the post, do make sure it is well protected.

Care of seedlings

If a proportion of seed in a tray sown in early summer germinates before autumn, the seedlings are left *in situ* unfed until the spring germination of their fellows. In cold climates these youngsters would need protecting from severe frost. But once the spring germination is under way I give all seedlings weak liquid feeds every 10–14 days to encourage them to develop quickly with the lengthening hours of daylight and increasing temperatures. Well-nourished seedlings will always re-establish more quickly than starved ones when they are transplanted. It is a good idea to move them into individual containers as soon as true leaves start to develop, since they will already have a substantial root system which, if left, can soon become tangled with that of neighbouring seedlings and result in breakages when potting up. The earlier the disturbance is carried out, the sooner the plant can establish itself and take advantage of the main growing season. One advantage of using perlite in the sowing medium is that it definitely aids the separation of the roots of seedlings. If possible, a fungicide should be incorporated into the potting compost, or young plants treated with a drench after potting.

The treatment of seedlings intended as rootstocks for grafting is covered later. I suggest that if plants are intended for the garden, seedlings should be put in a pot of 7–9 CM diameter. After an initial period of shading to aid establishment, the young plants should be given plenty of light to encourage sturdy growth. From my commercial angle, I aim to grow on species I produce from seed for two seasons. They remain in a 7 CM pot for the first growing season, so they do need some liquid feeding to maintain healthy growth. From the gardener's point of view, once your young plant has filled a 7 or 9 CM pot with root, which it may do in six to eight weeks, it will benefit from potting on or planting out. Which you do must depend on the circumstances, but I am convinced that species with a fine, deep-growing root system, such as *D. alpina*, *D. giraldii* and *D. oleoides*, resent pot cultivation and should be planted out as soon as practicable. The stronger-growing types may need pinching or stopping to produce a well-shaped bushy plant.

Storage of seed

As well as germination, the storage of daphne seed was also studied by Dourado, Ellis and Hong (2000). They discovered that, contrary to popular opinion, daphne seeds show orthodox storage behaviour, surviving drying to a low moisture content of 5 percent after which they can be safely stored at low temperature. Seed from fully ripened fruits stores best. Once cleaned it should be dried to a low moisture content, for example in equilibrium with silica gel, and placed in an airtight container. A domestic refrigerator or freezer is then suitable for long-term storage.

Layering

For someone without propagation facilities who may just require the odd extra plant, it would be well worth trying to layer those daphnes whose pliable growth and/or semi-prostrate habit makes them particularly suitable for this method; I never have, but in our garden *Daphne arbuscula*, *D. petraea* and the *D.* ×*susannae* hybrids have all layered themselves without any encouragement. It follows that stems of tired old plants of the right habit could be pinned down, if necessary, and top-dressed with some good compost, which should encourage them to make root and rejuvenate. The technique is well covered in many books.

Grafting

Woody plants have an area in which the cells remain capable of dividing after the cells in the surrounding areas of tissue have reached maturity. This area is called the cambium, and in simple terms is the thin green layer (seen as a ring when the stem is cut) located between the wood and the bark. A successful graft brings the cambium of the piece of plant to be propagated, known as the scion, into contact with the cambium of the rootstock. The cells of both cambiums divide and unite to form a callus or union. Most daphne species I have worked with seem perfectly compatible, in that a scion and stock from different plants make a strong, long-lived union. However, in a few cases there seems to have been partial incompatibility; although a union seems to develop, the scion does not make growth and slowly declines. Examples are mentioned later.

The technique of grafting tends to be viewed with trepidation by the average gardener. I accept that there are genera like *Acer* and *Betula* which may need special treatment to graft successfully, but daphnes are very straightforward. By no stretch of the imagination can I be classed as a handyman, in fact quite the opposite, with my club thumbs and arthritic fingers! So with a little practice, anyone should be able to graft daphnes and achieve a high rate of success. If you happen to have surplus seed-raised plants which could be used as stocks, why not try a few grafts just for fun?

More practical reasons why one may wish to graft are various. I have often been presented with material of a daphne I would like to grow that almost certainly would not root from cuttings, but has grown well as a graft. In some cases, where there is only a small amount of material, I prefer the near certainty of success with grafting to the higher risk of taking cuttings. Provided that you have noticed the problem early enough, the total loss of a plant suffering from root problems can be averted by grafting a piece of the top growth. In the case of slow-growing species such as *D. petraea*, a plant of reasonable size can be produced in two or three seasons—less than half the time it would take if grown on its own roots. Some named clones of species like *D. bholua* are difficult to root from cuttings, so grafting is required. From a commercial view, grafting can produce a plant of saleable size in a much shorter time, and a well-fed grafted plant of one of the smaller species of daphne will quickly make a mother plant for cutting material. Lastly, I feel that if the aim is to grow some of the smaller species and hybrids in pots on a long-term basis for showing or to enjoy under glass, then many are easier to manage on the roots of *D. longilobata* or *D. mezereum* than on their own; this applies especially to *D. arbuscula*, *D. cneorum* and *D.* ×*hendersonii* cultivars.

Choice of rootstock

Rootstocks for fruit trees such as apples are clonally propagated because trees grafted onto seed-raised stocks show great variation in characteristics such as vigour, fruit bearing and drought tolerance. I have never conducted any trials to see if the same principles apply to seed-raised rootstocks for daphnes, but there is certainly variation in the growth habits of a crop of plants seed-grown to provide rootstocks, which may cause the growth and flower production of the scions to vary. However, no species I have used as a rootstock has proved superior in terms of growth, flower production and longevity—although choice of rootstock can influence a species' tolerance of drought and extremes of temperature.

Daphne mezereum

The fact that this species reliably produces good quantities of seed and is hardy puts it at the top of the list as a choice of rootstock. It will generally take two growing seasons to produce a stem of suitable thickness to use with thicker types of scion, but those seedlings which germinate in the same season as sowing will make a stock of about 0.3 CM in diameter by the end of the following year, which is adequate for the smaller types of daphne. A proportion of seedlings are liable to make two or three shoots of equal vigour. I tend to use those for growing on to saleable size, but if they are to be used as rootstocks, excess shoots should be removed as early as possible to leave a single stem. My one complaint about *D. mezereum* is that the cambium exposed by the transverse cut made before grafting often produces adventitious shoots, a problem which does not arise in other species I have used as rootstocks. This is a particular nuisance when small scions such as *D. petraea* forms are concerned, as it is difficult to rub out these shoots without knocking the scion out of place. Once the scion has made some growth, and possibly exerts some hormonal dominance, this problem ceases. There is no difference in performance between the pink- and white-flowered forms of *D. mezereum* when used as a rootstock, and I have never noticed any sign of an evergreen scion variety losing foliage in the dormant season due to being grafted onto a deciduous species. Plants grafted on *D. mezereum* come slightly later into growth than those on *D. longilobata* (see below); a useful characteristic in areas where late frosts occur.

Daphne longilobata

In the U.K. this species has been confused with *D. acutiloba* (see p. 21). The stock plants I grow for seed production have the protection of an unheated tunnel in order to stop the birds taking the fruit, but *D. longilobata* does also have a reputation for not being totally hardy, and should therefore be treated with caution as a rootstock in areas where the ground is liable to freeze for long periods. Good quantities of seed are reliably set over a period of two to three months. The earliest seed will germinate reasonably well by autumn if sown fresh, and these seedlings, potted on in the spring, will make considerably sturdier stocks in one season than would *D. mezereum*, suitable for grafting scions up to 0.3 CM in diameter. However, it is worth noting that these young stocks have a thick cortex, and the cambium layer is thus relatively near to the centre. This is not a problem if a slender-stemmed scion like *D. petraea* is to be used, but if the scion stem is of the same diameter as the stock, cambiums may be difficult to match. A further season's growth produces a stem with the cambium in a more conventional position and with a diameter up to 0.9 CM—rather large for thinner scions, but ideal for species like *D. bholua*. When grafting early in the season it is noticeable that scions on *D. longilobata* are much quicker into growth than those on *D. mezereum*. I find that *D. arbuscula* and *D. calcicola* do not grow well on *D. longilobata*, possibly indicating partial incompatibility. *Daphne longilobata* has softer wood than *D. mezereum*, and when its stems are less than about 0.4 CM in diameter they are also much more pliable, which can make it more difficult to tie in the graft with materials like tape or rubber strips.

Daphne tangutica and *Daphne retusa*

These are readily obtainable species that reliably produce seed. It is just possible to produce a plant of *D. tangutica* in one season which would be suitable for a slender scion, but generally two years are required; *D. retusa* definitely needs two years' growth before grafting. *Daphne arbuscula* and *D. calcicola* grow well when grafted on this species. I have no experience of temperatures low enough to damage *D. tangutica*, or the closely related *D. retusa*. Henry Taylor reports that *D.* ×*hendersonii* 'Rosebud' grows well in Scotland grafted on *D. retusa*, and produces larger flowers of a better colour than when grown on its own roots. I have never tried grafting a vigorous species like *D. bholua* onto *D. tangutica*, but I suspect that the rootstock would have a dwarfing effect. This might produce a plant more suited to container cultivation than one on its own roots or grafted on *D. mezereum* or *D. longilobata*.

Daphne laureola

This needs a minimum of two seasons to make a stock of workable size. It makes a good stock for *D. glomerata* and *D. calcicola*.

Daphne giraldii

Although this is sometimes recommended as a rootstock, I find it difficult to raise from seed and grow on in pots in the same way that I produce stocks of *D. longilobata* and *D. mezereum*. I therefore cannot recommend this species as a rootstock. I suspect there may be some confusion between *D. giraldii* and other yellow-flowered daphne species from China (see also p. 60).

Rooted cuttings

Theoretically, there is no reason why a well-established cutting cannot be used as a stock for grafting, so long as it is free from disease, particularly virus. I have grafted clones of *D. arbuscula* onto rooted cuttings of the same species and see no reason why *D. bholua* could not be used in the same way; however, the big advantage of a seed-grown stock is juvenile vigour and freedom from disease.

Production of rootstocks

Unless a friend has some to spare, you will need to produce your own stocks from seed for grafting purposes. When potting on seedlings which are going to be used as rootstocks, try to keep the cotyledons well clear of the surface of the compost. By doing this, when you come to cut back the stock for grafting, the length of stem most likely to produce shoots or suckers will be kept to a minimum. It seems to be a characteristic of daphne roots that they cling to the sides of pots. As a result it can be difficult to remove a young plant from its pot and, when you do succeed, it is galling to see so many root tips—the most important part of the root system—left adhering to the sides of the pot. To facilitate easy removal and reduce root damage, I use a 7 CM semi-rigid pot for my rootstocks that is coated on the inside with a product containing copper hydroxide, which has the effect of repelling root growth. As this product may not be available to the average gardener, I suggest that the stocks are potted in relatively flimsy, semi-rigid pots. By gently pinching opposite sides of the pot in turn, a plant can be removed with far less trauma than from a rigid pot. Care needs to be taken over the period of rootstock production to prevent undue rooting through the bottom of the pot, especially if the pots are plunged. Standing them out on woven landscape fabric or coarse gravel helps to prevent this problem.

During its second season *D. longilobata* can make vigorous top growth, well in excess of 30 CM. I like to keep a balance between root and top growth, so I cut back this growth to approximately 20 CM in June. If possible, use stocks one season old for dwarf types of daphne, particularly *D. petraea*. The main reason for this is that after two seasons in a small pot, the root system of a stock can become very congested, or pot-bound. It seems that putting a very small scion on such a stock may not provide enough stimulus and carbohydrates to the root system to encourage it into growth strong enough to re-establish in new compost when put into a larger pot. The net result is an apparently healthy-looking scion in a static condition. This problem does not seem to occur when scions of more vigorous varieties such as *D. bholua* or *D. caucasica* are grafted on stocks of a similar age.

Choice of scion

Growth at the tip, or apex, of a stem can be used as the scion material, or a section of stem, which can be several years old. The ripeness of the wood and its diameter are the key factors to keep in mind.

If you have a choice of scion material, then growth of nearly equal diameter to, or thinner than, that of the rootstock is best. Avoid stems of greater diameter than the rootstock. Choose well-ripened wood; even in early spring, wood towards the tips of the previous season's growth may be green and unripened on species such as *D. bholua* and *D. odora*, while in late summer many varieties will not have ripened wood towards the tips of their new (or "maiden") shoots.

If wood is ripe enough to use a scion from the apex of the current growth, remove the apical bud, as this may contain flower buds or, if it is a vegetative bud, will produce one strong shoot which must be stopped to encourage a bushy plant. For scions of smaller species such as *D. cneorum* or *D. petraea*, two- or three-year-old wood is preferable to maiden wood, as it produces a bushier, stronger plant; however, it does mean cutting a sizeable portion from the donor plant.

For the smaller species, I do not use a scion longer than 3.7 CM. The scion for more vigorous types should have two to four buds and should not exceed 7.5 CM in length. Using too long a scion will result in a leggy plant, as only the buds near the top of the scion will grow. Leaves may still be present on the scion; in the case of large leaves, as in *D. bholua*, I leave two or three in place, but reduce them by half. Foliage of the smaller-leaved types is left uncut on the top portion of the scion. Although some scions may shed their leaves after two or three weeks in a closed propagating case, I think they will still have benefited the scion by producing carbohydrates for growth before they fell. It is important to remove these fallen leaves to prevent fungal infection.

The process of grafting

The time of grafting does not seem critical. For convenience, most of mine is done towards the end of January and a small proportion in mid-August, but I have been presented with pieces of daphne to graft virtually from March to August, and I have never failed to get at least a few to grow; however, if you have a choice, I would recommend February, March or August. If grafting in January, I bring my rootstocks into the glasshouse about six weeks beforehand, give them a drench with fungicide and encourage them to break dormancy by maintaining the daytime temperature above 10°C (50°F). Our recent succession of mild winters barely makes this process necessary, but it would certainly be helpful in areas which experience colder winters should you wish to graft early in the year.

The best advice I can give to anyone attempting to graft daphnes for the first time is to practise cutting with your knife before attempting the real thing. A mature plant, or perhaps the top growth from a rootstock plant, provides ideal material with which to practise preparation of the scion. The sharper your knife, the easier it will be to use, and the less likely you are to cut yourself. I use a knife with a replaceable blade.

Unless a method is devised to hold the pot containing the rootstock firmly in place, you will find making the graft and tying it difficult, and you may well wish for a third hand. To keep the rootstock's pot steady, I use a plank of wood 10 CM wide by 1.2 CM thick, secured in a vertical position. At a comfortable

My contraption for holding a rootstock secure for grafting.

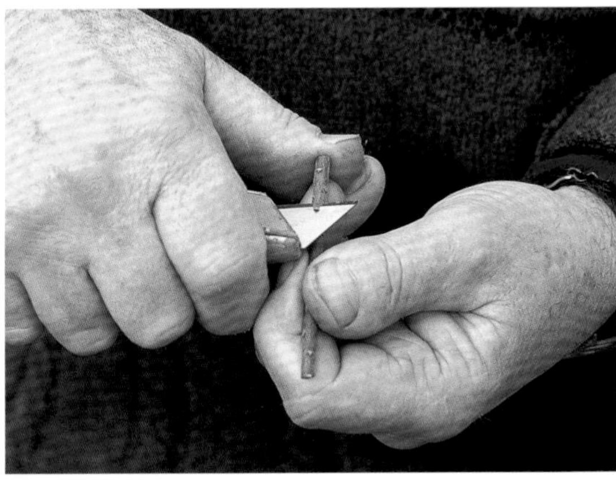

Preparing the scion. Note arms held close to body.

Making the vertical cut in the rootstock. Note left-hand fingers support the stock and hold the prepared scion.

working height, I attach to the plank a rigid pot of similar diameter to the rootstock's pot; string and staples seem adequate for this. The pot of the rootstock will fit snugly into the secured pot, leaving both hands free for grafting and tying. A simple alternative if you just have a few stocks to graft is to embed an empty pot of the same size as the pot containing the stock in a larger pot filled with sand. I would put a 7 CM pot into a 15 CM pot of sand. Doubtless there are other ways of holding the rootstock firm, but do make sure it is at a comfortable working height.

Before cutting back the growth of the rootstock, clean the surface of the compost. As well as removing any moss or loose material, I take away 0.6–1.2 CM of compost to allow the graft to be made as low on the neck of the rootstock as possible.

If you are not used to working with a knife, it is important that you work with your arms held close to your body so that you have full control of your knife; this will reduce the chance of a mishap to the scion, or to the hand holding it! Irrespective of the size of the scion in relation to the stock, I have never used any style of graft other than a simple wedge (see Figure 3A). This involves cutting the stem of the rootstock down to 1.8–3 CM above soil level, and rubbing off any buds left on the stem below the cut. Within reason, the longer the piece of stock left, the easier it is to graft and tie, but more stem area that could produce suckers will be left, and the dwarfer types look incongruous on a long "leg" of rootstock.

Next, I prepare the scion by slicing down either side of its base to create a wedge shape (see Figures 3B, 3C). The length of this wedge will depend on the thickness of the scion material. The wedge of a thick stem, for example of *D. bholua*, may be up to 2.5 CM long, compared to perhaps 0.6 CM for *D. petraea*. For the latter you would do little more than shave off the bark. A gently tapered cut exposes a larger area of cambium at the upper part of the wedge (see Figure 3D), which is good. Try to make a straight rather than a curved cut, and make sure the cuts meet at the tip of the wedge. If I have to prepare a scion with a much smaller diameter than the stock, I tend to

Figure 3: Grafting

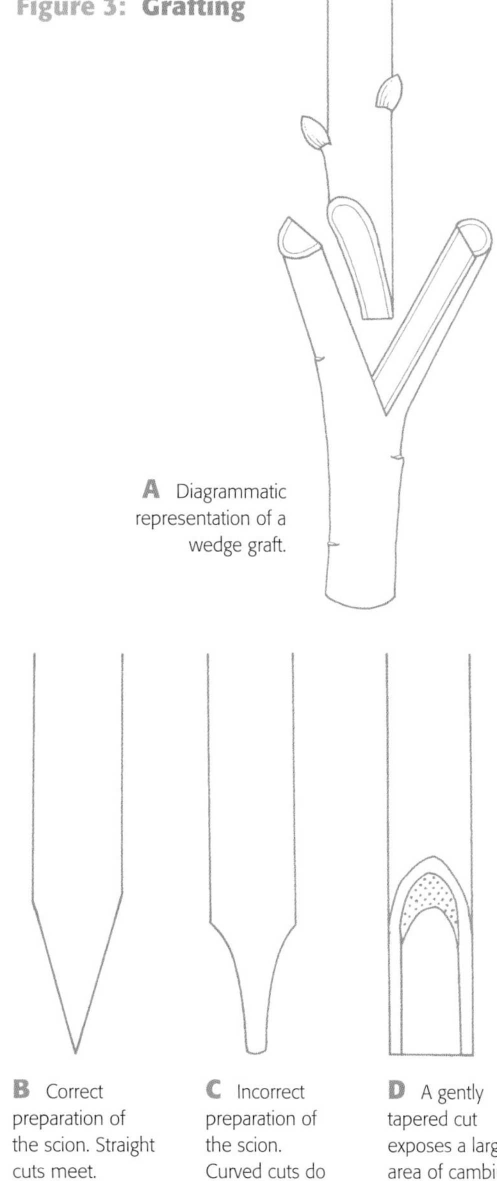

A Diagrammatic representation of a wedge graft.

B Correct preparation of the scion. Straight cuts meet.

C Incorrect preparation of the scion. Curved cuts do not meet.

D A gently tapered cut exposes a larger area of cambium (shaded).

make one side of the wedge thicker than the other. This thicker side is put to the outside of the stock.

Having prepared the scion, irrespective of its diameter in relation to that of the stock, make a vertical cut down the centre of the rootstock (see photo on p. 170); it should be longer than the length of the wedge of the scion. Align the cambium of at least one side of the scion with the cambium of the stock and push the scion firmly in until all the cut surface of the scion is below the top of the stock. If it is not, remove the scion and make a deeper vertical cut in the stock. This is because the uppermost part of the wedge cut will have the broadest area of exposed cambium, and this should unite with the cambial area of the stock even if the cambiums of the main cut areas are incorrectly aligned.

The graft can be secured by peg, raffia or tape.

Securing the graft

There are several ways of securing the graft; inspired by his lack of a third hand, Harry Jans has developed a novel method using small pegs of the type available from craft shops, used for hanging greetings cards on a line. Standard clothes pegs can be used for thick grafts. I have tried this simple procedure; it works perfectly, and is particularly useful when grafting on stocks of small diameter. It is to be recommended to the amateur who may not have access to alternative tying materials. Harry plunges his completed grafts in moist peat, burying the graft to keep it moist. However, grafts I have secured with a peg and placed in a shaded, closed polythene frame have taken well without going to this trouble. For stocks with a diameter above 0.4 CM I use Buddy-Tape™, a Japanese product that comes in a roll which tears into sections 6.5 CM long by 3 CM wide. This is too wide, and so I cut it in half lengthwise. After a little practice, I have found this tape is easy to use and an efficient tying material; I particularly like the fact that the cut top of the rootstock can be covered because the tape is easily stretched and distorted. Although I have not tried them, rubber grafting ties would be an alternative.

Starting position for my raffia tie.

Stocks with a diameter of 0.4 CM or less, particularly of *D. longilobata*, are very pliable, so they will not remain steady enough to use grafting tape without a high chance of disturbing the scion's position. I therefore use raffia, which has been soaked in water for a minimum of two hours, for all my small, awkward grafts. Soaking the raffia makes it much more pliable and easy to use, and as it dries it contracts, and so tightens the bound graft. I cut the raffia into 20 CM lengths and split these lengthwise to produce strips around 0.5 CM wide; anything wider is more awkward to use. I have an unconventional method of tying, in that I place the middle of the piece of raffia at the bottom of the graft on the side farthest from me, and bind clockwise with the right hand and anticlockwise with the left, to the top of the stock, finishing with a half-hitch. This is different to several methods of tying that I was taught on nurseries, but has three advantages over any of these. First, tying off with two ends is easy. Secondly, tying off can be done equally well on either side of the stock. Thirdly, during the process of binding the forces on the graft and stock are applied from both sides evenly rather than one-sidedly, which greatly reduces the chance of distorting the stock or displacing the scion.

For many years I have used an old supply of grafting wax on my grafts tied with raffia, but recent experiments have shown that it is not necessary provided that the grafts are kept in an enclosed environment. This is just as well, since this product is no longer obtainable! But I shall miss the smell of the hot wax.

Aftercare of grafts

My grafts are stood in shaded polythene frames, but any type of propagator would be suitable. Bottom heat is set at around 18°C (65°F), and the plants are given a spray with a general fungicide. A humid atmosphere is maintained for four to six weeks, after which ventilation is increased and shading reduced. Once the union between rootstock and scion has formed, the scion will make vigorous growth, particularly from spring grafting. Regular attention is needed to create a balanced, well-shaped young plant by pinching strong extension growth. Failure to pinch young growth on grafts of prostrate varieties such as *D. cneorum* and *D. arbuscula* may result in a plant with a bare centre. Cutting back into old wood will become necessary to correct this. Grafts tied with raffia need to have the raffia cut soon after removal from the closed frame to avoid constriction of the stem; this is unnecessary if a material which degrades naturally is used. Early-season grafts are potted on in April or May; August grafts remain as they are over winter and are potted on in spring once there are signs of root activity.

When potting on a graft of one of the more vigorous cultivars, for example of *D. bholua* or *D. caucasica*, I raise the compost level to just below the union. I do not do this with small types such as *D. petraea* and *D. striata* which are better with plenty of air circulation around the base of the plant, so reducing the risk of fungal infection and dieback, nor with naturally prostrate plants such as the dwarf forms of *D. cneorum*, which soon hide the union as they grow. If necessary for aesthetic reasons, the neck of the stock can be hidden with a top-dressing of coarse gravel when planting out or potting on.

Stem cuttings

Producing a new plant from a cutting is so satisfying; I still get a kick from it! Apart from planned propagation, pruning for shape or accidental breakages may provide material at what may seem unsuitable times of the season to take cuttings, but it is always worth having a try. Given patience, you may be surprised at what will root.

Types of cuttings

In some cases, there may not be any choice of material for cuttings, but where possible, choose material from young, healthy, strong-growing plants. Cuttings taken from tired old plants lack juvenile vigour; they will be more difficult to root, and less likely to make a worthwhile plant. Material from a plant in that sort of condition should instead be grafted. I try to maintain special "mother" plants as a source for my cutting material; they are given five-star treatment, and replaced at the first sign of loss of vigour or disease.

Softwood cuttings

Growth produced early in the season which has not started to ripen or turn woody will provide material for soft stem cuttings. Misting and the newer fogging systems may be used when rooting this type of material. However, as I have no experience of either of these methods, and as neither is readily available to amateur growers, I shall not go into detail. Without the above-mentioned facilities, soft growth of daphnes should be regarded as the least suitable for a gardener to try to root, because despite its ability to root quickly if managed correctly, it is not easy to keep in good, turgid condition and is more prone to infection by fungi and bacteria.

Semi-ripe cuttings

In my situation I find semi-ripe growth ideal for cuttings. Growth in this condition has formed a terminal bud at its apex, while the base is firm and probably brownish in colour. Most of my stock plants have the protection of unheated polythene tunnels, which gives me an early start, with cuttings from *D. jasminea* ready to be taken in mid-May, and then the majority, such as *D. arbuscula*, *D. petraea*, *D.* ×*hendersonii* and *D.* ×*susannae*, available in early to mid-June. Obviously, plants growing outside will be several weeks behind in growth; I have stock plants of *D. blagayana*, *D. cneorum*, *D. tangutica* and *D.* ×*burkwoodii* outside and cuttings from these are taken from the middle to the end of July. I try to take cuttings early, because from a commercial viewpoint I want strong rooted cuttings before winter, but it is the physical state of the material rather than the time of year which is the most important point for gardeners to consider.

Figure 4: Cuttings

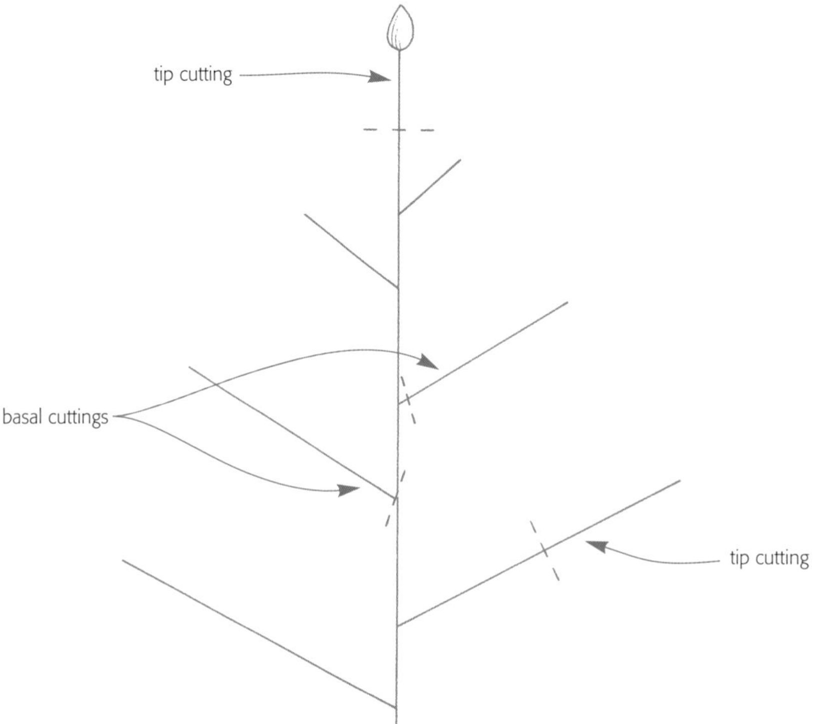

Two different types of cutting can be made from semi-ripe material: tip cuttings, or basal cuttings (see Figure 4); I include heel cuttings with the latter. I favour basal cuttings for the smaller types of daphne, except for *D. jasminea* and *D.* ×*whiteorum* cultivars, for which I use tip cuttings. To take a basal cutting, you would generally select an axillary growth, or sideshoot, and cut it, preferably with a sharp knife, at its origin from the main stem. A basal cutting from terminal growth is cut where the current season's growth started. This area has numerous minute bud initials, originating from the base of the scales that enclosed the overwintering bud from which the new growth developed. These bud initials produce growth hormones, or auxins, which can encourage the cells of the cambium to divide and ultimately produce roots. It is interesting to note that when *D. arbuscula* layers itself, roots are only produced from these basal areas of the stem growth.

A heel cutting is essentially a basal cutting obtained by pulling an axillary growth off a main stem. It has the attributes of the basal cutting plus a well-ripened, lignified base to protect against infection, and may well be the best type of cutting for rooting in a cold frame without bottom heat. The disadvantage of heel cuttings is the amount of growth that has to be removed from the stock plant in order to obtain them.

Semi-ripe tip cuttings are taken with their lower cut above the basal area. I use this type of cutting for *D. bholua*, *D. blagayana* and *D.* ×*burkwoodii*, where a basal cutting would often be too long for ease of handling and the production of a well-proportioned plant. Additionally, young plants of hybrids such as *D.* ×*hendersonii* 'Ernst Hauser' and *D.* ×*whiteorum* 'Beauworth' and cultivars of *D. cneorum* tend to make very vigorous shoots in their first few seasons of growth, and these need stopping to produce a bushy plant. If this process is delayed until the growth is semi-ripe, the resulting material can be used as tip cuttings.

Hardwood cuttings

When a cutting is made from material which has fully ripened or matured, it is referred to as a hardwood cutting. In the past I have had reasonable results from hardwood cuttings of *D. blagayana*, *D. cneorum* and *D.* ×*burkwoodii* taken at the end of August or early September and from *D. odora* cuttings taken in March. A recent article in the Daphne Society Newsletter also describes successful propagation on a commercial scale of *D.* ×*burkwoodii* 'Carol Mackie' from hardwood cuttings taken in October. The rooting process is generally much slower than with younger material, but this type of cutting is easier to manage, without high summer temperatures to worry about, and good reserves of carbohydrates to produce a root system. Hardwood cuttings can be tried in a simple cold frame or even under a cloche in the open ground.

Preparation of cuttings

Preparation of daphne cuttings is no different from those of other woody species. The base of a torn-off heel may need trimming. If a sharp knife or secateurs are used to remove basal cuttings there should be no need to make any further cuts. Tip cuttings, which should be taken from the parent just above a bud, may need another cut at the base to just below a bud. Wounding the base of ripe or semi-ripe tip cuttings does seem to improve rooting. This involves removing a thin sliver of bark at one side of the base which exposes an area of cambium cells and provides a larger area to absorb hormones if a rooting powder or dip is used. Cuttings of most of the smaller types of daphnes seldom need to be more than 5 CM long; I remove lower leaves until those that remain will be clear of the surface once the cutting is inserted in the rooting medium. If the lowest leaves of a cutting sit on the compost they invariably rot and provide infection points for *Botrytis*. Cuttings of species with larger leaves, like *D. odora* and *D. bholua*, should have their leaves reduced in size by about half. The aim is to reduce the area of leaf which will lose water, in order to maintain the cutting's turgidity, but to leave enough leaf area to manufacture the carbohydrates which the cutting needs for root growth.

The biggest problem I have with many daphne cuttings is the development of flowers or soft growth, or both, in the cutting frame. The terminal buds of virtually all types taken from mid-June to mid-July will develop flowers if left on, therefore I remove them when preparing the cuttings. Both soft shoots and flowers are undesirable because their development will divert the cutting's food reserves from root production, and they are also the most likely parts to be infected with *Botrytis*. Cuttings can be treated with a hormone dip or powder, but it is not essential. Certain species seem to be sensitive to hormones and can be damaged by them; these are mentioned in their individual descriptions. I generally use a combined talc of 0.5 percent indolbutyric acid and 0.1 percent napthylacetic acid.

Compost for cuttings

Various combinations of the ingredients discussed in Chapter 5 can be used to create composts in which daphne cuttings will root successfully, though of course their management may differ. The aim must be for a balance between good aeration and moisture retention that also takes into account the environment the cuttings will be in; better drainage is required for cuttings under mist than in a cold frame, for example. I use a compost which consists of 50 percent coarse sand, 25 percent peat and 25 percent propagation bark, this being made up of particles less than 6 MM in size. My advice would be to stick to any compost or mix you have had success with. If you are a beginner, experiment with several combinations using an easy-to-root woody subject before trying your precious daphne material.

Care of cuttings

Juggling a number of critical factors is the key to rooting cuttings. Success depends upon getting the right balance of light and humidity to the top part of the cutting, and moisture, aeration and warmth to the bottom part. If any one of these key factors is wrong, rooting is jeopardized. In England's variable climate it is difficult to maintain this balance without automated environmental controls, but I get by with basic materials such as clear or milky polythene, fleece and shade netting. If you are going to propagate on a regular basis, do try to keep records of what you do and whether it is a success or failure, and note any weather patterns that may have affected results.

My cuttings are inserted into standard plastic seed trays which are placed in polythene-covered frames built on benching in a glasshouse. The bench has warming cables that maintain bottom heat at 15–17°C (59–62°F). During the summer the glasshouse is shaded, and the tops of the frames have moveable netting for additional shading in hot weather. The cuttings are hand-misted at intervals to maintain a damp leaf surface. After insertion, the cuttings are given a thorough watering to settle the compost around their base. I then follow this with a drench of fungicides against *Botrytis* infection of the top growth, and pathogens such as *Pythium* and *Rhizoctonia* which can destroy a whole tray of cuttings. Routine fungicidal sprays are needed to prevent *Botrytis* infection while rooting takes place.

I cannot compare this with any other method as this is the one that I have always used; in most years there are some inexplicable failures, probably because the critical balance mentioned above is bound to vary from year to year with my relatively simple propagation setup. On a domestic scale there is no reason why a cold frame with a glass or polythene cover, a windowsill propagator, or a flowerpot with a polythene bag cover cannot be used successfully.

The time it takes to root cuttings is variable; under my conditions hybrids of *D.* ×*susannae* and *D.* ×*hendersonii* are well rooted in six weeks, while *D. bholua* and *D. calcicola* may take three or four months. Many of the new hybrids seem in general to root better than forms of species such as *D. cneorum* and *D. collina* of gardens; this is probably due to their juvenile genetic condition. The use of soil-warming cables or a small electric propagator to provide bottom heat does speed up the rooting process. In the summer my main concern is to keep the cuttings cool, but as the days shorten bottom heat is useful—though not essential—and light must be maximized by removing shading. While avoiding direct sunlight, try to provide as much light as possible in the short winter days.

If cuttings have been rooted in an artificial environment of extra humidity and warmth, they will need to be weaned to the normal climate when they are moved. This is a greater problem with cuttings taken in June and July, which will have rooted by August or September, when the sun is still powerful enough to cause damage. Generally, these early cuttings will have made soft, weak top growth in the frames, which I reduce by at least 70 percent and then place the trays in a cool, shaded area where they can be covered with fleece for a few days and damped occasionally in hot conditions. Although it is accepted practice for many woody subjects, I do not recommend adding slow-release fertilizer to cuttings compost for daphnes because I know of instances where this has caused damage. I always liquid-feed rooted cuttings, and attempt to increase light intensity as quickly as possible to discourage weak new growth.

Gardeners should remember that daphnes were successfully propagated from cuttings long before the days of mist, soil-warming cables and polythene; it just took a little longer. Prior to rooting, the base of a cutting or the wounded area generally forms a callus which is produced by cells of the cambium dividing. This should be followed by the production of roots, but it is not unusual for cuttings, particularly those taken after July, to form a callus by autumn, but not to produce roots until the increasing day length and light intensity of the following spring, so keep looking after cuttings so long as they remain healthy.

It is my aim to produce a saleable plant as quickly as possible, so all cuttings that can be rooted and weaned by early September are potted up into 7 CM pots and grown on in a tunnel which can be kept just above 0°C (32°F) in winter. Beyond mid-September, all cuttings still in their trays are kept there until the following spring before potting up. I treat the potting-up and establishment of rooted cuttings with great care, as it is a stage in the propagation process where large losses can occur. Newly potted cuttings are shaded with fleece until established, after which unbranched growth can be pinched to encourage a bushy plant.

Root cuttings

This method of propagation is unlikely to be used much deliberately, because few people will want to dig up cherished daphnes and chop off pieces of root. However, several species of daphne are known to produce adventitious shoots from their roots. If you are repotting, a few pieces of root could be removed without causing damage, and this method tried. Alternatively, if a plant has to be moved in the garden and pieces of root are left behind in the ground, or you move a container-grown plant which has rooted into the substrate below, look out for young plants the following season which may arise from the broken roots. Obviously, it is essential to know that your plant is not grafted, or a plant from the less desirable rootstock will be obtained.

I have never deliberately propagated from root cuttings, but pieces of root left in the benching grit when container-grown plants were moved have produced shoots. This has happened with *D. genkwa*, *D. mezereum* and *D. sericea.* The *D. genkwa* were potted up and eventually made saleable plants. Some clones of *D. bholua*, *D. calcicola* and *D. jezoensis* that I have grown produced adventitious shoots from their roots, which indicates that root cuttings might be successful. To make a root cutting, a healthy piece of root should be cut into lengths approximately 3.7 CM long, with a transverse cut to the top end of the root and a slanting cut at the lower end. Fill a pot to within 2.5 CM of the top with a standard cuttings mix and insert the cuttings with the transverse cut uppermost and level with the top of the compost. Cover with 1.2 CM of sand or grit. A cold frame, or a covered frame or propagator with gentle bottom heat would be a suitable environment for the cuttings. Traditionally, root cuttings were made in the dormant season to fit into nursery schedules, but timing may not be that critical.

I have noticed that when thick roots of *D. mezereum* and *D. genkwa* are exposed to the light, they are far more likely to produce adventitious shoot growth (see photo p. 58). It would therefore seem feasible to propagate from well-established, healthy plants of these species by carefully scraping away the soil from an area around the plant to expose some root, thus encouraging shoots to develop. I suspect the removal and establishment of a section of root with shoots might be difficult, but it certainly would be worth a try. It would also be worthwhile with these species to try laying root cuttings horizontally in a tray of compost, with their upper surface exposed to light.

5 Cultivation

In this chapter I hope I can provide some guidelines for the successful cultivation of this wonderful genus of plants. I have had my fair share of failures over the years, and these still happen, but these days I do have a better idea of the reasons for a plant's failure. It is completely wrong to assume that daphnes are naturally short-lived or contrary. While I accept that this genus is susceptible to attack by several lethal fungal pathogens over which control is difficult, if they are given the right environment and treatment, daphnes are long-lived plants worthy of a place in every garden. What is true is that daphnes are unforgiving of mismanagement; "perverse" and "unpredictable" are two adjectives used by Dr. A. M. Amsler (1953) and Elliot Hodgkin (1961), noted daphnephiles of the 20TH century—I think a little harshly. To most of us, growing daphnes is a challenge which makes success that much sweeter.

The most important advice I can give to anyone who would like to grow daphnes is to make sure you have the right conditions and a suitable site prepared in which to grow them before you obtain any plants. It is all too easy to make an impulse buy when faced with the temptation of an attractive, fragrant plant on display in a nursery or garden centre, but your problems will start early if you plant a daphne in an unsuitable site. Moreover, plants kept in their pots for weeks or months until a suitable area is prepared for planting them are vulnerable to neglect and disease.

Growing without protection

For the average gardener, unless extremes of weather dictate the need for winter protection or summer shade, daphnes will be happier and require less looking after if they are grown in the open ground.

Soil drainage and aeration

One point about the cultivation of daphnes which is generally agreed on is that the growing medium needs to be well drained but moisture-retentive. While this may sound contradictory, it can be achieved by various methods. Of course, some species are more tolerant than others of the two extremes of very dry or wet root conditions, and the properties of the growing medium may need to be adjusted according to the local rainfall pattern and whether it will be possible to provide irrigation.

It is my impression that daphnes are very dependent on a well-aerated growing medium, or in other words, a plentiful supply of oxygen to the roots. Hence the need for good drainage, because if the minute spaces between soil particles are full of water, air is excluded, and roots suffer from lack of oxygen. It is important to understand that plants respire—not in the way that animals breathe, but still absorbing and using oxygen for many of their metabolic processes. A good supply of oxygen is essential at the growing point at each root tip, which is where nutrients and water are absorbed. Poor drainage also encourages root disease.

Providing well-drained conditions inevitably increases the risk of the growing medium drying out, so careful watering is needed to aid establishment of all species. The challenge is to provide a soil or a made-up medium with the right balance between moisture retention and drainage, particularly for those daphnes less tolerant of drought. The soil in the gardens of many modern homes is poorly drained due to the use of builders' heavy machinery, which destroys the structure of the soil and creates a "pan"—a compacted layer impervious to water. The greater the clay content of a soil, the greater this problem is likely to be. Sandy or silt soils may also have pans, created by various chemicals cementing mineral particles together. Thorough cultivation deep enough to break up a pan is essential for good drainage. In a newly made garden, keep in mind also that soil may have been brought in to adjust levels, and that it will almost certainly have been dumped on compacted soil, so a pan may be quite deep in these circumstances. Further ways of improving soil structure can be put into practice once you have a good understanding of your soil type.

Soil types

Assuming that most people will want to grow their daphnes in the garden, a basic understanding of soil is essential. Put simply, soil is a mixture of rock particles of various sizes, decayed plant material known as humus, various minerals and a wide range of living organisms ranging from microscopic bacteria, viruses and fungi to invertebrates such as nematodes, mites and earthworms. I shudder when I hear soil referred to as dirt! Treat it with care and respect and you will get ample reward in the shape of healthy, well-grown plants.

Soils are variable, so make sure you find out what type you have. Clays and silts are fertile, but need careful cultivation and are often poorly drained. Sandy types or thin organic soils over chalk will dry out quickly and be low in nutrients. Deep organic soils occur where woodland has been felled or marshy areas drained and will have a high humus content; they are also more likely to contain harmful fungal pathogens.

From a gardener's point of view, soil can be divided into topsoil and subsoil. The latter is of little use to daphnes, other than to provide anchorage and a moisture reserve in dry periods. Topsoil is the area which plants colonize with their feeding roots to extract the nutrients and water required for healthy growth. A depth of topsoil of between 20 and 30 CM is what we all need to grow plants well. The depth of a shallow topsoil can be increased by breaking up the subsoil and incorporating large quantities of organic matter. It takes time and effort, but all plants will benefit. Do not be discouraged if your garden has sandy or thin chalky soil. Some of the choicest daphne species, such as *D. arbuscula* and *D. petraea*, inhabit cliffs or rocky areas where little soil exists. They have to send their roots down into crevices to colonize pockets of decayed organic matter and weathered rock that have accumulated through time. I suggest, therefore, that many of the smaller species and hybrids can be grown successfully in what may at first seem a poor site.

Heavy clay soils, which are generally badly drained unless a lot of work over a long period of time has gone into improving them, should however be regarded as unsuitable for daphnes. No matter how many times we have seen it done on television, it is not good enough simply to dig a hole and incorporate some grit and humus. The surrounding area remains poorly drained, so a sump is created which fills with water and drowns the roots of the plant therein. The creation of raised areas or container-growing is the best way to approach growing daphnes if your ground is poorly drained.

Soil structure

An essential point to understand about soil is that it has a structure that can be destroyed by compaction caused by heavy machinery, or by cultivation when it is too wet. A soil's structure is the way its components have been arranged over time by soil organisms and weathering. Soils with a good structure will have plenty of spaces between their particles to allow free passage of air and water; a characteristic essential for the good growing of daphnes. Once lost, soil structure cannot be regained quickly; the ground must be broken up by deep cultivation and large quantities of organic matter incorporated. Organic matter can consist of any plant material, such as peat, bark, garden compost, leafmould, spent mushroom compost or farmyard manure. The cultivated ground should then be left to the weathering action of frost and rain and it is most important not to cultivate or tread on it when it is wet. On heavy ground where the pH is neutral or acid (see below), adding lime helps clay particles to bind together which increases drainage and aeration.

If you can afford to be patient, regular incorporation of organic matter is the best way to improve the structure and fertility of any soil, not just clay. Shallow chalky soils and light sandy ground are improved because the water-holding capacity is increased, and the organic matter decomposes to create humus, which prevents leaching—the washing away of plant nutrients as water drains. Organic matter also encourages the buildup of the important micro-organisms that improve the structure and fertility of the soil.

We started our first plant nursery in an old walled garden. Previous generations of gardeners had cultivated the ground solely by hand or by horse, no doubt adding generous quantities of farmyard manure. This had resulted in deep, fertile topsoil with an excellent structure. *Daphne blagayana*, *D.* ×*burkwoodii* 'Somerset' and *D. cneorum* cultivars grew wonderfully planted in this ground without any special preparation. Unfortunately, when we moved to Kilmeston we were faced with heavy clay. What structure the garden soil once had had been destroyed by builders' machinery, so I have created special raised areas for all the daphnes I grow outside.

Soil pH—acid or alkaline?

Referring to previous publications on daphnes results in conflicting opinions as to whether it is important to provide an acid or an alkaline growing medium for any particular species. If I had a choice, I would always pick the latter, though I believe *D. jezoensis* and *D. odora* to be two species that may grow better in a neutral or slightly acid soil—but they can be grown in alkaline conditions with a little extra care. Apart from these, I have yet to come across daphnes that show a preference for growing in a soil of a particular pH value. The pH is a measure of acidity within a material. The pH scale measures from 1 to 14, with 7 being neutral. Below 7 is acid and above 7 is alkaline. Because it is a logarithmic scale, an increase in one unit of pH represents a tenfold decrease in the level of acidity. Various testing kits are available which enable the pH of a soil or compost sample to be read.

Daphne odora does seem slightly calcifuge; particularly as they get older, plants may show signs of chlorosis in alkaline soils. Symptoms of chlorosis are poor growth, yellowing of leaves due to lack of chlorophyll, and premature dropping of leaves. These symptoms are similar to those caused by a virus infection (see p. 217), so take care to make an accurate diagnosis. Plants can often be restored to health by treating with a chelated iron compound, a mulch with organic matter and an application of a balanced fertilizer. If you grow *D. odora* under alkaline conditions it is an even better idea to carry out the above operations every second year before the plant shows signs of distress.

I do not know of any instance of a daphne species which grows naturally in alkaline soil failing to grow well in an acid soil. However I would favour adding some lime to very acid soils, below pH 5.5 for example, because pathogenic fungi known to attack daphnes, such as *Thielaviopsis basicola* and some species of *Phytophthora*, prefer acid conditions.

Composts

I use the word compost in this instance to mean the growing medium made up to fill a raised bed, trough or pot in which daphnes are to grow. The materials discussed are also those which can be used in different proportions to root daphne cuttings.

There is no secret formula for successful daphne compost that I can reveal to you. There is a wide range of materials that may be used, and very few people will agree on the same combination. What must be aimed for is a balance between the plant's various requirements. Physically it must be well drained, and therefore well aerated, but moisture-retentive. Chemically it must supply all the essential minerals and facilitate their easy uptake by the plants. The importance of water retention will depend on how often you can check your plants' water requirements, or whether automatic irrigation is available. For instance, I have grown daphnes very well in pure grit, but I live and work on site, so they can receive daily attention when it is needed.

The aeration of compost can be assessed in terms of air-filled porosity (AFP). This is the proportion of the volume of the compost which contains air after it has been saturated and allowed to drain, expressed as a percentage. Compost with a low AFP of, say, 5 percent will hold a large quantity of water after draining and so will be poorly aerated. Compost with a high AFP of 25 percent will be well aerated, but will not hold large reserves of water. I aim for an AFP of 30 percent for daphnes, and suggest that 25 percent should be the minimum requirement. You can calculate the AFP of your compost mix by filling a pot of known volume and soaking it in a bucket of water for at least five minutes. The drainage holes at the bottom of the pot should be taped up to prevent loss of compost while in the bucket. On removal, take off the tape and collect and measure the volume of water that drains out of the compost within an hour. The volume of the drained water expressed as a percentage of the volume of the pot will provide the AFP.

Most keen growers of alpine plants in containers will be using compost with a high AFP. Over the years they will have developed it to suit their particular growing methods and conditions. Experience will have taught them how to manage the plants in their compost mix. I feel sure that daphnes would grow well in such composts, and it would be wrong to change from compost you know how to manage without first experimenting to see how well daphnes grow in it. Compost ingredients likely to be used are discussed below.

Sand and grit

Fine sand with a large proportion of particles below 0.7 MM is unsuitable. Fine particles block air spaces and impede drainage. Grit or sand with particles that range in size from 0.7 to 5 MM is ideal. The grit I used for many years came from a stone crusher, so it was very sharp textured; daphnes loved it and cuttings rooted well in it. These materials should improve drainage and aeration; they also add stability by virtue of their weight when used in containers, and aid re-wetting of dry mixes, particularly those with a high organic content. Make sure that sand you use is of horticultural quality, and thus does not contain high levels of harmful chemicals or salts.

Loam

Loam is topsoil. Its fine particles retain water and minerals by adsorption, keeping the latter from being leached out of the compost by rain or watering. The addition of loam to a compost mix increases its "buffering capacity". This refers to the ability of a growing medium to resist changes in pH, thus reducing the risk of damage to roots from a high concentration of fertilizer salts, such as might occur if a slow-release fertilizer was used in a compost that was subjected to excessive heat—a situation which can arise in black plastic pots under glass or polythene, or if exposed to direct sunlight in the open.

Convention dictates that loam should be sterilized before use in a compost to avoid problems with weed seeds and harmful micro-organisms. However, I feel there is still much to be understood about the relationship between plants and beneficial micro-organisms. These may be fungi or bacteria which can help roots to take up nutrients, sometimes in a symbiotic relationship with the plant; there are others which protect from infection by suppressing or attacking harmful pathogens. There is room for experiment here, and if you have access to a good source of friable loam there may be an advantage in not sterilizing it.

For long-term cultivation of daphnes in containers, I recommend a loam-based compost rather than a loam-free one, because I think its physical nature will be more stable and the nutritional status will be easier to maintain.

Peat

My experience relates solely to sphagnum moss peat of medium-grade milling. I believe that young peats such as those from northern Europe, which are fluffy in texture, need different management, but can grow plants well.

Peat provides a source of organic matter of regular quality with the ability to hold large quantities of water while remaining aerated, provided that it is not compressed. As peat decomposes to humus its colloidal nature increases, improving nutrient retention in the compost and uptake by the plant. Peat has a low, acid pH, generally between 4.0 and 5.0, so lime should be added to increase the pH. The recommended level for maximum nutrient uptake is 5.5–6.0, but a more alkaline mix may have benefits for daphnes by reducing the activity of harmful fungi. I suggest adding a minimum of 450 G dolomitic lime per 100 litres of peat.

Sphagnum moss peat has the properties necessary for making good compost, but avoid sedge peat, the structure of which is unsuitable. Proprietary peat-based (loam-free) composts are suitable for short-term cultivation, such as one or two seasons, in containers. However, some additional drainage material such as grit or perlite should be added at a rate of at least 25 percent by volume.

One of the main disadvantages of using compost with a high peat content is the difficulty in re-wetting it evenly if it is allowed to get dry; I believe this to be a common cause of plant failure after planting out. Peat can also introduce fungal pathogens such as *Phytophthora cinnamomi* and *Thielaviopsis basicola* to compost.

Bark

It is important to use bark that has been correctly processed for potting composts by maturing. This removes substances such as tannins and resins which could be toxic to plants. Matured pine bark can be obtained in different particle sizes; the potting grade I use has very few fine particles, with 3 to 15 MM being the normal range. This is an excellent material for increasing the AFP of composts. I use a finer grade for my propagation compost, with particles of up to 6 MM, and there are bark products available which can wholly or partially replace peat. The use of bark in composts can lead to nitrogen deficiency, but I have found that adding a small amount of ammonium nitrate at mixing compensates for this. On a smaller scale, liquid feeding would be an alternative way of solving this problem.

As well as the good physical properties of processed pine bark, there is evidence that the phenolic compounds in it give some control of pathogenic fungi such as *Pythium* and *Thielaviopsis basicola*. The pH of potting bark is between 4.5 and 5.5, so I add 225 G of dolomitic limestone per 100 litres of bark.

Pumice and perlite

Pumice is a volcanic rock which is widely available in various sizes in some areas of the United States of America, particularly the west. It is chemically inert but absorbs water, and so it is a good material for improving the drainage and aeration of composts.

Perlite is made from expanded volcanic rock, and is available in various-sized particles. It adds excellent drainage and aeration properties to potting and seed composts. Being inert and of neutral pH it has no effect on plant nutrition. I find that the use of perlite in my seed composts facilitates parting the roots of seedlings for pricking out or potting up.

Additional advantages to using a material of this kind in compost for container-grown plants are its ability to aid re-wetting of the compost when it is very dry, and the fact that it reduces fluctuation in compost temperatures. One disadvantage is that, since these materials are very light in weight, the stability of tall plants in containers can be a problem.

Calcined clay

This material has been heated to fuse the small clay particles into larger aggregates. On a large scale, material of this sort may prove expensive, but it has the good properties of clay without the bad ones, in that it can improve aeration as well as retaining water and nutrients. I have used this type of material for terrestrial orchids successfully, and do not doubt that daphnes could be grown well in compost based on it.

Wetting agents

I do add a material to my compost to aid re-wetting. This is particularly useful for plant production under protection, where the compost surface can get quite dry while the compost at the base of the pot still has all the moisture the plant requires. Without the use of this agent, there would be a danger that when water was given it would run off the surface of the dry compost rather than be absorbed.

Fertilizers

The type of fertilizer and the amount you use has to be a personal choice. I use a slow-release fertilizer at less than the recommended rate. If necessary, I supplement with a liquid feed, but I seldom find I have to for my container-grown sales plants. Plants which are in containers long-term are liquid-fed with a material containing nitrate, phosphate and potassium (NPK) at a ratio of 1:1:1, plus trace elements. To compensate for any nitrogen deficiency caused by using bark, I add ammonium nitrate at a rate of 85 G per 100 litres.

My composts

My daphne composts are primarily geared to commercial production over two growing seasons rather than long-term growth in containers. I pot rooted cuttings into proprietary peat-based compost, to which I add seed-grade perlite at the rate of 25 percent by volume. My compost for potting on plants to grow to saleable size consists of one part by volume coarse sand, one of potting bark, one perlite, three peat and one half of a part loam. I add dolomitic limestone to create a pH of between 7.0 and 7.5, which is higher than recommended for container growing.

If you decide to create your own compost recipe, try to make sure that the ingredients you use are going to be easily available in the future, and will be of the same quality every time you replenish your stock.

Raised areas

Improving poorly drained ground takes time and hard work. An alternative approach is to create sites suitable for daphnes by making areas raised above ground level, in the form of banks, rockeries or raised beds.

In a garden such as ours, which has heavy clay as the basic soil, this was the way I made sites which I hoped would suit daphnes. For example, a sunny, west-facing bank created with good woodland loam when our road entrance was put in has suited *D.* ×*burkwoodii* cultivars very well for many years without any special preparation before planting (see photograph, p. 108).

More sophisticated raised areas can be constructed in the form of rockeries or raised beds surrounded by a retaining wall built with stone, brick or timber such as railway sleepers. My first raised areas consisted of two T-shaped beds with dry-stone walls, approximately 60 CM high. Experience has shown me that, since there was no provision for watering here in dry spells, I filled these beds with compost that was too free-draining for most daphnes to thrive, although *D. alpina* and *D.* ×*mauerbachii* 'Perfume of Spring' have grown well there for more than ten years. Had I paid more attention to providing water in dry summer periods, I am sure other daphnes would have survived. I made the walls without cement between the stones to allow for growing plants in the crevices, but rodents soon moved in and dug out large quantities of compost through unplanted gaps. My advice therefore would be to cement at least the bottom few courses of stonework, leaving an occasional gap in which to put plants. When I remake these beds, I will top them with a layer of at least 10 CM of gravel, since this has been very successful in my "daphnetum" (see p. 10), but increase the water-holding capacity of the compost below.

I think a raised bed should be a minimum of 45 CM high, and higher if practical. This provides for a deep but well-drained rooting area. It also makes bending down to smell your daphnes a lot easier as you get older!

Railway sleepers, which generally measure roughly 25 CM × 2.5 M, are very useful for making raised beds when they can be obtained; though they may not be as aesthetically pleasing as stone, I have used them with great success.

Since my ground was so poorly drained, but sloped sufficiently to allow for surface drainage, I did not dig into the clay area on which my beds were constructed because I think it would have resulted in an area where water collected at the base of the bed.

Container growing

Many of the smaller daphnes can be grown successfully outdoors in suitable containers. I regard containers with a capacity of less than 10 litres as unsuitable for long-term cultivation in the open, because they are too vulnerable to temperature and moisture fluctuations. Those made from clay or stone are preferable to plastic ones because they are less likely to overheat in strong sun. Pots are discussed further in the section on growing under cover (see p. 203). Old stone troughs or glazed sinks, which can be covered with a mixture of sand, peat and cement called hypertufa, make excellent containers for a selection of daphnes or for a mix of alpine plants which can include one or two daphnes. *Daphne arbuscula* and some of the dwarf forms of *D. cneorum* are particularly good for growing over the side of such a container (see photograph, p. 49).

In areas that experience prolonged periods of freezing during winter, container growing would be unsuitable without providing protection in the colder months, because even species that may be hardy grown in the ground are more likely to suffer from dehydration once the container compost is frozen (see below). Be sure to choose a container which has one good-sized or several smaller drainage holes. Do not stand containers directly on the ground, as worm activity can soon block their drainage holes. Raise them on bricks or on "pot feet".

Winter survival

Damage to daphnes caused by freezing temperatures falls into two categories: mechanical damage, and dehydration. The former is caused by ice crystals forming within the cells of the plant. The cell walls may be ruptured by expansion of the ice or by osmotic pressure due to an imbalance of sap concentration at the time of thawing, a situation which is aggravated when thawing is rapid due to direct sunlight falling on the frozen areas. Dehydration can be equally lethal; when the root zone is frozen, water lost from top growth cannot be replaced, a typical situation when temperatures are well below freezing without snow cover to blanket the ground, and plants are subjected to sun or wind. Evergreen species are particularly vulnerable to this kind of damage, and the larger the leaves, the more likely it is to happen. *Daphne bholua* and *D. odora* may survive unscathed by night temperatures as low as –17°C (0°F) provided that day temperatures are above freezing (Smithers, 1995). However, periods of several days where the temperature stays below freezing both day and night can result in severe damage to these species through dehydration unless plants can be protected.

Naturally, plants try to prepare for winter cold spells; stored carbohydrates increase the concentration of cell fluids, and growth made in the summer ripens, a process that involves the cell walls being strengthened by the formation of lignin. Ripe wood is much firmer to the touch, and the green bark of soft new growth becomes grey or brown. Species which originate from areas that have cold winters may drop their foliage, or, if it is retained, the leaves will be small with a thick waxy coating to prevent water loss. The evergreen species from Asia which have large, soft leaves are the least hardy. Some alpine species may rely on an insulating blanket of snow to protect them from low temperatures, so hard frost without snow cover may damage them.

Sometimes, the foliage of *D. petraea* shows signs of superficial damage after the first frosts of winter. The cuticle, which is a waxy coating of the leaf, is lifted, creating an air space between it and the cell walls. This gives the normally dark green leaves a pale green appearance. Damage occurs mostly on the strong growth of young plants, and does not appear to harm the plant unduly, although the damaged leaves will be shed by spring. This characteristic has been passed on to the hybrids between *D. petraea* and *D. jasminea* (*D.* ×*whiteorum*) and some of the hybrids between *D. petraea* and *D. cneorum* (*D.* ×*hendersonii*).

It is difficult to define just how hardy a given species of daphne may be, so my suggestions in Chapter 2 should be treated as a guide only. For example, a species' distribution in the wild may include a range of altitudes and latitudes, and plants sourced from the higher altitudes or northernmost latitudes of this range are likely to be the hardiest. Not only provenance but other variables such as nutrition, age of plant, garden microclimates and timing of a cold spell in relation to the plant's growth cycle may all influence hardiness and explain why a plant may survive low temperatures at a particular time of year, but be killed by similar temperatures occurring at a different time. I have experienced *D. genkwa* being killed by –5°C (23°F) when it was just coming into flower, with sap freely flowing, but this species reliably withstands temperatures of –29°C (–20°F) when dormant. Thus hardy deciduous species such as *D. caucasica* and *D. genkwa* which are adapted to the low winter and high summer temperatures of a continental climate may not cope well with the fluctuating winter temperatures of a maritime climate.

Precautions against cold damage

Plants that have been overnourished are more vulnerable to cold damage. Too much fertilizer, particularly nitrogen, encourages soft growth which may not ripen before the onset of cold winter weather. Nitrogenous fertilizer should always be balanced by potassium, and should be applied sparingly early in the growing season. Judicious withholding of water in late summer can also help to slow growth and encourage it to ripen; yet another reason for choosing well-drained ground in which to grow daphnes. Young plants full of juvenile vigour, one or two seasons planted, are more likely to make excessive growth which does not ripen in time to resist frost. They are also more likely to be killed outright in a situation where an older plant may simply be cut back by low temperatures. It is therefore well worth while taking special care of young plants of borderline hardiness for their first few winters. Materials like fleece, burlap or bubble film can be used to protect top growth. As well as keeping the plant warmer, any covering material protects against the desiccating effects of wind and sun if the root zone is frozen. Mulching the root zone with material such as bracken, leafmould, straw or gravel may protect the roots from freezing which is important to reduce the risk of dehydration.

All gardens have microclimates—areas which may be colder or warmer than average. Avoid planting vulnerable plants in frost pockets, which are caused by the coldest air, which is the most dense, collecting in hollows or flowing downhill and building up against barriers such as fences and hedges. A difference of one or two degrees in temperature may be critical to a plant's survival. Cold, draughty spots are particularly lethal to evergreen species.

The sun can be a plus or minus in the hardiness equation. Plants that catch the early morning sun will be subject to rapid thawing of frozen leaves or flowers, which is more likely to result in damage than gentle, slow thawing. This is a particularly important point to consider when siting winter- or early spring-flowering species such as *D. bholua* or *D. odora*. However, sunlight and warmth help to ripen growth, which will increase its resistance to frost. The growth of *D. genkwa* or *D.* ×*hybrida* can be helped to ripen by the stored and reflected heat from a brick or stone wall, while growing *D. jasminea* or *D.* ×*whiteorum* cultivars against or over sunny rocks has the same effect.

Snow and wet

Winter survival may not simply be a question of cold tolerance; long periods of mild, damp conditions can also create problems. Species native to mountain areas may be used to snow cover, and plants under snow remain dry. In their natural habitat cliff-dwellers such as *D. arbuscula* and *D. petraea* enjoy a buoyant atmosphere which rapidly dries their leaves after rain, as well as super-fast drainage in the root zone. These are very different conditions than those they have had to put up with in my garden over the last few winters, where weeks of rain and dank, gloomy days may have been the cause of apparently healthy leaves suddenly falling from plants of *D. arbuscula*, *D. glomerata* and *D. petraea*, all evergreen species. There is no obvious reason for this behaviour, but it may be that the leaves of species adapted to conserve water suffer from oedema in excessively wet conditions. While they do leaf up again the following spring, some loss of vigour is inevitable. In addition, pests and diseases which are killed or inactivated by cold winter weather remain active in our mild winter months; in particular, the short hours of weak sunshine fail to dry the top growth of plants which makes them vulnerable to attack by *Botrytis* and *Marssonina*.

A blanket of snow may be of benefit to plants with a low-growing habit, but taller-growing daphnes such as *D. bholua*, *D. ×burkwoodii*, *D. caucasica* and *D. odora* are prone to damage from the weight of wet snow accumulating on them and breaking off limbs or splitting main stems. Careful pruning to create a strong system of main limbs can help prevent this.

Although I have suggested the minimum temperatures species and hybrids may survive in earlier chapters, I hope the contents of this section indicate that a daphne of borderline hardiness in your climate may be grown successfully with a little extra care. The exchange of information made available by joining local garden clubs or societies such as The Alpine Garden Society and The Royal Horticultural Society in the United Kingdom, or the North American Rock Garden Society and the Daphne Society in the United States, is invaluable in helping to find out how hardy a particular plant may be in a given area. And if you can purchase your daphne from a local supplier, they should be able to give you helpful advice.

Planting and aftercare

My impression as a retail nurseryman is that many daphnes simply fade away after planting without ever getting established. Given that daphnes are intolerant of mismanagement, thorough preparation of the chosen site according to the principles already outlined in this chapter must be followed by careful planting and aftercare.

Aspect

Several of the more important points relating to aspect have been discussed in the section on hardiness. A further point to consider is getting the right balance between sun and shade. Too much shade can result in lax growth liable to wind or snow damage, a poorly shaped plant and less flower production. Just how much shade is too much will depend on the latitude of the site. A plant that needs shade in Italy or Turkey may be happy in sun in England. The more sun a shade-loving species used to monsoon rains like *D. bholua* receives, the more important adequate water in the growing season becomes. As a general rule, all of the deciduous and the smaller-leaved evergreen daphnes should be sited in full sun. Large, evergreen leaves are an indication that a species' natural habitat is shady, but not dry.

It is important to site some daphnes so that they are protected from high winds. The vigorous growth of young plants of species such as *D. acutiloba*, *D. bholua* and *D. odora* is soft and lax, making it vulnerable to wind damage, especially when wind is combined with rain. As some of these larger plants mature, shelter from high winds is also important to maintain stability, since their root system does not seem equal to supporting the top growth. In some cases staking or hard pruning may be required.

Time of planting

Modern container production of plants has resulted in year-round availability of plants, but planting at certain times of the year should in many areas be approached with caution. Key factors to consider are the likelihood of very high or very low temperatures, and the availability of water and some way or someone to apply it as required.

If winter temperatures are unlikely to fall below –17°C (0°F), late summer or early autumn planting is probably the best option. The ground is still warm, which aids rapid establishment of the root system, while the sun's power has reduced enough to avoid damage to the soft growth a young plant may have made. Planted at this time, plants should have established well enough to cope with dry spells during the following spring or summer.

In areas that experience very low winter temperatures, spring planting may be best. In areas with hot summers but mild winters it may be possible to get away with planting for nine months of the year, avoiding the hottest three months, provided that water is available to keep spring plantings alive. Apart from its value in protecting plants from cold in the winter, fleece is an excellent shade material with which to protect recently planted daphnes from hot sun until they have established.

Planting

All purchased plants should be well established in containers. I advise against buying bare-root or rootballed daphnes. Before planting, immerse the plant in its container in a bucket of water until all air bubbles cease, and then remove the pot. It is an irritating characteristic of many daphnes that their roots cling tenaciously to the inside of the pot in which they have been grown, which can make it difficult to remove the plant from the pot. Provided that the container is pliable, simultaneous pressure on opposite sides will bow out the other two sides, so detaching the roots. Moving the pressure points round 90 degrees will have the same effect on the other two quarters of the pot, so that the root ball comes out evenly when the pot is inverted. I have never been in favour of teasing out a fibrous root system before planting, since it is an operation which will break many of the delicate white root tips that absorb the nutrients and water which the plant requires. I think it can do more harm than good. I accept that *D. mezereum*, often used as a rootstock, characteristically has one or more roots much thicker than the rest, which can get tangled when restricted in a small pot. While this would not affect establishment, it may jeopardize the future stability of tall-growing plants, so if curled-around roots can be disentangled without disturbing the root ball a great deal, particularly when planting in the dormant season, it may be worthwhile.

Trying to adjust the depth of planting to bury the union of a grafted plant to encourage the scion variety to make roots is not necessary. My advice is to plant so that the surface of the root ball is just below the level of the soil surface. Then, a mulch of grit for small types, or organic matter for larger ones, helps to conserve moisture and provide a cool root run. Assuming that the planting site has been well prepared, the soil or made-up compost will be in an open, friable state, so it is essential to get the root ball firmly in contact with the growing medium, and this is best done with the heel of the foot, followed by a thorough soaking. Failure to achieve good contact between root ball and soil is, in my opinion, a major cause of plant losses.

Watering and feeding

It is frequently stated that all daphnes are intolerant of drought; I am among those guilty of this slander! I am sure that more daphnes are killed by too much water than by lack of it. I suggest that the species from Asia are less tolerant of dry conditions, as they may be used to frequent summer rainstorms or monsoon conditions, and they do not seem to have such a deep root system. Many of the European species are used to rain or snow melt, or both, while they flower and make a flush of growth in early summer, but through the summer they often have to tolerate high temperatures and low rainfall until autumn. Their wide-ranging root system is adapted to cope with drought, so if they are provided with a deep root run and given enough water to establish their roots, they will tolerate dry spells as well as most shrubs. The death of a plant in a dry spell is too often blamed on the species' intolerance of drought, when in fact poor soil preparation and/or winter waterlogging has destroyed much of its root system with fatal consequences during the first dry period of summer.

A common cause of failure is lack of water after planting. The majority of commercially produced container plants are grown in compost containing a high proportion of organic matter; this type of compost can be very difficult to re-wet if it is allowed to dry out. After planting, two or three hot or windy days can completely dry out a root ball even though the area surrounding it may still be moist. If the roots have not had time to grow out of the root ball, they cannot get to the moisture. This situation may not be obvious to the average gardener who will give what may seem a good watering, but not re-wet the root ball because the dry organic matter actually repels water when it is applied too quickly. In such a situation, water must be applied in small amounts over a longer period, but try to avoid this problem by regular watering for several weeks after planting. Drip-fed irrigation systems are a very good way of establishing new plantings, and a dry root ball can also be successfully re-wetted by piercing a small hole in the bottom of a plastic bottle filled with water and standing it at the base of the plant.

Once they are established, however, it is important not to water daphnes little and often as this will encourage surface rooting, which is liable to make plants vulnerable to drought. A thorough soaking to a good depth with a long period between applications will encourage the daphne roots to do what they would in the wild—grow deep in search of water.

As well as the obvious signs like drooping of young growth or curling of leaves, drought symptoms to watch out for in older plants are bright green foliage changing to dull, olive green, and flowers drooping at the perianth tube or not opening properly. Keep in mind that these symptoms could also indicate root death.

Daphnes definitely respond to careful feeding; the older they get, the more beneficial it is likely to be. Particular care is necessary in a plant's early years not to overfeed, because long, lax growth, if left unpinched, results in a poor shape and bare stems at the lower part of the plant in varieties such as *D.* ×*burkwoodii* and *D. odora*, while *D. cneorum* may develop a central area of bare wood. All daphnes should produce a flush of vegetative growth from spring to early summer immediately after they flower. If they do not, or the growth is weak or of a poor colour, they are either lacking in nutrients or lacking in young feeding roots to absorb nutrients. The ideal time to feed is just as the first flowers of the season are developing; feeding too late in the season may produce soft growth liable to wind and frost damage. When and how much to feed will only be learned with experience of your own soil, compost or growing conditions.

Open-ground plants in my garden are given a dressing of a balanced NPK granular fertilizer around mid-March. Plants in troughs are liquid-fed about once a fortnight between March and June from the second season after planting.

Species such as *D. collina* of gardens, *D. arbuscula* and *D. tangutica* and the majority of hybrids will follow the first flush of bloom on their previous season's wood with a flush of vegetative growth which produces flowers in July and August; balanced feeding encourages this.

Moving established plants

This operation is fraught with danger, but with care can be successful. Young plants which have only been in the ground for a season or two move relatively easily, but the older the plant, the greater the risk of loss. Try to time the move to spring or autumn, when the sun is less strong, but the soil warm. Making spade cuts down two sides of the root zone several weeks before the move reduces the shock and allows the cut roots to make fibrous new growth which aids re-establishment. Make sure a thorough soaking is given a day before moving, and in dry conditions, add plenty of water to the bottom of the new planting hole. Top growth can be cut back to balance the reduced root system if required, and any soft growth should be removed as a matter of course. In hot weather shading with fleece and light spraying of the foliage with water in the evenings will be appreciated for a couple of weeks after transplanting.

Routine maintenance

To produce a well-shaped plant it is advisable to monitor the growth made by a young daphne in the first few years after planting. Pinching or stopping strong extension growth will result in a bushy plant without bare stems at the base. Most cultivars of *D. bholua* and *D. odora* are not naturally bushy as young plants, and it is difficult to get them to branch even after removing the tips of strong growth. Cutting back to a bud at least six leaves back from the apical bud can be more successful.

Species such as *D. cneorum*, *D. genkwa* and *D. odora*, together with some of the more vigorous *D. ×burkwoodii* cultivars, are prone to developing large areas of bare stem at the base or in the centre of the plant, particularly if they are poorly managed or incorrectly sited. Provided the root system is healthy, and the plant receives some form of fertilizer afterwards, hard pruning to within a few inches of the base will usually result in a rejuvenated, bushy plant. The best time to do this would be immediately after spring flowering. To prevent infection from fungal spores after such drastic treatment it is advisable to paint the cut surfaces with a wound protectant.

The only regular maintenance necessary for the larger daphnes in the garden is inspection for the pests and diseases detailed in Chapter 6. In particular, early removal of any dieback by cutting back to healthy growth is essential. Wherever possible, accumulations of dead flowers should be removed to reduce the chance of fungal infection. This is especially important during the shorter days of spring and autumn, when dead material may remain moist for long periods. When removing dead flowers in spring, care must be taken not to damage the new shoots which on many species and hybrids will be emerging from the base of the inflorescence.

The naturally prostrate and dwarf, bushy species and hybrids clothe the ground with their growth. Over time, a thick layer of dead leaves and flowers builds up underneath this growth and the lowermost twigs, deprived of all light, die. Fungal infection of this material can easily transfer to basal growth of the plant unnoticed. Once infection has reached the main stem it generally proves fatal. This is a common reason for the apparently inexplicable sudden death of a healthy plant. Evergreen daphnes drop most of their old leaves in early summer at the time of the main flush of new growth; since this coincides with maximum dead flower drop, May and June is the best time to have a really good tidy up at the base of plants. It is also the most likely time that new suckers will be showing from the rootstock of plants that have been grafted. Soft shoots are best peeled off, but if larger sucker growth has turned woody, it should be cut off as close as possible to its point of origin.

Cultivation under cover

If winter-flowering varieties such as *D. bholua*, *D. jezoensis* and *D. ×hybrida* are grown in containers, they can be kept outside for much of the year and brought into a conservatory, garden room or porch for flowering. Blooming for at least two or three months if kept cool, their scent is a joy in the dark days of winter. But as a nurseryman, for me the big advantage of growing daphnes under protection year-round is the early availability of propagation material, which allows for cuttings to be rooted and potted by autumn, and in this unpredictable climate it does also make control of water so much easier; this has to be one of the keys to successful daphne cultivation. Our winters of late have been getting milder and wetter, which many of the smaller daphnes grown in the open seem to dislike. If you really want to enjoy your daphnes at their peak time of beauty—April, in my case—it is an advantage not to have rain dripping down your neck every time you bend down to sniff a flower. Protection from wind, rain, hail and frost preserves the blooms from damage, and a warm atmosphere improves the scent; however, high temperatures reduce the life of the blooms.

Type of protection

In my case, protection has mainly consisted of unheated clear polythene tunnels, where daphnes grow planted in raised beds made from railway sleepers or in clay pots plunged in sand. A glasshouse which is kept just frost-free in winter and heavily shaded in summer to facilitate propagation by cuttings is also home to daphnes grown in pots, some plastic, some clay, but these are not plunged. My glasshouse contains far too many genera, some tender, for ease of management, so I would not heat it for the sake of the daphnes since, with protection from winter wet and freezing winds, most should survive night temperatures of –10° to –15°C (14° to 4°F) when dormant. Winter protection could also be provided by cold frames; the aim should be to allow maximum light while protecting from wind chill and wet.

All my plants remain under cover year-round, but I suspect that most of my daphnes in pots would be just as happy, or happier if they were moved outside for the summer, and in areas that have hotter summers than Hampshire, it would be a necessity. My plants under clear polythene do have some protection in summer with shade netting.

Pots

Plastic and clay are the most common materials used for the manufacture of pots. Unglazed clay pots are porous and allow water to evaporate through them, which is a cooling process, and daphnes do like to have a cool root area. Clay pots are also beneficial in aiding drainage and aeration of the compost. The disadvantages of clay containers are cost, weight, rapid drying out, and possibly the chance of breakage from frost damage. I have never grown daphnes in a pot with a glazed finish, but provided it has adequate drainage holes, I see no reason why one could not be used. Plastic pots and the compost within them can get very hot if exposed to direct sunlight. I know that daphne roots avoid growing into the compost at the side of a pot which receives direct sun; so it is fair to assume that if the whole bulk of the compost gets too hot, the plant may suffer. High compost temperatures also cause excessive release of salts by slow-release fertilizers, and this can cause root damage and encourage infection by fungal pathogens. Temperature problems can be avoided by plunging pots into sand or soil.

Whether raised from seed, cuttings or grafts, cost dictates that I use plastic pots for all my daphnes for the first two or three years of growth. Apart from cost, the other advantages of plastic are ease of handling, less need for watering, and the ease with which plants can be turned out, either for planting or root inspection. Plants I intend to keep for display are transferred to clay pots after two or three years.

My growing routine

In my glasshouse, plants in both clay and plastic pots stand on benches covered in a 5 CM layer of 6 MM grit. They are well spaced, but would get better air circulation if stood on wooden slats or wire mesh. However, this would increase water loss, so I think my method a suitable compromise. Plants soon root into the bench grit if left unmoved for long in the growing season, but regular turning prevents this and maintains even development of the plant.

The clay pots in which daphnes grow in my clear polythene tunnel are plunged in sand to three-quarters of their depth. The sand is kept moist in summer, but dry in winter. Not plunging the pot to the rim allows for some cooling evaporation of moisture and encourages plenty of air circulation around the base of the plant.

Once a pot is filled with roots, the plant will benefit from potting on. This is an annual event for me until a pot size of 22.5 or 25 CM is reached. Potting on after that results in handling problems. I try to pot on in March or April when the root system is active and will have all of the growing season to colonize the new compost.

Once plants have been in their final size pots for several years, I may have to prune them to keep them to a manageable size; I shear them around their margins in a very brutal way immediately after the spring flush of flower and apply a weak liquid feed at fortnightly intervals up to the end of June. This routine results in a second flush of flower in July and often a third in September. The fact that I have a plant of *D. petraea* 'Grandiflora' over 20 years old (which I have never sheared!) and teenaged *D. jasminea* and *D.* ×*hendersonii* indicates that daphnes can be long-lived in containers, but keep in mind that pot-grown daphnes do need a lot of attention in the growing season. I am lucky to have a "plant sitter" to look after them when I am away.

Growing daphnes under cover in the summer increases the risk of infestation by red spider mite. It can be a serious threat and is difficult for the amateur to control with chemicals, though biological controls are available. Plants under cover are less likely to suffer from leaf spot diseases and dieback unless poor ventilation is coupled with overhead watering. I do spray with a fungicide in autumn as a preventive measure, since this is the most likely time for infection. In addition my plants receive regular fungicidal drenches against root disease. The chapter on Pests and Diseases (p. 207) contains further discussion of this and all the other problems above.

Raised beds under cover

When I built a raised bed for daphnes at the southern end of a clear polythene tunnel, I made the sides two railway sleepers high to create a bed about 50 CM high. As this area had originally been a potting shed, the base of the bed was concrete. Pot-grown daphnes had shown their liking for growing into bench grit in the glasshouse and this prompted me to fill the bed to one sleeper high with a mix of peat, loam and grit, on top of which went a 20 CM layer of 5–6 MM grit. All planting was therefore into the pure grit. Without exception, daphnes planted into this bed grew well for a number of years, whether grafted or on their own roots (see photograph, p. 25). These included numerous forms of *D. arbuscula* and *D. petraea* and a wide selection of hybrids, of which 'Bramdean', 'Cheriton', 'Meon' and 'Tichborne' soon outgrew their allotted space. This bed required regular liquid feeding, and watering was difficult to judge correctly, particularly during the winter, but it was a great success, and I would recommend a construction along similar lines to anyone wanting to grow a collection of daphnes purely for enjoyment.

I have also made a raised bed in a tunnel that is just one sleeper (25 CM) high. The base is poorly drained heavy clay, so I left this uncultivated to avoid creating a drainage sump under the bed. The bed is filled to within an inch of the top with a mix of peat, bark, grit and loam, and top-dressed with 6 MM grit. I do not rate this as successful as the bed two sleepers high, but grafted plants of *D. petraea* and plants of *D. calcicola* and *D. genkwa* on their own roots have grown well.

Provided you can cope with watering and provide plenty of ventilation, growing daphnes in a raised bed under polythene in our climate seems to provide them with what they like; a deep, cool root run, warmth for their top growth and protection from our increasingly wet winters. In areas which experience colder winters, the extra warmth available under polythene and the facility to control water supply should provide the ideal conditions for ripening growth to withstand the cold.

6 Pests and Diseases

Pests

To the best of my knowledge, unless they transmit a virus, no pest in the United Kingdom causes life-threatening damage to daphnes, so use chemical control with caution as a last resort. There is an ever-increasing concern that chemicals used for pest control cause harm to the environment. The majority of chemicals used by the professional grower are no longer available to the gardener; since different countries have banned or plan to withdraw various chemicals, I shall avoid making many specific recommendations for control by pesticides. Regular inspection of plants through the growing season is important since it enables you to identify a pest attack before it builds up to serious proportions and makes control easier. In many cases birds and predatory insects will prevent a major buildup of a pest. Biological control is rapidly becoming available to gardeners for a number of major pests. This involves buying a supply of an insect, mite, nematode, bacteria or fungus which is a predator, parasite or pathogen of the particular pest species that may be attacking your plants (see Useful Addresses for suppliers). This form of control is particularly effective when used on plants grown under protection. Strict hygiene pays handsome dividends when it comes to preventing plant problems. This includes weed control, as many common species of weed harbour pests and viruses.

Aphids

Although I have come across attacks by these sap-sucking insects on the soft new growth of some daphnes, particularly *D. jezoensis*, *D. longilobata* and *D. mezereum*, it is not a common occurrence on the nursery or in the garden. The fact that aphids are a principal vector of viruses is the main significance of this pest.

Control

Natural control by birds and predatory insects such as ladybird or lacewing larvae and parasitic wasps should prevent any large buildup of aphids. On a small scale they can be brushed off with a paint brush. Spray with soft soap or a contact or systemic insecticide. Biological control using ladybirds, lacewing larvae and parasitic wasps is available.

Plant bugs

Members of the family Miridae are major pests of daphnes in my garden, primarily in the form of capsid bugs, but shield bugs also cause damage. In the United States the tarnished plant bug (*Lygus lineolaris*) and the garden flea hopper (*Halticus bracteatus*) may well cause similar damage. Both nymphs and adults use their piercing mouth parts to feed on plant sap. They attack the growing points of the plant and as growth continues, the developing leaves have a tattered, necrotic appearance and flower buds often abort. The adults are at their most active in May and June, so the new growth and, most importantly, the summer flush of flowers can be badly damaged. Following attack, growth may be erratic, particularly in young plants—resulting in poorly shaped specimens. Dead tissue is vulnerable to attack by *Botrytis cinerea*. Daphnes with medium-sized and large leaves seem more vulnerable to attack than smaller-leaved types. These insects also spread virus.

Control

Mirids are not easy to control as the insects may well have left by the time the damage is noticed. Close and frequent inspection in spring will reveal the first signs of attack. It is difficult to use contact insecticides effectively, so systemic sprays may be required to control severe attacks.

Leaf hoppers

There are many species of these small, pale green insects, most just less than a centimetre long. Their life cycle involves eggs, young (nymph) stages which are wingless, and the flying adults. The hornbeam (*Carpinus betulus*) hedges in my garden make an ideal breeding ground for them, and they tend to attack the larger-leaved daphnes such as *D. bholua* and *D. odora*, leaving small, pale green areas on the leaves. The damage they cause here is relatively insignificant, but may be more serious in other locations. They are important vectors of viruses.

Control

Natural control by birds and predatory insects, particularly of the nymph stages, is generally effective. Alternatively, spray with a contact or systemic insecticide.

Thrips

These small insects show a preference for attacking the leaves of *D. jezoensis* and *D. mezereum* when grown under protection, and various species cause problems outdoors in the United States. Youngsters are wingless, but the adults fly, and so it is possible that they could spread viruses. Thrips feed by puncturing cells and sucking up the sap; the empty cells fill with air, revealing the damage as small silvery patches on otherwise green leaves.

Control

Control measures should only be necessary in a case of severe infestation. Control by spraying with chemicals may be ineffective. Biological control for use under cover is available, using predatory bugs and mites. In small enclosed areas, sticky traps can be used to keep numbers down.

Caterpillars

Although it is not an annual occurrence, I have from time to time had problems with the larvae of one of the tortrix or leaf roller moths. The larvae tie or "glue" leaves together at the tip of the stem to form a nest. They then feed on the youngest leaves and the apical bud within. Damage is evident from September onwards. Plants in the garden and under protection have been attacked; *D. bholua*, *D.* ×*burkwoodii* and especially *D. tangutica* are the most likely to be damaged.

Control

Since the caterpillar is well protected in its nest, sprays are not effective, and birds do not seem to recognize a potential meal. Pulling the leaves apart to remove the dark grey larva or pinching off the whole nest is the only way I know of controlling this pest.

Red spider mite

These mites are a significant pest of daphnes grown under the protection of glass or polythene, but I have never experienced problems in the garden. Plants grown in warmer climates may well be attacked in the open. Severe attacks can cause defoliation and seriously debilitate a plant, rendering it more vulnerable to attack by fungal pathogens. These tiny mites are difficult to see without a magnifying glass, and generally build up their numbers on the underside of leaves, so the first noticeable sign of an attack may be a faint yellow speckling on otherwise green leaves as their chlorophyll is destroyed by the feeding mites. Population buildup can accelerate rapidly as summer temperatures rise. On my nursery some species attract red spider mite more readily than others; *D. bholua*, *D. blagayana*, *D. jezoensis* and *D. mezereum* are most regularly attacked, while I have never seen mites on *D. odora*, and Joe Blue of Briggs Nurseries Inc. reports that *D.* ×*transatlantica* 'Eternal Fragrance' growing alongside badly infested plants of *D. cneorum* 'Ruby Glow' was not attacked.

Control

Red spider mite thrives in hot, dry, crowded conditions so its increase can be reduced by spacing plants out and spraying with water. Chemical control is virtually impossible for the amateur grower, but effective biological control in the form of predatory mites is available. Where daphnes are overwintered under protection, moving them into the open in late spring will reduce the chance of severe infestation.

Slugs and snails

These creatures are seldom considered a serious pest of woody plants, but they can cause considerable damage to daphnes, particularly to young plants. In my garden, much of the damage occurs during mild spells in the dormant period, so daphnes grown in areas that experience colder winters may escape attack. Leaves of evergreen species, dormant axillary and terminal buds and flower buds are attacked. During the growing season the flowers of many species may be preferred to the vegetative parts. I list here the varieties most likely to be attacked in order of tastiness: *D. caucasica*, *D. jezoensis*, *D. blagayana*, *D. bholua* and *D. glomerata*.

Control

I do need to protect *D. jezoensis* with slug pellets if I am to see any flowers in spring, and young plants of vulnerable varieties may need similar protection in areas prone to snail and slug activity. Environmentally friendly control measures include night-time patrols with a torch; beer traps; inverted grapefruit or orange skins; and the encouragement of song thrushes and hedgehogs.

Parasitic nematodes are an effective alternative to chemicals for control of slugs and one application will provide six weeks of protection. These parasitic nematodes are available in the United States, Canada and the United Kingdom.

Vine weevil

The larvae of this beetle have become a major pest of a wide range of plants over the last 30 years, particularly those grown in containers. They feed on the roots or basal area of the plant. Since this pest has such a wide host range, I have to incorporate a chemical control into all my potting composts, but I am pleased to say that to date I have never found one of the cream-coloured, C-shaped grubs in a daphne pot, nor seen any sign of the U-shaped notches on leaf margins made by adult beetles feeding. This may be because my nursery contains many tastier items for them to attack! I will cautiously say that daphnes do not suffer from vine weevil problems, but it is possible that a population of weevils could develop a taste for them if alternative host plants were not available.

Control

Chemicals are available which can be incorporated into composts. Biological control using parasitic nematodes can be used when temperatures are above a certain level. Adult weevils can often be found by torchlight.

Bumblebees

I am not going to suggest that anyone should take measures to kill such useful insects; I simply want to record the fact that certain species of bumblebee have caused a lot of damage to the flowers of some of my daphnes. This damage occurs more often, or is more noticeable, under glass or polythene cover. The problem is that the "tongue" or proboscis of the bee is not long enough to reach down to the nectar at the base of the long perianth tube of a daphne flower, so it uses its mandibles to cut a hole in the side. This often causes the flower to bend or droop at the point of damage. Varieties regularly damaged in this way are *D. arbuscula*, *D. jasminea*, *D. petraea* and *D.* ×*whiteorum* cultivars. Holes bitten into the perianth tubes of *D. retusa* and *D. tangutica* do not seem to cause the same damage, perhaps because the flower parts seem to have a thicker texture.

Deer and rabbits

Since I have no experience of my daphnes suffering attack from either of these animals, I am relying on reports from my customers in the United Kingdom and members of the Daphne Society in the United States. In the U.K. both deer and rabbits will eat daphnes, but not as a first choice. The problem does not seem as bad in the U.S., but it should be assumed that deer will eat anything if they are hungry enough.

Control

Other than fencing, I cannot recommend any control.

Diseases

In the chapter on cultivation I explained in some detail the importance of routine maintenance and hygiene in the prevention of disease. Prevention rather than cure should be the aim. Correct choice and preparation of the site should result in strong, healthy plants which are less likely to succumb to pathogen attack. Regular inspection of plants allows problems to be tackled before they become life-threatening.

Fungi reproduce by minute spores which are distributed by wind and/or water movement. Under favourable conditions of temperature and humidity these spores will germinate when they come into contact with a suitable host. Under adverse conditions, fungi can also enter resting phases which are capable of surviving for many years. Thus any control programme must include speedy removal of all infected material. Do not plant a susceptible species in any area where root disease has occurred.

Leaf spot

This disease is caused by the fungus *Marssonina daphnes*, a name synonymous with *Gloeosporium mezerei*. As with many of these leaf spots, this fungus is specific to daphnes, and attacks have been reported from North America and Europe as well as the United Kingdom. *Daphne mezereum* is reputed to be particularly susceptible and nurseries in North America have had problems with *D. cneorum* 'Ruby Glow'.

In my own experience, *D. collina* of gardens is the most susceptible plant in the garden, and this trait has been passed on to hybrids made between it and *D. arbuscula*, *D. caucasica* and *D. cneorum*. Given adequate ventilation, plants growing under cover are rarely attacked. Infected plants develop dark, circular spots, followed by leaf yellowing and dropping. Severe attacks may include infection of young stems and dieback. The fungus is encouraged by long periods of cool, wet weather. Spores are mainly spread by water droplets in the form of rain or overhead watering.

Control

Choose an open, sunny site where plants receive good air circulation. Avoid night-time or overhead watering. Tidy all fallen leaves from infected plants, and prune off any infected stem growth. Once infection has been identified, chemical control in the form of repeated spraying at 7–14-day intervals, depending on weather conditions, may be required to control the fungus. I have no experience of spraying daphnes with fungicides containing copper, but they are recommended for this problem and should be available in some form to everyone. For the gardener, any fungicide marketed for the control of powdery mildew and black spot of roses would be worth trying.

Botrytis cinerea

It is common to hear or read of apparently healthy, well-established daphnes suddenly collapsing for no apparent reason; in the United States this has been named "daphne sudden death syndrome". I am confident that in the majority of cases the cause is infection by the fungus *Botrytis cinerea.* If a daphne has grown and thrived for a number of years it is fair to assume the site must be free of the fungal pathogens which cause root rot; this leaves *Botrytis cinerea* as the only known fungus which commonly kills daphnes suddenly. Also, death by root disease tends to be a slower process. Most of the small, evergreen daphnes have a bushy habit which may extend to soil level; over a period of years the lowermost stems near the centre of the plant become deprived of all light and die. Dead leaves and flowers which fall and accumulate at the base of the plant provide the ideal situation for *Botrytis* to develop and infect the dead stems. There will be no leaf discoloration to alert the gardener to this infection; once it has spread to the main stem, collapse and death will occur in a few days.

Given the lethal outcome of many infections, it may seem strange to state that *Botrytis cinerea* is a weak parasite. What I mean by this is that when a spore germinates it is a relatively weak organism and cannot readily gain entry into healthy living tissue. It needs to either find a wound for entry or grow on dead material to build up enough strength to infect healthy tissue. A wound may be caused by snow, frost or storm damage, careless handling, or animal or insect activity. Dead material is generally in the form of old flowers, but damage caused by capsids on young foliage and accumulated dead leaves at the base of the plant are also readily infected. Even when *Marssonina daphnes* (see Leaf Spot) has infected a plant, dieback is more likely to be caused by secondary infection by *Botrytis* via stem lesions or through scars left by the fall of infected leaves.

Botrytis has such a wide host range that it should be taken for granted that spores are present in the air most of the year. The ability of these spores to germinate is governed by temperature and humidity, and most damage occurs in cool, damp conditions. Temperatures between 10°C (50°F) and 25°C (77°F) and a wet plant surface or a relative humidity above 95 percent provide ideal conditions, but spores may germinate slowly at temperatures as low as 5°C (41°F) provided that there is adequate moisture. Once the fungus gains entry to the plant it soon builds up strength and will travel down a stem until it makes contact with a major limb, resulting in the common daphne problem of dieback. Failure to remove infected material may have fatal results.

The main points to watch for to recognize *Botrytis* infection are grey mould on dead flowers or other dead material, most likely after a period of humidity, or an area of leaves on a healthy green plant turning olive green, then brown.

Control

Botrytis cinerea is an extremely variable organism, some strains being more virulent than others, and some now resistant to a range of chemicals used to protect against infection, particularly older formulations. This fact, together with the shrinking range of chemicals available to combat the fungus, dictates that cultural control is very important.

Avoid positioning plants where the atmosphere may be stagnant for long periods and maintain plenty of ventilation when growing under protection. Do not water overhead or late in the day and do not overwater. Excessive use of fertilizer, particularly nitrogen, or feeding late in the growing season, encourages soft growth vulnerable to infection.

Do not allow dead leaves to accumulate at the base of plants, particularly those with a lower-growing habit. Remove as much dead blossom as practical, particularly from late summer onwards.

Keep a watch for the first symptoms of dieback and cut out any infection well below discoloured wood. Protect obvious wounds with a wound paint or spray.

Chemicals can be used to protect against infection. My cuttings are sprayed routinely at 10–14-day intervals and I spray mature plants several times in late summer when areas of the plant and dead flowers are likely to remain wet for longer periods. It is important to alternate different chemicals in a spray programme to avoid resistant strains of fungus developing.

Root rots

In my experience root rots are more likely to cause problems where daphnes are grown in containers rather than the open ground. The type of well-drained soil that daphnes require does not suit root-rotting fungi such as *Phytopthora* and *Pythium*; they prefer stagnant conditions and their spores are largely spread in water. On the other hand, many container composts are poorly drained and may be overwatered. I also believe that there are many beneficial fungi and bacteria in the soil whose presence and functions are not fully understood. They may attack or inhibit parasitic fungi which attack daphne roots. Thus, by putting container plants into sterile compost, or one with an incorporated fungicide, are we denying them the protection of the naturally occurring organisms? There is scope for experiment here, and I am adding a product to my compost which contains *Trichoderma*, a soil-borne fungus which is claimed to be antagonistic towards some plant pathogens, and drenching containers with *Bacillus subtilis*, a naturally occurring microbial inoculant; through its presence the population excludes or competes with harmful micro-organisms. To date, trials show that this procedure is at least as effective as incorporating a fungicide in the compost or using fungicidal drenches. Provided that the plant material is healthy to start with, the *Trichoderma* can prevent infection, but it will not control any infection already within the plant. This type of plant health management is in its infancy, and I hope that more work with beneficial fungi and "compost teas" will provide safe ways of protecting daphnes that are readily available to gardeners.

It may prove hard to identify which of the several lethal fungal pathogens has killed your plant. The only way to be certain is to send specimens to a diagnostic laboratory. Although the amateur grower may find that difficult, this information is essential for efficient protection of other daphnes you may have. In the United Kingdom, the Royal Horticultural Society provides a diagnostic service for members.

Thielaviopsis basicola

This fungus causes black root rot. It has a wide host range, attacking major crops such as cucumber, tomato, tobacco, bedding plants and pot plants in both the United Kingdom and the United States. I have sent dead container-grown plants to a laboratory for technical analysis several times; in each case *T. basicola* has been identified. This fungus normally survives by living saphrophytically, not parasitically, on organic matter in the soil and so may be present in peat or leafmould used in cuttings or potting composts. However, in certain circumstances the balance in the soil changes and the fungus then infects plants. This infection is encouraged by warm temperatures, high moisture levels, a fertile growing medium and an acid pH—all conditions likely to be found in the compost of container-grown plants. Symptoms on daphnes are first a loss of vigour; the foliage then changes to a dull, pale green, and gradually most of the older leaves drop off. Examination of the root system will reveal that all the small feeding roots have rotted. *Thielaviopsis basicola* is mainly spread in drainage water and infected organic matter, or by fungus gnats and sciarid flies.

Control

It is important to exercise cultural control and maintain strict hygiene. Use well-drained, alkaline compost and avoid overwatering. Research has shown that the use of composted pine bark as a compost ingredient added at the rate of 40 percent by volume can suppress fungal attack.

Few chemicals are available against *T. basicola*. I have found regular drenches with compounds containing the active ingredients prochloraz or hydroxyacetic acid may be effective, while thiophanate-methyl is registered for use in the United States.

Phytophthora

Species of this group of fungi, such as *Phytophthora parasitica*, *Phytophthora cinnamomi* and *Phytophthora cactorum*, are known to cause daphne fatalities on both sides of the Atlantic. Symptoms include yellowing of leaves, partial dieback of branches and death of roots close to the stem. These fungi are more likely to be a problem in poorly drained ground. Their spores are spread in drainage water, and they are capable of forming a resting phase which can survive for many years in the ground.

Control

Never transplant infected plants into clean land. Prevent pots or ground from becoming waterlogged. Avoid excessive watering and manuring. Effective chemical controls are not available to amateur growers.

Rhizoctonia and *Pythium*

There are records of attacks by species of these fungi on daphnes. They are more likely to occur under propagation or container-growing conditions, attacking the base or new roots of cuttings and causing damping-off disease in seedlings.

Control

The cultural control regime outlined for *Thielaviopsis basicola* should be the best way of avoiding infection. *Pythium* exists in so many different strains which constantly mutate that chemical control is likely to be difficult for amateur growers. Copper-based compounds may give some control, and the use of sterilized container compost will help avoid infection. Most chemicals which control *Pythium* will not control *Rhizoctonia* and vice versa.

Honey fungus

Armillaria mellea, also known as the bootlace fungus, is common in wooded areas, or areas which were once woodland and may contain woody remains on which the fungus can exist as a saprophyte. The fungus has an extremely wide host range, but while most daphnes can be attacked, I suspect the woodland species such as *D. laureola* and *D. pontica* may be resistant, since they are thriving after several years in my armillaria-infested woodland. Grafting a susceptible variety on to a rootstock of one of the resistant species would be a solution if *A. mellea* is known to be present in the ground.

Plants killed by *A. mellea* characteristically have a fan-shaped pattern of thin white fungal growth on or under the bark. The fungus also produces long, black rhizomorphs like a black bootlace, which survive on any dead, woody material. It is therefore important to remove as much root as possible of any dead plant.

Control

Control is virtually impossible, so when the fungus is known to exist, avoid planting susceptible varieties.

Virus

Several different viruses have been isolated from daphnes; cucumber mosaic virus is particularly common. These microscopic organisms have a large host range. They can be spread over wide areas by plant-feeding insects and nematodes. Thus an aphid could infect a daphne with a virus by moving from a common weed such as chickweed (*Stellaria media*) or fat hen (*Chenopodium album*), since both are known hosts of virus. Symptoms of infection are often yellow mottling of the foliage, small leaves and stunted growth, and early leaf fall. Leaf mottling is more obvious where foliage receives sunlight, and it may not show when shaded. Infection is believed to render daphnes more susceptible to frost damage. There is no cure and any plants suspected of having virus infection should be removed and burned to avoid the spread of infection. When propagating by grafting or cuttings, care must be taken to use only healthy material, since viruses can easily be spread by knife, secateurs or hands. *Daphne jezoensis*, *D. mezereum* and *D. odora* seem the most susceptible to virus attack. Control of insect vectors such as aphids, capsid bugs and leaf hoppers is important.

7 Garden Use

Scent

For me, scent has to be the major contribution that daphnes can make to a garden. I realize that gardeners living in harsher climates or in areas with a shorter growing season than mine may be without a daphne to savour for two or three months of the year, but the repeat-flowering habit of some of the hybrids and the increased availability of winter-flowering species allows me to have a daphne flower to nose most of the weeks of the year.

The first two months of the year are covered by *D. bholua*, *D. jezoensis* and *D. mezereum*; then in March and April *D. blagayana*, *D. odora* and *D. acutiloba* link to the main spring flush of species and hybrids which lasts to the end of May. June can be a lean month, but *D. giraldii*, *D. longilobata* and *D. striata* will oblige, while *D.* ×*transatlantica* 'Jims Pride' and 'Eternal Fragrance' should have flowers by the end of the month. By early July, flowers are appearing on the new growth of a few of the species and many of the hybrids, a display which lasts to the first frosts in many cases. In November and December *D. bholua* 'Darjeeling' and *D.* ×*hybrida* see the year out. There are so many wonderfully scented daphnes that unpleasantly scented species like *D. glomerata* and scentless ones like *D. jasminea* may be put near the bottom of a wants list in spite of their attractive appearance.

As you acquire more daphnes you will notice that many have subtly different fragrances, although there is quite a large group that I would simply class as sweetly scented; *D. arbuscula* and *D. petraea* fall into this category. Some of the more distinctive scents, according to my sense of smell, are: *D. acutiloba*, spicy citrus; *D. blagayana*, narcissus; *D. caucasica*, sweet garden pinks, which it passes on to its hybrids; *D. jezoensis*, freesia; *D. laureola*, honey; *D. longilobata*, gardenia, but only in the evening; *D. odora*, wonderfully citrus—the best of all, I think. When sniffed close up, the scent of *D. cneorum* can be almost overpowering, but wafting on the air it is delicious!

To enjoy the full benefit of daphne scents, you should give thought to planting positions; winter flowers should be accessible for easy sniffing without getting muddy or diving into the shrubbery. Low-growing types can be put into raised beds or planted in troughs mounted on stones to make bending down to them easier. The pleasure of sitting out in the garden on a summer evening will be enhanced if the scent of *D.* ×*burkwoodii*, *D. tangutica* or *D.* ×*transatlantica* is drifting around.

Plants that produce scented flowers in the months of winter and early spring are particularly valuable. Apart from the pleasure they give in the home and garden, species such as *D. bholua*, *D. mezereum* and *D. odora* are excellent subjects for the winter borders of parks and botanic gardens open to the public.

Winter-flowering species may not produce much scent in cold conditions, and many daphnes produce more scent towards evening, presumably to attract moths, which are important pollinators of their long-tubed flowers. Plants suffering from drought or with root systems reduced by disease or waterlogging will be noticeably less fragrant.

Foliage and winter structure

The compact evergreen habit of many of the dwarf daphnes such as *D.* ×*napolitana* and *D.* ×*rollsdorfii* varieties can provide winter structure to low-planted areas like raised beds and rock gardens in much the same way as a dwarf conifer or hebe would. Larger evergreen shrubs such as *D. bholua*, *D. laureola* and *D. pontica* also provide useful winter structure to borders or open woodland areas, but try to avoid planting in heavy shade or where there is too much competition from tree roots; this results in weak, straggly growth and little blossom production. These species associate well with other spring-flowering shrubs such as sarcococcas and skimmias.

Over many years, variegated sports of several species and hybrids have been selected and propagated. Some may not be particularly strong growers due to lack of chlorophyll, and others may not be to everyone's taste, but there are some whose combination of variegated evergreen leaves and fragrant flowers makes them valuable garden plants. There are numerous named forms of *D.* ×*burkwoodii* with variegated leaves, some merely variations on a theme; cultivars 'Carol Mackie' and 'G.K. Argles' have a narrow cream or gold edge to their leaves, with plenty of chlorophyll still available to produce vigorous growth; 'Briggs Moonlight' has a narrow green edge to an otherwise cream leaf, and 'Golden Treasure', with gold to lime green leaves outlined in dark green, is proving a first-rate plant in my "daphnetum" (see photograph, p. 114).

Although *D. odora* 'Aureomarginata' is popular in the United Kingdom because it seems hardier than clones with plain green leaves, the narrow cream edge to its leaves is hardly spectacular, but selections such as *D. odora* 'Geisha Girl' and 'Mae Jima' from Japan are worth garden space for their foliage alone (see photographs, p. 87). The former has a combination of green, grey-green and pale yellow variegation, while the latter has leaves with a broad margin of deep yellow.

Among other variegated daphnes of note are *D.* ×*napolitana* (?) 'Stasek', a wonderfully free-flowering plant of good habit with a narrow cream edge to its leaves; *D. longilobata* 'Peter Moore', with leaves in a pleasing combination of pale cream and grey-green; *D.* ×*mantensiana* 'Audrey Vockins', a small, free-flowering evergreen with a gold edge to its dark green leaves; and *D.* ×*transatlantica* 'Beulah Cross', which has attractive cream-edged foliage and produces fragrant flowers for six months of the year.

Purple foliage may not readily spring to mind when thinking of daphnes, but *D.* ×*houtteana* 'Louis Van Houtte' and *D. mezereum* 'Kingsley Purple' fall into this category. The former is best treated purely as an evergreen foliage plant as its flowers are insignificant and largely hidden by leaves, but *D. mezereum* 'Kingsley Purple' produces strongly fragrant pink flowers in early spring before the leaves develop, and a crop of bright red fruits in June. To achieve the best foliage colour both these varieties need sun for at least half the day.

Fruit

Provided that birds allow them to ripen, the following species of daphne reliably produce an attractive crop of fruits: *D. alpina*, *D. domini*, *D. giraldii*, *D. longilobata*, *D. mezereum*, *D. oleoides* and *D. tangutica*.

Rock gardens and containers

There is a large group of the smaller daphne species and hybrids that can be classed as dwarf shrubs. These are ideal for rock gardens, raised beds or large containers such as troughs or sinks. Provided they are grown on their own roots, *D. arbuscula*, the small forms of *D. cneorum* and *D. petraea* can be planted in crevices between rocks or the dry-stone walling of a raised bed. *D.* ×*hendersonii* cultivars and *D. petraea* are particularly suitable for troughs.

Low-growing plant associations

Many daphnes show resentment of neighbouring plant growth mingling with their own in the form of browning of the foliage or weak, straggly growth.

However, the more vigorous forms of *D. cneorum*, such as 'Eximea', 'Velky Kosir' and f. *alba*, do associate well with other rambling or prostrate growers such as *Lithodora diffusa*, *Genista sagittalis*, × *Halimiocistus sahucii* and *Thymus serpyllum* varieties. Combinations like these make effective edges to sunny beds, or they can be planted near the edge of paved paths or patios to grow over the paving or around focal points such as a sundial or statue.

Winter interest under cover

For a number of years our winters in Hampshire have been much wetter and duller than they used to be, so it is a joy to go into the glasshouse on these dismal days to admire and sniff plants of *D. bholua*, *D.* ×*hybrida* and *D. jezoensis*. A garden room, conservatory or glasshouse can be used to enjoy container-grown plants of winter-flowering daphnes; come late spring they can be moved outside.

In winter and early spring large plants of *Daphne bholua*, *D. mezereum* and *D. odora* can provide material for a vase. They will fill a warm room with their scent for a considerable time as their flowers open in succession.

Useful Addresses

Plant societies

The Alpine Garden Society
AGS Centre
Avon Bank
Pershore WR10 3JP
United Kingdom

The Royal Horticultural Society
80 Vincent Square
London SW1P 2PE
United Kingdom

The Scottish Rock Garden Club
Hazel Smith
Harrglayock Salsgirth
Dollar
Fife FK14 7NE
Scotland

The Daphne Society
Membership Secretary Shelley Herlich
43 Greenfield Lane
Commack
NY 11725
USA

The North American Rock Garden Society
Jaques Mommens
P.O. BOX 67
Millwood
ny 10546
USA

Where to see or buy daphnes

Always check on availability of plants and opening times of the nursery before visiting and check with the owner of a garden that it is convenient to visit.

Where to see daphnes in North America

John Bieber
185 8TH Street
Bethpage
NY 11714
USA
5166814885

Marleen Neil
5233 SW Hewett Blvd.
Portland
OR 97221
USA
503 297 9477
marleeninc@worldnet.att.net

Maria Galletti
1182 Parmenter Road
Sutton Quebec
Canada J0F 2K0
450 243 5354
alpinemtecho@endirect.qc.ca

Nickolas Nickou
197 Sunset Hill Drive
Branford
CT 06405
USA
203 488 4936

Planting Fields Arboretum
P.O. BOX 58 Planting Fields Road
Oyster Bay
NY 11771
USA
516 922 8600
vsimeone@juno.com

The New York Botanical Garden
Bronx
NY 10458 –5126
USA
718 817 8057

Where to buy daphnes in North America

Arrowhead Alpine Nurseries
P.O. BOX 857
Fowlerville
MI 48836
USA
517 223 3581

Maria Galletti (see above)

Richard Lupp
28111 112TH Street
Graham
WA 98338
USA
253 847 9827
rlupp@aol.com

Environmentals Nursery
Donna Messina
P.O. BOX 23
Cutchogue
NY 11935
USA
631 734 6449

Siskiyou Rare Plant Nursery
2825 Cummings Road
Medford
OR 97501
USA
541 772 6846
srpn@wave.net

Where to see daphnes in the U.K.

Mr M. Baron
Brandy Mount House
Alresford
Hampshire SO24 9EG
01962 732189
NCCPG Collection Holder

Mrs D. Field
42 Park Lane
Hartford
Northwich
Cheshire CW8 1PZ
01606 75642
NCCPG Collection Holder

Blackthorn Nursery
Kilmeston
Alresford
Hampshire SO24 0NL
01962 771796

Where to buy daphnes in the U.K.

Blackthorn Nursery (See above)

PMA Plant Specialities
Junkers Nursery
Lower Mead
West Hatch
Taunton TA3 5RN
01823 480774

Wisley Plant Centre
RHS Garden
Wisley
Woking
Surrey GU23 6QB
01483 211113

The Alpine Garden Society and The Scottish Rock Garden Club stage a series of shows around the United Kingdom where container-grown daphnes can often be seen in flower, and young plants purchased from nurserymen attending with sales stands.

Suppliers of biological control agents for the amateur market in the United Kingdom

Biowise
Graffham
Petworth
West Sussex GU28 0LR
01798 867574
post@biowise-biocontrol.co.uk

Defenders Ltd.
Occupation Road
Wye
Ashford
Kent TN25 5EN
01233 813121
help@defenders.co.uk

Harrod UK Ltd.
Pinbush Road
Lowestoft
Suffolk NR33 7NL
01502 505300

Supplier of composted pine bark in various grades

Melcourt Industries Ltd.
Boldridge Brake
Long Newnton
Tetbury GL8 8RT
United Kingdom

Glossary

absorption the uptake of substances or water by plant cells.

adsorption the physical binding of substance particles to the surface of another by adhesion.

adventitious growing from an unusual position.

aff. abbreviation of *affinis*, near to.

apical dominance a condition whereby the stem apex prevents development of lateral branches. It is controlled by auxins (growth hormones).

apiculate describes a leaf apex terminated with a short point.

auricle ear-like appendage at the base of leaves or petals.

axillary borne in the axil i.e. where a leaf or small stem joins a stem.

caducous soon dropping off.

calcifuge a plant species not generally found growing in alkaline soils.

capillary action the process in which moisture moves through fine channels in soil or plants under surface tension forces.

capitate with a knob-like head.

chelated iron iron is an essential element for plants, which calcifuge plants fail to absorb in the presence of high calcium levels. Chelation provides iron in an organic form which makes it available to calcifuges.

chlorophyll the green pigment in plants which enables them to photosynthesize (create carbohydrates in the presence of sunlight and carbon dioxide).

chlorosis a condition caused by lack of chlorophyll generally due to iron or magnesium deficiency.

clone a group of genetically identical organisms.

colloid either of mineral (clay) or organic (humus) origin. They provide surfaces with high mineral exchange capacity.

compost tea a term devised in the United States to cover various liquid products obtained from composting or brewing plant material. These products have been shown to help prevent and/or control a wide range of fungal diseases.

coriaceous leathery.

cortex tissue below the epidermis, but outside the vascular bundles.

cotyledon seed leaf.

dimorphism sexual differences within a species, such as types of flowers in dioecious plants.

dioecious possessing male and female flowers on separate unisexual plants.

drupe a fleshy fruit containing one seed.

fleece a finely woven fabric for horticultural use with good insulating properties.

glabrous lacking hairs.

glaucous having a bluish green colour, or waxy, bluish green bloom.

fasciation a malformation in which shoots are flattened and may occur in masses.

hermaphrodite applied to plants which carry male parts (stamens) and female parts (the pistil) on the same plant.

involucre a whorl of bracts.

leaching removal of soil materials in solution by downward percolation of water.

lignin a complex polymer which is deposited in cell walls, giving them a rigid, woody structure.

metabolism process in an organism or single cell by which nutritive material is built up into living matter.

mucronate describes a leaf apex with a distinct point.

mycelium a mass of hyphae, which are the minute threads which make up the vegetative body of many fungi.

necrosis dead plant tissue.

obtuse blunt or rounded.

oedema a physical condition caused by the inability of cells to control their water content.

pathogen an organism which produces disease.

pericarp the fruit wall.

photosynthesis the series of metabolic reactions whereby solar energy absorbed by chlorophyll combines with carbon dioxide to synthesize carbohydrates.

polythene tunnel hoop house.

pubescent covered in soft hairs.

raffia strips of dried leaf from the raffia palm traditionally used in place of string as a tying material.

retuse notched.

ripe wood that part of woody stems where secondary thickening has occurred and cells have become lignified.

sap the liquid contents of the vascular system of a plant.

saprophyte an organism which gains nutrition from dead organic matter.

sessile lacking a stalk.

sport a sudden deviation from type, a mutation.

stool the permanent base of a coppiced, woody plant.

sucker an underground shoot arising adventitiously from a root or the base of the stem. Refers to shoots from a rootstock where relevant to a grafted plant.

symbiosis the situation in which dissimilar organisms live in close association to their mutual benefit.

tissue culture in simple terms the reproduction of plants by culturing meristem tissue in a sterile medium.

trace element a chemical nutrient essential for successful growth, but only in minute quantity, for example, zinc, copper and boron.

vegetative propagation the propagation of plants without involving the re-combination of genetic material. The resulting plants will be clones.

whorl the arrangement of plant parts in a circle.

Bibliography

Amsler, A. M. 1953. *Journal of the Royal Horticultural Society* 78: 5–18.

Bieber, J. 1999. *Daphne genkwa, The Daphne Society Newsletter* 1: 1: 7–8.

Brickell, C. D. and B. Mathew. 1976. *Daphne*, The genus in the wild and in cultivation. Alpine Garden Society.

Brickell, C. D., and B. Mathew. 1976. *Journal of the Royal Horticultural Society* 101: 550–551.

Brickell, C. D., and A. R. White. 2000. A Quartet of New Daphnes. *The New Plantsman* 7 (March): 6–18. The Royal Horticultural Society.

Brickell, C. D., 2000. Daphne Part 2: Hendersons' Daphne. *The New Plantsman* 7 (June): 114–122. The Royal Horticultural Society.

Brickell, C. D., and A. R. White. 2000. A Further Trio of New Daphne Hybrids. *The New Plantsman* 7 (December): 236–248. The Royal Horticultural Society.

Dourado. A., R.H. Ellis, and T.D Hong, 2000. Breaking Dormancy. *The Smaller Daphnes*, proceedings of 'Daphne 2000': 12–14. The Alpine Garden Society in association with The Royal Horticultural Society.

Erskine, P. 1990. Tufa in the rock garden. *Bulletin of the Alpine Garden Society* 58: 275 – 279.

Grey-Wilson, C. 2002. A–Z genera. *Bulletin of the Alpine Garden Society* 70: 321.

Halda, J., and Z. Zvolanek, 1982. Vichren Daphnes. *Bulletin of the Alpine Garden Society* 50: 267–270.

Halda, J. *The Genus Daphne.* SEN, Dobré 2001.

Hodgkin, E. 1961. *Journal of the Royal Horticultural Society* 86: 481–488

Jans, H. 1993. A free standing tufa wall. *Bulletin of the Alpine Garden Society* 61: 196–199.

Jans, H. 2000. Grafting Daphnes. *The Smaller Daphnes*, proceedings of 'Daphne 2000': 15–16. The Alpine Garden Society in association with The Royal Horticultural Society.

Kummert, F. 1990. Some notes on the genus daphne. *Bulletin of the Alpine Garden Society* 58: 266–268.

Melcourt Industries Ltd. 1993. *The Professional Growers Guide.*

Rolfe, R. 2000. *Daphne cneorum*, a discourse. *The Smaller Daphnes*, proceedings of 'Daphne 2000': 25–35. The Alpine Garden Society in association with The Royal Horticultural Society.

Smithers, Sir Peter. 1995. *Adventures of a Gardener.* The Harvill Press with The Royal Horticultural Society.

Stearn, W. T. 1996. *Botanical Latin* 4th edition. David & Charles.

Ward, T. 2002. Field Notes. *The American Nurseryman.* January 94.

Index of Daphnes

Figures in **bold** indicate the main plant entry. Those in *italics* indicate illustrations.

Conversion Tables

Millimetres (MM)	Inches
1	0.04
2	0.08
3	0.1
4	0.2
5	0.2
6	0.2
7	0.3
8	0.3
9	0.4
10	0.4
12	0.5
15	0.6

Centimetres (CM)	Inches
0.1	0.04
0.2	0.08
0.3	0.1
0.4	0.2
0.5	0.2
0.6	0.2
0.7	0.3
0.8	0.3
0.9	0.4
1.0	0.4
1.1	0.4
1.2	0.5
1.3	0.5
1.4	0.6
1.5	0.6
1.6	0.6
1.7	0.7
1.8	0.7
1.9	0.8
2.0	0.8

Centimetres (CM)	Inches
2.2	0.9
2.4	0.9
2.5	1.0
3.0	1.2
3.2	1.3
3.5	1.4
3.7	1.5
4.0	1.6
4.5	1.8
5.0	2.0
5.5	2.2
6.0	2.4
6.5	2.6
7.0	2.8
7.5	3.0
8.0	3.1
9.0	3.5
10.0	4.0
12.5	5.0
15.0	6.0
20.0	8.0
22.5	9.0
25.0	10.0
30.0	12.0
35.0	14.0
40.0	16.0
45.0	18.0
50.0	20.0
60.0	24.0
70.0	27.5
75.0	30.0
80.0	32.0
90.0	35.0

Metres (M)	Feet
1.0	3.3
1.2	3.9
1.3	4.3
1.4	4.6
1.5	4.9
1.6	5.2
1.7	5.6
1.8	5.9
1.9	6.2
2.0	6.6
2.5	8.2
3.0	9.8
5.0	16.4